COERCION

NOMOS

XIV

N O M O S

N O M O S   X I V

Yearbook of the American Society for Political and Legal Philosophy

COERCION

Edited by

J. ROLAND PENNOCK *Swarthmore College*

and

JOHN W. CHAPMAN *University of Pittsburgh*

Aldine · Atherton, Inc. · Chicago/New York · 1972

First published 1972 by
Aldine • Atherton, Inc.
529 South Wabash Avenue
Chicago, Illinois 60605

ISBN 0–202–24116–5
Library of Congress Catalog Number 71–169505

Printed in the United States of America

PREFACE

Hard upon *Privacy* comes *Coercion,* Volume XIV of the NOMOS series. Of the fifteen papers presented here, those by Samuel Cook, Robert Jervis, William Riker, Howard Sobel, and Robert Paul Wolff are revised versions of papers or remarks delivered at the meetings of the American Society for Political and Legal Philosophy, held in conjunction with those of the American Political Science Association in September, 1969. The program for these meetings was prepared by a committee under the chairmanship or Oran R. Young of Princeton University. The other chapters of the book were arranged for by the editors.

While the chapters of NOMOS XIV do not divide neatly into three (or any other whole number) parts, certain groupings do make sense, and it is only fair to give the reader some indication as to what is to come.

An introductory chapter by one of the editors is followed by four chapters that are primarily definitional and concerned with usage.

Among other issues, they raise the question whether an offer, as well as a threat, may be coercive. Virginia Held (joined on this issue by Donald McIntosh, in another part of the volume) maintains that it may, as opposed to the position taken by Michael Bayles and Bernard Gert and (in another part of the volume) Alan Wertheimer. Michael Weinstein introduces the notion that coercion relates to the use of space, using this idea to distinguish coercion from both oppression and repression.

While the contributors generally agree that coercion is bad, the next three papers, by, respectively, Robert Faulkner, Samuel Cook, and Robert Wolff, are concerned especially with the moral aspects of the subject, Faulkner dealing with the topic *via* a detailed elucidation and commentary on Books III and V of Aristotle's *Nicomachean Ethics.*

In the succeeding three chapters, William McBride, William Riker, and Howard Sobel discuss the problem of the avoidability of coercion. Alan Wertheimer also has something to say on this subject, although his contribution deals primarily with the question of whether coercion interferes with political obligation. He contends that it does not.

Finally, the last three papers, in part or in whole, deal with the role of coercion in international relations. Donald McIntosh considers coercion by means of game theoretic analysis, noting that a country may influence the behavior of other countries by shaping their evaluation of the results of a specific negotiation or interaction. Robert Jervis, in analyzing bargaining tactics, also makes use of game theory. It is the game of "chicken" rather than either the "prisoners' dilemma" or Riker's less familiar "couples game" that he finds most applicable to international affairs. Lastly in the concluding chapter, John Chapman adds a historical perspective and argues, as does McIntosh, that the dynamics of national and international politics are more alike than is generally supposed.

If we may hazard a generalization it would seem to be that coercion, like the poor, is always with us. Some two hundred years ago, political thinkers complained about the more direct and personal forms of coercion, as did Rousseau in his revulsion against "personal dependence." He recommended dependence of all upon "the City," which for Hegel meant the State. And no doubt the modern state does free men from forms of coercion by which they had been plagued. But now we hear—and not only from Marxists—complaints about systemic coerciveness, both national and international, from which the institutions of sovereignty and democracy had been presumed to relieve us. Coercion appears to be the phoenix of the human condition.

J. R. P.
J. W. C.

CONTENTS

CONTRIBUTORS

MICHAEL D. BAYLES
Philosophy, University of Kentucky

JOHN W. CHAPMAN
Political Science, University of Pittsburgh

SAMUEL DUBOIS COOK
Political Science, Duke University

ROBERT K. FAULKNER
Political Science, Boston College

BERNARD GERT
Philosophy, Dartmouth College

VIRGINIA HELD
Philosophy, Hunter College

ROBERT JERVIS
Political Science, Harvard University

WILLIAM LEON MCBRIDE
  Philosophy, Yale University

DONALD MCINTOSH
  Political Science, City College of New York

J. ROLAND PENNOCK
  Political Science, Swarthmore College

WILLIAM H. RIKER
  Political Science, University of Rochester

J. HOWARD SOBEL
  Philosophy, University of Toronto

MICHAEL A. WEINSTEIN
  Political Science, Purdue University

ALAN P. WERTHEIMER
  Political Science, University of Vermont

ROBERT PAUL WOLFF
  Philosophy, University of Massachusetts

COERCION

NOMOS

XIV

1

COERCION: AN OVERVIEW

J. Roland Pennock

"Coercion signifies, in general, the imposition of external regulation and control upon persons, by threat or use of force and power." So says the *Dictionary of the Social Sciences.* As the reader will discover for himself, this definition does not meet with universal acceptance. In particular, the distaff member of our team takes issue, arguing that more subtle forms of influence than force and power may qualify. By any definition, however, "coercion" invites contrast with "liberty" or "freedom," as in the title of Bernard Gert's chapter. Is one the obverse of the other? Indeed, it might even be suggested that in discussing one of these concepts much or all of what it would be appropriate to say about the other has already been covered.

Ten years ago the annual volume of NOMOS was devoted to "Liberty." Perhaps no great significance attaches to the differences in their tables of contents. Different editors and changed times may largely account for the differences in subjects discussed. Moreover, on that earlier occasion, the Society, at its annual meeting, had been marking the centennial of the publication of "On Liberty." Half of the chapters and slightly over half of the pages were devoted in whole or in part to John Stuart Mill. Even without the occasion for celebration, this distribution would have seemed only mildly disproportionate in a volume devoted to this topic.

"Coercion," however, has no patron saint. No name stands out as demanding discussion in the present volume. Defenders of "authority" are numerous; and the name of Hobbes, in this connection, eclipses even that of Mill. Yet authority is by no means the same as coercion. Moreover, although Hobbes is no great defender of liberty, authority is not for him its opposite. Rather liberty's opposite, according to Hobbes, is that which hinders a man from doing what he has the strength, wit, and will to do. And if this is not the definition of coercion (as it would appear to be if we were to accept the *Dictionary of the Social Sciences* definition), it at least includes coercion.

"Liberty" is a "virtue word": for some more than for others, but it generally has a positive connotation; coercion, the reverse. It may contribute to understanding to compare the two terms more carefully, not directly in terms of their definitions (as is done in the four immediately succeeding chapters) but in terms of the problems, similar and dissimilar, to which consideration of their meanings gives rise.

I

Let us begin with a series of situations in which the definitional problems seem to be similar, if not identical, supporting the idea that the two terms are logically related by opposition. Take the case of physical laws, gravity, for example. We do not normally say that a person who accidentally steps off a cliff is coerced into falling to the base below, nor that he is thereby deprived of freedom. Peripheral usages may be found. We might say that the invention of the airplane freed man from being confined to the surface of the earth. We would hardly say that, previously, he had been coerced to remain on the earth's surface. Possibly the difference arises out of the fact that in the case of liberty we have our attention mainly on what is liberated (since the word refers to the condition of the being that is freed) and hence are less likely to notice that the liberating factor is of a kind (a physical law) not usually thought of as affecting liberty. The concept of coercion, on the other hand, directs attention to the source of the coercion (since it refers to the *use* of force rather than to its effect), and hence to the fact that the human element, usually associated with coercion, is here lacking. (Bayles maintains that coercion is necessarily an interpersonal relation.)

Now let us shift to the case of coercion that is human but not deliberate (at least as far as concerns its coercive effect). We may speak sometimes of being forced to do something by "the logic of the situation." Take the case of "cutthroat" competition. The competitor who cuts his prices down to the level of his direct costs is not trying to coerce others to do the same. In fact he would much prefer that they did not. But they are likely to do so. And they will feel coerced.[1] And the coerced party will also feel that his liberty has been curtailed.

Yet these are borderline cases. Suppose we shift the situation to a busy street intersection, or, rather, to one where the traffic is virtually constant on one of the streets but only sporadic on the other. The traffic light has ceased to function, with the consequence that the people on the cross street find it virtually impossible to get where they want to go. Are they being coerced? One would hesitate to say so. Is their liberty being curtailed? I think one would hesitate to use this terminology, as well; although perhaps it would be a trifle less forced than to say they were being coerced. If there is a difference here, it probably goes back to the point made above about the ways in which attention is directed by the two words. It is more difficult to think of the drivers of the cars on the main road exercising coercion in this situation than it is to think of the others as being deprived of liberty, for the latter are indeed frustrated. Again we seem to be operating at the borderline of the commonly understood meanings of both terms. Perhaps the distinction I sense is between the price-cutter, who is departing from his previous behavior pattern and who is aware of the effect of his action on his

---

[1] I believe this usage is widely shared. Bayles contends, however, that the coercer must have intended the effect produced upon the person coerced.

competitor—even though he does not intend it—and the driver, who does not change his behavior and may not even know that the light is out of order.

Take a case of social necessity the results of which are favorable to me. Being brought up in an English-speaking community, I am (in one sense) compelled to learn the English language. This is perhaps no less a matter of the "logic of the situation" than the cases discussed above. Yet one would hesitate to say either that I was coerced or that I was deprived of liberty. The two cases seem to be on a par in this respect; and the crucial difference from the preceding cases is that here there is no question of going contrary to my wishes. Furthermore, I am actually *more* free, or at least I have more options than would otherwise have been the case. What I am in a sense required to do is essential to the fulfillment of my needs and desires.

Similarly, the structure of the situation may produce the effect in question in more subtle ways. Take the case of an Amish community located in the midst of a society growing ever more unlike it in ways of which the Amish disapprove. Are they coerced? Are they unfree? (I exclude cases of legal compulsion.) How we would answer these questions may be in some doubt, but I believe the answer, whatever it was, would be the same in each case.[2] More generally, it is the prevailing ideology that is at issue and that suggests that one of our terms is the counterpart of the other.

May one be coerced by disapproval, say by the disapproval of society? And if so is one's liberty limited? It would seem that an affirmative answer is called for in each case. Mill of course was greatly concerned about the pressure of society toward conformity. One can certainly imagine cases where the pressure to conform was stifling to liberty. And in such cases I suspect one would say that society was exercising coercion, even though it was not deliberate. But note, if the price of nonconformity is not great, we may hesitate to say that liberty is curtailed. Under these circumstances, we may say that people who conform against their preferences or convic-

---

[2] In this example, it is the matter of coercion by a social situation that I am considering. From another point of view, if the Amish hold fast, they are not coerced in any case, by Bayles's definition. This point will be discussed below.

tions are either fools or weaklings. They are perfectly free to do as they please, we might say. Moreover, no one is coercing them. Here, if there is any difference, we might be a little more inclined, in my opinion, to say they were being coerced than that they were not free. (This conclusion accords with Gert's definition of coercion "in the wide sense.")

In general, the question raised by this situation relates to both liberty and coercion: it is whether all restraints and constraints are to be counted as constituting coercion or limiting liberty, or whether only restraints of a certain kind and degree count as being coercive and as interfering with liberty. (The case of an unsuccessful threat, implicit here, will be discussed below.) While for the most part the question of degree seems to affect our usage of the two terms in like fashion, I believe one can note divergences in two directions. In the case just considered we may be more inclined to qualify our judgments about liberty by reference to some standard of reasonableness than we are in the case of coercion, although in at least one kind of situation Virginia Held would not agree. (Again the emphasis is on the human object of action and hence upon subjective factors—here "reasonableness.") To shift once more to traffic controls —but here a properly functioning rather than a malfunctioning light—we might be more ready to say that a red light is coercive than that it deprives of liberty. If so, I would suggest that the reason for this asymmetry of usage is because, in the case of liberty, we are more apt to judge the particular situation in terms of the whole system of which it is a part. Thus we might not consider a red light as depriving us of liberty because we realize that on the whole it makes for less frustration than would otherwise be the case. In the case of coercion, where the emphasis is on the act rather than the condition, the broader context is less relevant.

Finally—and this is the question on which Bayles, Gert, and Wertheimer are aligned against Held and McIntosh—must the incentive, the sanction, be negative? The first three authors mentioned contend that it must: a promise of benefit is never coercive, they maintain. Held and McIntosh argue on the other hand that this is not the proper test. Rather, the question is whether the incentive (or disincentive) is one that a normal person might reasonably be expected to resist. The point to be made here is that precisely the same issue arises with respect to liberty. Most writers probably would argue that a bribe does not interfere with liberty, but Stanley Benn takes the opposite point of view.[3]

II

Thus far we have reviewed a series of problems that one encounters in defining coercion and we have found that the same problems usually arise in defining freedom. Generally, they tend to support the picture of coercion and freedom as opposite sides of the same coin, although even here we have noted certain qualifications. Now we turn to a set of problems that seem to bring out differences rather than similarities between the two concepts. First, two general points. Coercion is what someone does. It is an exercise of power. Freedom, on the other hand, is a condition.[4] The two terms are not parallel. But this does not mean that they cannot be counterparts. The condition might always result from coercion or its lack. Liberty might always be describable in terms of the presence of coercion; and coercion might be definable in terms of its effect on liberty. The second general point arises from the fact that coercion is a form of the exercise of power. As is well known, the relation between liberty and power is ambiguous, or at least debatable. It should not be surprising, therefore, that this ambiguity shows up in some of the cases to be discussed below.

Even if coercion always interferes with liberty—at least with a specific liberty—does its absence always result in liberty? In other words, is coercion the only thing that interferes with liberty? Not if we accept the notion of "pyschological freedom."[5] According to this concept any psychological state that interferes with harmony between basic motives and overt behavior is an interference with liberty. Bernard Gert argues, however, (Chapter 3) that this concept of liberty is too broad—that it comes from collapsing the distinction between "liberty" and "power." Moreover, it should be

[3] Stanley I. Benn, "Persuasion and Freedom," *Australian Journal of Philosophy,* 45 (December 1967), 267.
[4] This is another way of putting the point made above that "coercion" directs attention to the actor while "liberty" relates more to the effect of the action.
[5] Cf. Christian Bay, *The Structure of Freedom* (Stanford, Calif.: Stanford University Press, 1958), Chap. 3, esp. 83-88, and Chap. 4.

noted that Bay himself, for whom liberty is certainly the supreme good, declares that coercion is "the supreme political evil."[6] So perhaps the difference just noted between coercion and the opposite of liberty is not so great after all. In fact, it may disappear entirely if we limit the discussion to "political" liberty or even to the broader concept of "social freedom."

Another somewhat puzzling case is that of "manipulation," meaning by that term conditioning or otherwise influencing behavior by controlling the content and supply of information. Here again something other than coercion may affect a person's freedom in the very broadest sense of that term. This is what Bay calls "potential freedom." Again the difference between coercion and freedom's opposite appears only where "freedom" is used in an extended sense. It once more appears, however, that the words "liberty" and "freedom" have a certain elasticity, a certain tendency to be stretched beyond their usual meanings that is less true of "coercion."

This same tendency is noticeable in connection with the idea of being "forced to be free." Rousseau's famous, or notorious, concept clearly could not be identified with the *absence* of coercion, since it itself involves coercion. Nor can freedom coerce. Again we are made aware of the fact that "freedom" is often used less precisely than "coercion." Even Rousseau, when he spoke of being forced to be free, would probably have admitted that any forcing, any coercion, entailed some limitation of freedom or limitation of *some* freedom, even though freedom *in the large* might be increased. One is reminded of Green's concept of "hindering hindrances," which clearly involves coercion and the limitation of someone's liberty in behalf of a greater or more important liberty. Although most would agree with Bay that coercion is evil, other things being equal, the evaluative connotations do not seem to have rubbed off onto the word itself to the same extent that the positive connotations of freedom have.[7] Thus some may say (perhaps rather carelessly) that

---

[6] *Ibid.,* 92.

[7] One might speculate that a change may be occurring in this regard. Today's younger generation seems to be unusually sensitive to "coercion" as well as to "authority." When even "tolerance" can be regarded as "coercive," the latter term is surely being enlarged. (The reference is to Herbert Marcuse, "Repressive Tolerance," in Robert Paul Wolff, *et al., A Critique of Pure Tolerance* [Boston, Mass.: Beacon Press, 1965].)

"bad" liberty is not really liberty (possibly, it is "license"), but the parallel statement that "good" coercion is not really coercion, or even that it does not "really" interfere with liberty, does not occur.

Perhaps most people would agree that both of the terms under discussion admit of degree. However, in one respect Michael Bayles, in his chapter below, does not agree. (On this point he is in disagreement with Bermard Gert and Virginia Held.) A person who is threatened unsuccessfully is not coerced, he argues. Note too, that it is certainly true that we say "He tried to coerce me into doing X, but I refused." He only tried; he did not succeed. Yet, in the case of liberty, I would suggest, we are a little more tender. If I feel it more difficult to live according to my preferred life style because of the ill-concealed disapproval of my neighbors, even though I do not allow myself to be influenced by them I might consider moving to someplace where I would feel more free to do as I please. I might not say I was coerced, and yet I might contend that my freedom was being infringed upon. What that example brings out is not only that freedom is more a matter of degree than is coercion but also that it has its subjective side. Some might say that a man is as free as he feels; and conversely, that he is not free if he does not feel free. Several years ago, Pitirim Sorokin sought to make this point (and at least one other) by means of a simple formula. Freedom, he asserted, can be reduced to this formula:

$$\text{Freedom} = \frac{M}{W},$$

where M stands for the sum of the means available (including lack of restraint) and W stands for wants or desires. His primary point was that one could increase one's freedom as well by limiting his desires as by increasing his opportunities to satisfy his desires. Many might object that, carried to its logical conclusion, the end result of the former process would be death, the very negation of liberty. Yet we do seem to accept the idea that a multiplicity of wants, out of all proportion to the possibility of fulfilling them, is frustrating and that frequently the frustration can be better removed by eliminating the wants than by trying to satisfy them. We might thus think of limiting wants as a way of increasing freedom, since freedom is so closely linked with frustration. Coercion does not seem to enter this picture at all. Yet perhaps this very connection is misleading us here. Gert would protest (and so would many others) that Sorokin's formula is too inclusive—that the variable of "means" should be limited to the absence of restraints. This point introduces the well-worn argument as to whether "freedom" should be defined "positively" or whether this extension blurs an important difference by confusing "freedom" with "power." Once more it is apparent that "coercion," in spite of the definitional arguments that attend it, is a much tighter, more precise concept than is liberty.

"Freedom $= \dfrac{M}{W}$" is not wholly satisfactory, as we have seen; but it does have some intuitive plausibility, deriving both from its emphasis on the subjective aspect of liberty and from our feeling that the liberty of the pauper, for example, is so hollow as hardly to merit the name. On the other hand, the formula "Coercion $= \dfrac{W}{M}$", derivable from the proposition that coercion and liberty are opposites, makes no sense whatsoever. However, it could be argued that *"Unfreedom $= \dfrac{W}{M}$"* and also that coercion may decrease M (thus increasing unfreedom). Seen this way, coercion is one way but not the only way of decreasing freedom.

III

Other things being equal, it seems to be generally agreed that coercion is bad, as it is similarly agreed that liberty is good. Coercion may be bad because it is physically or psychologically painful, or it may be bad because it interferes with individual autonomy. The latter point is of special significance and calls attention to the fact that the evaluations of the two terms just expressed may not be universally accepted. However, they must be accepted by all who subscribe to any philosophy that places the autonomy of the individual at the apex of its value hierarchy.

Introduction of the notion of autonomy also suggests that of equality; for if the autonomy of individuals is of supreme value it follows that in a most important sense individuals are equal. This equality affects the valuation of coercion in the following way. If one state coerces another the presumption of wrongdoing is strong. If, on the other hand, the United Nations does the same thing and with the same objective—even to a nonmember state—the presumption may even be reversed in favor of justification of the coercive action. Both actions are coercive; both are instances of interference with autonomy. But coercion of one state by another amounts to a claim of superior judgment of what is right, and thus to a denial of equality. On the other hand, coercion by an organization of states does not amount *per se* to a claim of superiority on the part of any *one* of them. In other words, a claim of legitimacy for a *collective* judgment against an individual does not deny the equality of individuals. It has already been suggested that the fact of interference with autonomy is not the only reason for calling coercion presumptively bad; it is perhaps even more obvious that in many situations coercion is justified. Hence the point being made in this paragraph is not a strong one. It does suggest, however, that our high valuation for individual autonomy and for equality, as well as for liberty, helps to explain why coercion by presumed equals is generally thought to be bad.

IV

But of course it is not only coercion among equals that is thought to be bad. Coercion of individuals by government is also felt to be undesirable, *ceteris paribus*. How then can it be limited? Where wills conflict in society? What are the alternatives to coercion? One way is to limit interaction. This approach, at least superficially, does not appear promising in a world of three billion people which is rapidly increasing in numbers. It is worthy of remark, though, that decentralization may be thought of as a move in this direction. The smaller the units within which harmony must be found, the less the likelihood that coercion will need to be resorted to *within those units*. That much is clear and no doubt accounts for the renewed popularity of decentralization in this period of heightened egalitarianism, when coercion is more than ever a swear-word. However, how much can be accomplished in this direction is a matter of considerable doubt. In many instances the costs will be thought to outweigh the advantages. Also, what is gained by increased harmony within the units of decision may be lost in inter-unit conflicts. In other words, one question will be whether interaction actually is limited or whether its incidence is merely shifted.

Primarily, one must look towards methods of finding or creating agreement. One means of finding agreement is to rely upon market mechanisms. By definition this device reduces governmental coercion. Hedged about with suitable safeguards against irresponsible and harmful exercises of private coercive power, this means of finding agreement is regaining popularity even in Socialist countries. Doubtless the parameters imposed upon individual action by the market are in some ways as restricting as are the legal regulations that may be substituted for them. But they do generally allow a greater measure of choice. If we can't have both a color television *and* airconditioning, we may at least be able to decide for ourselves which to choose. Moreover, market controls are not imposed upon us deliberately. The matter of autonomy enters again. If my actions must be limited, let it be by an impersonal and invisible force rather than by another "autonomous" man. Moreover, the constraint that allows a choice is better, *ceteris paribus,* than the coercive order or prohibition. Many examples could be offered of coercive governmental regulations, the removal of which would not only diminish the total amount of coercion in society but which would be beneficial from other points of view as well. Production controls and price fixing in agriculture and in the dairy industry in particular readily come to mind. Not only are the controls coercive, but it seems clear that the average consumer of the product the price of which is raised by the controls is less well off financially than is the average producer who is benefitted.

The democratic methods of avoiding coercion primarily have been either to find agreement by discussion or to create it by leadership. Actually, this way of stating the matter is oversimple. Discussion normally involves a relatively equal give-and-take. No single person dominates: it may result in a compromise, all parties realizing that it is worth something to them to obtain agreement. Better yet, however, discussion may lead to what Mary Parker Follett called "integration." Out of the group process may emerge a new idea, one that satisfies all parties, rendering compatible wants that had been thought to be incompatible. With leadership, of course, there is normally still discussion; but the emphasis here is on persuasion, whether by inventiveness, logical demonstration, or bringing about a reordering of priorities among some of the people concerned. A skilled leader may also minimize the need for resort to coercion by enlarging the areas of trust both between followers and leaders and among the group whose clash of wills was the subject of arbitration. William Riker's contribution to this volume argues that areas in which trust, unsupported by coercion, may be relied upon are substantially characteristic of the political arena. Howard Sobel points to the limitations of this strategy by demonstrating the logic of situations in which coercion is inescapable.

Perhaps the search for harmony, for means of avoiding coercion, must at least in part be moved back a stage. It may be that citizens must be conditioned, educated, or otherwise "manipulated" so as to make them less selfish, more public spirited. This of course is the line taken by Utopians of all sorts—and I do not use that term in a pejorative sense. Nor, of course, does it exclude Marxists, Marx to the contrary notwithstanding. The problems here are twofold. One has to do with human nature: to what extent can man's self-regarding demands be subordinated to his concern for society? We have it on the authority of no less a believer in man's aggressive characteristics than Robert Ardrey that certain animals take measures to warn the herd of approaching danger even though doing so diminishes their own chance of escape.[8] In this volume William McBride cautiously suggests that education may go a considerable distance in altering men's values in this direction. Whether man could be made both less self-seeking and at the same time productive, energetic, and innovative is another and unresolved question. Apart from what can be done is the problem of the means for doing it. Where does "education" leave off and conditioning or even "brainwashing" begin? Can the New Man be created without resort to the very coercion the solution seeks to avoid? And if not, could the coercion be limited to a generation? And in any case, as Skinner contends, would it be simply a substitution (perhaps even in lesser degree) for coercive forces operating but often unobserved in existing society?

V

Finally, quite apart from what men can do deliberately to limit coercion and find alternatives to it, one might consider the question (not taken up by any of the contributors to this volume)

[8] Robert Ardrey, *The Social Contract* (New York: Atheneum, 1970), 77-78.

of whether any trends are observable. Is there any tendency for coercion to increase or decline? It is not strange that none of the contributors to this volume have chosen to deal with this question, if only because of the multiplicity of kinds and locales of coercion and the difficulty if not impossibility of agreeing upon any way to measure it. Elsewhere many writers have dealt with the question of whether societies over the centuries have tended to develop forms and institutions that provide for greater individual freedom (and thus less coercion). Hegel can be cited on the affirmative side and Sorokin in opposition. Neither has sufficiently precise measures to prove his point. Recently, an interesting attempt has been made to deal with political coercion in quantitative terms.[9] The authors are able to compare a large number of polities with respect to five different complexes of measures of the coerciveness-permissiveness spectrum. At least a base has now been established. Perhaps in forty or fifty years a replication of the relevant part of this study might provide interesting data about trends. For shorter periods, it would be impossible to tell whether phenomena like the outbreaks of campus and ghetto violence of recent years represent ripples on the surface of the body politic or tidal movements.

Meanwhile one can only speculate and point here and there to straws in the wind. Criminology to date appears to have come up with few answers to the problem of crime. What does appear to be clear is that coercive punishment has failed as a deterrent. Moreover, among children at least, deviant behavior seems to yield better to trust, fairness, credibility, and affiliation than to coercion. Such evidence has led one pair of researchers to conclude that "Ultimately, the model of the persuasive socializer may achieve greater success than the coercive one."[10]

Looking much more broadly at the domestic social and political scene, it is quite possible to see a great increase in democracy and with it a minimization of coercion as functionally necessary in a highly industrialized society and, for that reason, as bound to come

[9] Ivo K. Feierabend and Betty Nesvold with Rosalind L. Feierabend, "Political Coerciveness and Turmoil, a Cross-National Inquiry," *Law and Society Review,* 5 (August 1970), 93-118.

[10] See June L. Tapp and Felice J. Levine, "Persuasion to Virtue, a Preliminary Statement," *Law and Society Review,* 4 (May 1970), 565-81, for support for the statements in this paragraph. The quoted sentence is at 581.

about. This view has been forcefully and persuasively put forward by Warren G. Bennis and Philip E. Slater.[11] They argue that "democracy becomes a functional necessity whenever a social system is competing for survival under conditions of chronic change." Among other things this will entail "a reliance on *consensus,* rather than the more customary forms of coercion or compromise" to manage conflict; and "a basically human bias, one that accepts the inevitability of conflict between the organization and the individual, but that is willing to cope with and mediate this conflict on rational grounds."[12] They do not make such optimistic statements as mere unsupported affirmations. They find much evidence—in the business world for instance—for the proposition that the changes they discuss are already going on. Perhaps even more to the point, they contend that under conditions of modern technology nothing else will "work."

Possibly this word "work" harbors a serious flaw in their argument. It may suggest an unrealistic degree of rationalism. People may both persist in old ways and react violently to change when it is not to their advantage to do so. The point needs no elaboration. Even if irrationality gives way to more realistic behavior in the long run, the run may be very long and the damage done in the meantime may be catastrophic.

Therefore, it is not surprising that other views of the world situation are less hopeful. Large parts of the world's population have recently been awakened from the sleep of tradition. They have been ruled easily, with a minimum of coercion. In our lifetimes, however, we have witnessed a tremendous increase in the awareness of the possibilities for change, or at least a great increase in the recognition of tremendous material and other disparities both within and among states. More frequently than not the resulting demands are frustrated by either the unwillingness or the inability of those in power to grant these demands. While and where these conditions exist an increase in coercive activities from both sides seems inescapable.

Other facts point in the same direction. The explosive growth of the world's population is threatening from several points of view.

[11] *The Temporary Society* (New York: Harper & Row, 1968).
[12] *Ibid.,* 4.

Perhaps most seriously, however, it merely compounds the forces let loose by the possibilities and demands created by modern technology. Whether from shortage of resources or from inability to dispose of wastes or from the threat that increasing use of energy will so heat the atmosphere as to melt the polar icecap and inundate the major cities of the world, it seems not unlikely that man will be forced to put brakes on the geometrically increasing rate of energy expenditure that makes possible the postindustrial society. One can only shudder when one thinks of the repercussions of such a development upon the billions of people within and without Western society. Can the counterforces which Bennis and Slater see already at work—the forces making for increasing democracy and increasing consensus—enable us to avoid the catastrophic developments that are otherwise indicated? Can they even confine the use of coercion to its more subtle forms? What a challenge for Professor Skinner's conditioners and manipulators, let alone for those liberal democrats who see Skinner's vision as a nightmare!

All of what has been said has been without direct reference to international conflict. Even Bennis and Slater condition their optimistic predictions upon "the (outrageous) assumption that war will somehow be eliminated during the next half-century."[13] In the concluding chapter to this volume John Chapman hazards the thought that the nature of strategic thought is changing, that it is becoming more "political" and less solely concerned with the imposition of one political entity's will upon that of another. Even such a view, however, stops far short of envisaging a great diminution of coercion in the international realm. To be sure, even in that realm the forces that Bennis and Slater find inescapable in the domestic sphere may be at work. But the sand in the top of the hourglass runs perilously low!

[13] *op. cit.*, 19.

2

A CONCEPT OF COERCION

Michael D. Bayles

Political, legal, and social philosophers still make moral judgments on occasion, although doing so is not as popular as it once was. Frequently the concept of coercion plays an important role in such judgments, for coercion in the Western moral and political tradition has two significant connections with moral principles. First, in law as well as morals, that one was coerced to act as one did is usually a defense or excuse.[1] That is, if a person has been coerced to perform an action he is thought to be blameless or less blameworthy. Second, the use of coercion is generally thought to be morally bad. Christian Bay goes so far as to call it "the supreme political evil."[2]

---

[1] For example, the New York Penal Law, §35.35, treats duress as a positive defense and defines it in terms of coercion.

[2] *The Structure of Freedom* (Stanford, Calif.: Stanford University Press, 1958), 92.

Whereas for scientific purposes one may define a concept in any manner that has theoretical value, for purposes of moral evaluation one should stick to the ordinary concept. For the ordinary concept, at least of coercion, is that which has developed strong moral significance. Various features of the ordinary concept of coercion have been overlooked or ignored by some recent social theorists who have, on occasion, been concerned to make moral judgments. Hence their theoretical accounts of coercion, with some risk of distortion, will be taken as pertaining to the ordinary concept. Attention here will be focused on three features of coercion. First, coercion involves both the success of the coercer and in some sense the voluntary action of the person coerced. Second, coercion is an interpersonal relation involving a complex intention on the part of a coercer. Third, coercion usually involves a threat of harm and never involves a promise of benefit. We will first consider these points and then the relations between coercion and suggested concepts of freedom and power.

THE ORDINARY CONCEPT OF COERCION

At least two kinds or varieties of coercion may be distinguished. In one type physical force is directly applied to cause behavior in another person. For example, one may clasp another's hand and force his finger to squeeze the trigger of a gun. Such "occurrent" coercion takes place infrequently and will not be discussed extensively. In a second variety, dispositional coercion, one man (the agent) threatens another (the victim) with a sanction if the latter fails to act as requested. This type of coercion occurs more frequently than the other and will be the main topic of discussion.

Sanctions may be intended to apply in either of two ways. First, a sanction may be applied simply to teach a victim a lesson. For example, a father might threaten to spank his son if he does not apologize to a little girl he hit. Second, a sanction may be imposed until a victim does as told. For example, a father might send his son to his room until he is willing to apologize. In either case, the initial attempt at coercion has failed if a sanction is imposed. The essence of successful attempts at coercion lies in getting persons to act by means of threats alone without having to impose sanctions. However, if a sanction is imposed until a victim does as told, initial failure may not signify complete failure. Complete failure ensues when, for example, a son outwaits his father and is let out of his room without having to apologize.

Two closely related features are characteristic of the ordinary concept of coercion. First, in dispositional coercion a victim's behavior is voluntary in a sense in which it is not voluntary in occurrent coercion. A man who is physically forced to squeeze the trigger of a gun does not do it voluntarily in any sense. But a man who fires a gun due to a threat does in one sense act voluntarily although he does not in another. The sense in which dispositionally coerced acts are voluntary and occurrently coerced ones are not appears to be that which G. E. Moore once suggested as a criterion of voluntary conduct. Moore at one time thought that "a person could have done otherwise" can be analyzed as "he would have done otherwise, if he had chosen."[3] In dispositional coercion, unlike occurrent coercion, a victim would have acted differently if he had chosen.

Even though a victim of occurrent coercion would not have behaved otherwise if he had chosen, his behavior must be of a type that is capable of voluntary control or performance. When a doctor produces a knee jerk by tapping a leg with a mallet, he may properly be said to make the knee jerk. But he cannot be properly described as having coerced someone to jerk his knee. Since so much behavior is capable of voluntary performance, forced involuntary behavior is rare. An example might be startling someone by sneaking up behind him and shouting.

A victim of dispositional coercion always has a choice. He can either do as told, or do something else and receive a sanction. Which choice he will make depends upon his beliefs about the comparative importance of not doing what he was told and of the threatened sanction. Obviously what kind and how great a sanction must be threatened to get a person to act in a certain manner depends upon his character and values. Thus, what may be coercive for one man may not be so for another. General judgments of what is or is not coercive, such as that duress is not a defense for murder, involve value choices. The choice made by law in this case is that no threatened harm to a person can be worse than the death of another human being and so coercive. Of course this judgment ignores

---

[3] *Ethics* (New York: Oxford, 1965), 12f, 90.

(as a jury probably would not) the possibility of having to decide between the death of several others, say, one's wife and children, and that of one man.

A closely related feature of "coercion" is that it is an achievement word; it denotes success. If X coerces Y into throwing a fight, then Y does throw the fight. If X threatens to expose Y as an adulterer if he does not throw the fight but Y wins anyway, then X has not coerced Y. The incidence of attempted coercion (whether or not successful) may have more moral significance than that of actual coercion. Nonetheless, the ordinary concept of coercion does not include unsuccessful attempts.

It is not clear whether or not actual coercion requires more than an agent's attempting to coerce a person and the person acting as the agent told him. If not, then a person can be coerced to do what he would have done anyway. Suppose a juryman has decided to vote for acquittal, and is then told his wife will be disfigured by acid if he does not vote for acquittal. He votes for acquittal. It seems odd to say he was coerced to vote that way. One would not hold the man less responsible for his decision since he would have so voted anyway. Of course the agent is not necessarily less blameworthy if one says he did not coerce the juryman but only attempted to do so. Hence, a further requirement for a person to be coerced is that he would have chosen differently had he not been threatened. This requirement stipulates the sense in which a victim of dispositional coercion does not act voluntarily and so provides grounds for his being excused. It is not, however, a sufficient condition for the removal or diminishing of responsibility. As noted above, coercion does not excuse or diminish legal responsibility for murder.

The second major feature of the ordinary concept of coercion is that it designates an interpersonal relation requiring a complex intention by the agent. Coercion is an interpersonal relation in which one person affects the behavior of another. This characteristic distinguishes coercion from force, "making," compulsion, constraint, and restraint. Physical conditions may force, compel, or make a person act in a manner in which he would not have chosen without the conditions, but they cannot coerce him. A storm forces, compels, or makes a captain return his ship to port, but it does not, properly speaking, coerce him into returning to port. Similarly, chains may constrain a man to stay where he is or restrain him from running away, but they do not coerce him to remain. A person who puts a man in chains, but not the chains, exercises occurrent coercion.

Coercion is an achievement word and suggests the involvement of intention on the part of an agent. Since coercion denotes success, an agent must be successful at doing something. He must be intending to do something if he is to succeed at it in a nonironic sense. Ironically, of course, a man may try to settle a dispute but only succeed in making it worse. On the other hand, Christian Bay maintains that coercion can occur without being intended by an agent, and cites overprotective mothers as instances.[4] Unfortunately, mere reference to overprotective mothers is not very convicing.

Various intentions which an agent might have must be distinguished. Bay might mean that an overprotective mother does not intend that her child act in a specific manner. Such a contention does not seem plausible, for an overprotective mother wants her child to act so as to avoid what she conceives to be possible harms. Bay might mean that she does not intend to inflict a deprivation on the child if he does not act as desired. This contention seems more plausible, for a mother may love her child too much to inflict a deprivation for disobedience. However, if the child does not act as she intends and she does not inflict the threatened deprivation, her ability to coerce may soon dissipate. Finally, Bay most likely means that such a mother does not have "coercing her child" as a conscious object of her intention. But an intention to coerce is an intention to get another person to act in a certain manner by use of threats or force. That a person engaging in such conduct does not think of it as coercion does not prevent it from being coercion or from being done intentionally. Usually a mother is aware to some degree that she is coercing her child. Some evidence for this belief is her preparedness to defend her actions as being done for the child's own good.

The type of intention common to all instances of coercion is that of the first sort above: an agent intends that a victim act (or not act) in a certain way. The notion of intention involved here is roughly interchangeable with desire. At least, an agent also desires

---

[4] Bay, 93.

that his victim act in a certain way, and he seeks to bring about that behavior as a result of his own action. Only this first type of intention relates to the success or achievement involved in coercion. An agent who carries out an intention to inflict a deprivation because a person did not act as desired has already failed to coerce. More significantly, the reason an agent inflicts a deprivation is that his first intention, that the person behave in a specific manner, was not achieved. And the absence of the third sort of intention or awareness that one is attempting to coerce does not indicate lack of success in coercing.

Dispositional coercion involves an agent's having a further intention to impose a sanction if the intended (desired) conduct does not occur. Three types of situations can make clear that this further intention is necessary for dispositional coercion, though only the intention that a victim act in a certain way is necessary for occurrent coercion. (1) As Y prepares to leave a party X tells him, "You should take a cab rather than walk home across the park because you would probably be mugged." Here X intends that Y behave in a certain way because he foresees harm to Y if Y does not so behave. In this sense of intend equivalent to foresee and sometimes used in law, X does intend harm to Y. But this sense of intend is not the ordinary one. Here X is not trying to coerce Y, rather he is giving advice. The sense in which X must intend the harm to Y in coercion is that he foresee and desire it as a result of his own conduct.

(2) X says to Y in an alley, "I'm going to beat the hell out of you!" In this case X intends (in the proper sense) harm to Y, but he does not intend that Y act in a specific way. There is no conduct which he wants Y to perform. He is simply threatening Y. Not all threats involve coercion; nor does all coercion involve threats, that is, occurrent coercion.

(3) X says to Y in a bank, "If you don't open the safe I'll break your arm." In this case both intentions are present. X intends that Y perform a specific action. He further intends to impose a sanction on Y if he does not so act. In this case X is coercing Y. Dispositional coercion is thus distinguished from mere threats by an agent's intent that a victim act in a specific manner. It is distinguished from advice in that an agent intends to impose a sanction on the victim if he does not act as the agent desires.

The third main point about dispositional coercion concerns the nature of sanctions to be imposed for noncompliance. Can sanctions only be deprivations and harms, or can rewards and benefits also be used? Several recent theorists such as Bay, following Lasswell and Kaplan, define sanctions in terms of both harms and benefits.[5] Thus, in their view dispositional coercion may involve either a promise of a benefit or a threat of a harm for compliance or noncompliance with a coercer's intention.

In such coercion three reasons may be given for restricting sanctions to harms. First, to consider benefits as sanctions obscures the distinction between coercion and bribery. If a female student promises her male instructor sexual indulgence for a grade higher than she deserves in a course, the instructor can hardly defend his conduct if he succumbs to temptation by claiming he was coerced. He was bribed but not coerced. His responsibility or blame is not diminished as it would probably be were he coerced. Bay suggests that whether one calls a sanction a reward or punishment depends on "which side of the coin is looked at."[6] While it does make sense to say that the instructor would be deprived of sexual pleasure by giving a lower grade, it would be odd to view this deprivation as his punishment or a harm. Further, one cannot say that the penal system rewards those who do not commit crime by not fining or imprisoning them.

Second, the relation between the conduct an agent intends and punishment or harm differs from the relation between such conduct and rewards or benefits. Rewards are given for compliance with an agent's wishes; punishments and harms are given for noncompliance. This difference is obscured or neglected if coercive sanctions include both rewards and punishments. And this difference is the logic underlying the previous distinction between coercion and bribery.

Third, there is a linguistic objection to including rewards as coercive sanctions. If one person attempts to coerce another, he is usually said to threaten him with a sanction. It is somewhat odd to speak of promising sanctions. One may promise to harm another, but properly speaking one cannot threaten to reward someone. To

[5] Bay, 98, 89; Harold D. Lasswell and Abraham Kaplan, *Power and Society* (New Haven: Yale University Press, 1950), 97.
[6] Bay, 89.

speak of promising harms or threatening benefits is usually ironic. "If you do that I'll leave." "Is that a threat or a promise?" Or, "If you do it I'll give you a kiss." "Is that a promise or a threat?" In short, coercion involves threats and threats refer to harms, not benefits.

Two final clarifications should be made of the point that dispositional coercion requires an agent to intend harm to a victim for noncompliance. First, loss of legitimately expected benefits may be a harm. Suppose an employee has been promised a pay raise, but then is told by his employer that he will not receive it unless he stops working for a political candidate. At first such a situation would appear to be an instance of dispositional coercion by use of a reward. But the loss of the legitimately expected benefit constitutes a harm. Suppose business had been bad and the employer was forced to withhold pay raises in order to keep operating. Surely an employee would be correct to say that bad business had hurt or harmed him because he had not received his expected pay raise. The denial of legitimate expectations is a form of harm arising in special circumstances. If an employee has no legitimate expectation of a pay raise and is promised one if he stops his political activity, then the offer may be considered a bribe rather than an attempt to coerce him.

Second, harm may be imposed by omission as well as by action. This form of imposing harm is a special case of failure to provide a legitimately expected benefit. Suppose a person refuses to help another in difficulty unless the latter does something for him in return. One may want to say that the former coerces the man in difficulty into acting as he does. In such cases one must distinguish coercion from making a good bargain. Usually the first man's difficulties must be great before one may speak of coercion. For example, failure to rescue a drowning man or give food to a starving one unless he steals would be coercion. Since a drowning or starving man could legitimately expect to be helped, these cases are instances of failure to fulfill legitimate expectations. Hence, legitimate expectations turn into harms failure to provide benefits and so turn good bargains into coercive acts.

To summarize, there are at least two types of coercion: occurrent and dispositional. Occurrent coercion involves the direct application of physical force to get a person to behave in a specific manner. For the more interesting and frequent dispositional coercion, if X coerces Y to do A the following conditions must obtain: (1) Person X intends that Y do A. (2) X further intends to harm Y if he does not do A. (3) X threatens Y with harm if Y does not do A. (4) Y does do A. (5) Y would have acted otherwise had he so chosen. (6) Y would have chosen otherwise had he not been threatened. Condition (1) distinguishes coercion from force, restraint, etc., and mere threats. Condition (2) distinguishes it from bribery, warnings, advice, and some other forms of exercising power over another. Conditions (4) and (6) establish the success of the threat as well as the sense in which Y's conduct is involuntary and less blameworthy. Condition (5) establishes Y's behavior as voluntary in one sense and thus an action. Condition (3) has not been mentioned previously, but is obvious. It transfers X's conduct from the realm of mere intention to that of overt action.

COERCION, FREEDOM, AND POWER

The concept of coercion has interesting relations to the concepts of freedom and power. Freedom, of course, traditionally has many senses and meanings. The best analysis of freedom to date is by Gerald C. MacCallum, Jr., and his analysis is essentially followed here.[7] He reconciles the disputed notions of positive and negative freedom by analyzing freedom as a three term relation. Person X is free from R to do A. If he is not free from R to do A, then R is a restraint. For X to have freedom of speech under the first amendment to the U.S. Constitution is for X to be free from Congressional laws (restraints) to speak. The names of some freedoms emphasize what a person can do, as in freedom of speech. Others emphasize what a person is free from, as in Roosevelt's freedoms from want and fear. But freedom always involves being free from something to do something.

As a corollary, a person's power with respect to his actions can be defined. A person has complete power with respect to an action, that is, he has the power to do A, if he is free from every R to do A. For a person to have the power to take a trip to Hawaii he has

[7] "Negative and Positive Freedom," *Philosophical Review,* 76 (July 1967), 312-34.

to be free from lack of funds, jail, work, etc., in order to go. There can be degrees to a man's power to perform an action. A person has less power to perform an action the more restraints there are to his performing it.

A complication must now be introduced. Some restraints upon a person's freedom and power are absolute; like chains, they absolutely prevent his performing an action. Other restraints are not absolute. Whether or not a person is free from a factor (restraint) may depend upon its importance to him. Suppose X and Y have ample funds to go to Hawaii, but have no vacation time coming and would lose their jobs if they did so. Further suppose that X likes his job very much and could not easily get another, while Y hates his work and could easily get another. X is less free from his work to go than Y. Thus individual restraints can have degrees, can restrain more or less. Hence, degrees of power and freedom depend not only upon how many restraints there are to a person's acting, but also upon how much they limit his performance of an action. Many restraints do not physically prevent a person from performing an action but do hinder his decision to perform it. Most restraints which limit by degrees are of this kind. But physical restraints can also have degrees; mud may restrain a man from running fast.

It can easily be seen how coercion deprives a victim of freedom. In occurrent coercion a person is not free from physical restraint to do as he desires. In dispositional coercion a person is not free from a threat of harm to choose (not) to do A. Hence, a victim of coercion is not free from a restraint to do A. If freedom is valued for its own sake, then coercion is inherently bad as limiting a person's freedom. Of course, one may not value freedom for its own sake. And coercion might produce goods of greater value than the freedom in question.

The analysis of power given so far has been that of power over one's own actions, but now an analysis must be given of the exercise of power over other persons and their actions. The concept of exercising power over another seems to have a broad and a narrow sense. The broad sense approximates the notion of affecting the behavior of another. X exercises power over Y (broad sense) if X's doing B leads Y (not) to do A. Based on this analysis, X's exercise of power over Y implies that Y would have behaved otherwise had X not acted as he did. Hence, except for instances of one per-

son physically moving another, power requires (1) that Y would
have chosen to act otherwise had X acted otherwise, and (2) that
Y would have acted otherwise had he so chosen. In the narrow and
more common sense of exercising power over another, besides the
requirements for the broad sense, X intends that Y do A. This
sense may be called controlling another.

The differences between the narrow and broad senses of exercising power can be seen in a practical example. Suppose the owner of
an appliance store, X, reduces the price of a television set fifty dollars. He may not intend that his rival, Y, also lower his price; in
fact, he may hope Y does not do so. If Y does lower the sale price
for the same model of set, then X will have exercised power over
Y in the broad but not the narrow sense. If Y does not lower his
price and Y's customers go to X to buy television sets, then (assuming he intended to attract Y's customers) X will have exercised power over them in the narrow sense. But he will not have exercised power over Y at all.

Coercion is thus a form of the exercise of power over another
(broad and narrow sense). The distinguishing characteristics of
coercion as the exercise of power over another indicate how other
forms might be distinguished. (1) X can exercise power over Y
without threatening a harm, but such a threat is necessary for coercion. Bribery is an instance of the exercise of power over another
wherein X does not threaten harm to Y but promises him a benefit. (2) X need not further intend to either confer a benefit or impose harm upon Y in order to exercise power over him. X may exercise power or influence over Y by warning him of a danger, or by
persuading Y of the immorality of his proposed action. Perhaps the
chief difference in the forms of exercising power over others is between those in which X further intends to something for or to Y
and those in which he does not. All the latter sorts of control or exercise of power appear to be forms of persuasion. While some of
the former sorts may be persuasion, many are not.

A final complication must now be added to the analysis of one
person's power over another. So far the discussion has been about
X's *exercising* of power over Y. But one is frequently interested in
whether or not X *has* power over Y. As a first step one might say
X has power over Y if and only if (1) X has the power to do B,
and (2) if X does B then Y will do A (which may be to omit an

action). Such an analysis is acceptable as long as one is only concerned with X having power over Y with respect to a particular action. But if one is concerned with X's having power over Y with respect to a class of actions or Y's actions in general, this analysis will not suffice. For X may have power over Y, but in a particular case in which X does B it may happen that Y does not do A. For a general analysis of power over another person dispositions probably need to be considered. Hence, X has power over Y with respect to actions of type A if X has the power to do actions of type B, and if he does so act Y is more disposed to do an action of type A. Again, of course, narrow and broad senses may be distinguished depending upon whether X is or is not required to intend that Y do A.

Some important aspects of freedom, power, and coercion can perhaps be illuminated by their application to a point in political philosophy. Social contract theory frequently has been rejected on the ground that a man is not free to leave, or is coerced to remain in, a country. For example, Robert Paul Wolff has written, "When a man has no real choice but to live in the country of his birth, the demand that he swear loyalty to it has the quality of a coerced promise which is morally worthless."[8] Wolff's point here applies strictly to requiring loyalty oaths, for he admits that a state may have the right to require such a man to obey laws. But he does claim that the point shows social contract theory to be inapplicable to contemporary society.

To say that a man "has no real choice" but to remain in a country apparently implies he is not free to leave. Wolff does not say from what a man is not free; presumably he has in mind the usual sorts of nonlegal restraints such as lack of funds, language difficulties, relatives, etc. Hence, such a man does not have the power to leave the country. However, it does not follow that anyone exercises power over him to prevent his leaving. One may not be able to point to any other person or group of persons and truly assert that if X did not do B, Y would leave the country. The legislature is not exercising power over him (at least in the narrow sense) by bringing about those conditions which keep him in the country. It would be exercising power over him if it made it illegal to leave. But Wolff does not seem to be thinking of that sort of case.

---

[8] *The Poverty of Liberalism* (Boston, Mass.: Beacon Press, 1968), 83.

Presumably the point is not that the man is coerced to remain in the country but that he is coerced to promise (swear) loyalty. However, the conditions of a double intention on the part of an agent are not clearly met. First, someone must intend that the man promise loyalty. Even waiving difficulties about ascribing intentions to legislatures, the legislature may not care whether or not the man promises loyalty.[9] It may simply make the promise a condition for engaging in some activity and be indifferent as to whether or not anyone engages in it. Indeed, the requirement could be used to discourage people from engaging in some activity. If the legislature does intend that he promise loyalty and he does, then the it exercises power over him in the narrow sense. If it does not so intend and he promises, it exercises power over him only in the broad sense.

Second, to be coerced the man must also be threatened with harm for not promising loyalty. Having to remain in the country is not a harm threatened for not promising loyalty, for it is already a condition the man faces. Nor can it be said that his promise is coerced because the promisee made it difficult for him to leave the country. No one exercises power over him to make him remain. In either case, his inability to leave the country does not make his promise coerced; it only makes the conditions under which he must decide more difficult. But promises made in hard situations are not morally worthless.

To summarize, to be free is to be free from R to do A. If a person is not free from R to do A, then R is a restraint. A person has power to do A if he is free from every R to do A. If, in the broad sense, X exercises power over Y with respect to action A, then Y would not have done A had X not done B. X has the power to do B, and Y is restrained from doing something other than A by X's doing of B. For X to exercise power over Y in the narrow sense it must also be true that X intends that Y do A. Coercion is one form of the exercise of power over another. It is distinguished from other forms by X's further intention of harm to Y if Y does not act as X intends. In other forms of the exercise of power over another

⁹ See Gerald C. MacCallum, Jr., "Legislative Intent," *Essays in Legal Philosophy,* ed. Robert S. Summers (Berkeley, Calif.: University of California Press, 1968), 237-73.

X either has no further intention or intends a benefit for Y if Y does as X desires. Coercion is the most morally offensive form of the exercise of power over others because the agent intends to affect the victim's behavior and uses or is willing to use physical force or harm to do so. Thus, victims of coercion are readily excused.

3

COERCION AND FREEDOM

Bernard Gert

Does coercion necessarily limit freedom? The natural inclination is to reply "Yes, of course," and to support this by stating a definition of coercion: viz., getting someone to do something by threatening him with some evil. But this reply is inadequate for it is not clear why threatening someone with evil limits his freedom. Consider what I shall call enticement:[1] viz., getting someone to do something by promising him some good. Does enticement necessarily limit freedom? If we say "Yes," then we are committed to the view that it is *prima facie* immoral to get someone to do anything by promising him some good. We are committed to this because it is *prima facie* immoral to limit anyone's freedom, that is, there is a

This paper was written while on a Fellowship from the National Endowment for the Humanities.

[1] Enticement normally suggests getting someone to do something immoral. I do not use it with this suggestion.

moral rule that prohibits depriving anyone of freedom.[2] If we say that enticement does not limit freedom, we must explain why threats of evil limit freedom but promises of good do not.[3] (Interestingly, no one takes the view that enticement limits freedom, but that coercion does not.)

The previous paragraph makes clear that we do not yet have an adequate account of freedom, or of what it is to limit or deprive of freedom. Before we can adequately answer the questions raised in the first paragraph of this paper, we must provide such an account. It will also be necessary to provide an account of coercion and enticement. Most of this paper will be devoted to providing an account of freedom, coercion, enticement, and related concepts.

TWO SENSES OF COERCION

In discussing coercion and freedom I shall make use of some concepts developed in the paper "Voluntary Abilities."[4] The most important of these concepts for present purposes are the concepts of reasonable and unreasonable incentives. Reasonable incentives are needed in order to define "the ability to will." Briefly, a man has the ability to will to do a kind of action if and only if there are reasonable incentives that would lead him to do that kind of action and reasonable incentives that would lead him not to do it.[5] Someone suffering from extreme claustrophobia does not have the ability to will to go into a small enclosed space, for there are no

[2] See Bernard Gert, *The Moral Rules* (New York: Harper & Row, 1970), Chapter 5.

[3] See J. P. Plamenatz, *Consent, Freedom, and Political Obligation* (London: Oxford University Press, 1938), Chapter 5. See also Thomas Reid, *Essays on the Active Powers of the Human Mind* Essay IV, Chapter VI.

[4] By Timothy Duggan and Bernard Gert, *American Philosophical Quarterly*, IV (April, 1967), 127-135, reprinted in *The Nature of Human Action*, edited by Myles Brand, 204-216. The present paper slightly revises some of the definitions provided in the earlier paper, but there are no substantial changes.

[5] More exactly: A has the ability to will to do x (a kind of action) if and only if it is possible to describe (or otherwise indicate) a state of affairs to A such that he would believe that there were reasonable incentives for doing x, and believing this would, at least sometimes, will to do x; and it is possible to describe (or otherwise indicate) a state of affairs to A such that he would believe that there were reasonable incentives for not doing x and believing this would, at least sometimes, will not to do x.

reasonable incentives that would lead him to do that kind of action. This is quite straightforward. However, it sounds somewhat para-doxical to say that such a man also does not have the ability to will *not* to go into a small enclosed space. But though paradoxical sounding, it is still correct; for if one does not have the ability to will to do x, it follows that one does not have the ability to will not to do x either. Thus the fact that one wills to do something does not show that he has the ability to will to do it. This comes out most clearly in the case of compulsive or obsessive acts. A compulsive hand-washer does not have the ability to will to wash his hands, for there are no reasonable incentives that would lead him to will *not* to wash them. Thus though he washes his hands intentionally he does not do so voluntarily for he does not have the ability to will to do what he does. An intentional action is voluntary if and only if the person has the ability to will to do what he does. It is sometimes said that a person who lacks a certain ability to will lacks a certain freedom. However, I prefer to keep distinct the concepts of "the ability to will" and "freedom."

In my view, only someone with the ability to will can act freely or can act under coercion, that is, only voluntary actions are done freely or under coercion. Unreasonable incentives are needed in order to define both of these concepts. A man acts freely if and only if he acts voluntarily and does not do so because of any unrea-sonable incentives. A man who acts voluntarily, but only because of some unreasonable incentives, does not act freely. If the unreasona-ble incentives were the result of a threat of evil by someone, then he acted under coercion. If the unreasonable incentives were the result of a promise of good by someone, then he acted under enticement.

The accounts of coercion and enticement given immediately above are not equivalent to the definitions offered in the first para-graph of this paper. The difference is easy to overlook, but it is im-portant not to do so. In the initial account, coercion was the result of a threat of evil; on the latest account it is the result of a threat of an evil which provides an unreasonable incentive. Everything that is coercion in the initial definition is coercion in the later account, but the reverse is not true. Not every threat of evil provides an unrea-sonable incentive. The same seems to hold true for the two ac-counts of enticement. Thus I will talk of the wide and narrow sen-ses of coercion and enticement. Coercion in the narrow sense is the result of a threat of evil that provides an unreasonable incentive, in the wise sense it is the result of any threat of evil. The wide and narrow senses of enticement should be understood in a similar way.

GOOD, EVIL, REASONS, MOTIVES AND INCENTIVES

A good is that which no rational man will avoid for himself unless he has a reason. An evil is that which all rational men will avoid for themselves unless they have a reason. Note that rational men need no reasons for not seeking goods, they need reasons only for avoiding goods or not avoiding evils. Reasons for acting are beliefs that can make rational avoiding a good or not avoiding an evil. All beliefs that count as reasons for acting are or involve beliefs that one's action will result in someone avoiding an evil or gaining a good. What gives content to these formal definitions is a list of those things which are good and evil. The goods are abilities, freedom or opportunity, and pleasure. The evils are death, pain, disability, loss of freedom or opportunity, and loss of pleasure. Anything else that is a good or an evil is so because it involves one of these goods or evils.

A motive is a belief which at the time of deliberating or acting the agent regards as, and which is, part of an acceptable explanation for his action. Someone's motive is revenge if he regards his belief that the victim of his revenge harmed him or someone close to him, as part of an acceptable explanation of his action and we also accept it. This kind of motive involves a belief that is not a reason, for it has nothing to do with anyone avoiding an evil or gaining a good as the result of one's action. When the belief that serves as a motive for doing x is a reason, then I say that one believes there is an incentive for doing x. To believe there is an incentive for doing x is to believe that the consequences of doing x will be that someone avoids an evil or gains a good, and to correctly regard such consequences as being part of an acceptable explanation for one's doing x.

Incentives are those consequences of an action which, if known, provide both a motive and a reason for doing it. Consequences that provide only motives but not reasons, or only reasons but not motives, I do not call incentives. Thus the fact that someone will suffer because of an action, though it can provide a motive for doing it, cannot be an incentive because it does not provide a reason. Also, whether consequences that do provide a reason for doing x are incentives or not sometimes depends upon who is doing x. What is an incentive for one man is not always an incentive for another. For though consequences provide reasons independently of anyone's attitude toward them, whether they provide a motive depends upon the agent's attitude toward them. If he does not regard the consequences as a part of an acceptable explanation for his doing x, then they do not provide a motive for him and so they are not incentives for him.[6]

UNREASONABLE INCENTIVES

An incentive is unreasonable if it would be unreasonable to expect any rational man in that situation not to act on it.[7] A reasonable incentive is an incentive that is not unreasonable. It would be unreasonable to expect any rational man not to act on certain consequences only if those consequences always provide motives for all rational men. If consequences are such that they provide motives only generally, but not always, to all rational men, then they cannot be unreasonable incentives for it would not be unreasonable to expect some rational man not to act because of them. Consequences which involve the gaining of a good only generally, but not always, provide motives to rational men. Therefore, consequences which only involve the gaining of a good cannot be unreasonable incentives. Consequences which involve the avoiding of an evil always provide motives to all rational men, for all rational men must seek to avoid any evil—unless they have a reason. This means that the belief that they will avoid an evil always serves as a motive for all rational men. Of course, not all consequences that involve the avoiding of an evil will be unreasonable incentives. The evils must be significant; usually only death, severe and prolonged pain, serious disability, and extensive loss of freedom will be unreasonable

---

[6] For a fuller account of good, evil, reasons and motives, see Chapters 2 and 3 of *The Moral Rules.*

[7] This definition of an unreasonable incentive is close to what Stanley I. Benn calls an irresistible temptation. He says, "A temptation is said to be irresistible only if a man *could not reasonably be expected* to resist it, even though others might actually have resisted it in the past." "Persuasion and Freedom," *Australasian Journal of Philosophy,* 45 (December, 1967), 267.

incentives. Only serious evils such as these provide motives that make it unreasonable to expect any rational man not to act on.

That unreasonable incentives must involve the avoiding of an evil and not merely the gaining of a good is a somewhat surprising conclusion, and thus needs more discussion. It may seem that this conclusion makes my use of the phrase "unreasonable incentive" so far removed from any ordinary sense that my entire discussion of coercion and freedom, which depends so heavily on the concept of an unreasonable incentive, is undermined. I shall show that this is not the case, that I have simply made explicit the concept of "unreasonable incentive" that has been used in most discussions of coercion and freedom dating from Aristotle. Aristotle recognized that when a man was faced with the possibility of death, he would do things that he would not otherwise have done. Actions done in these circumstances Aristotle called non-voluntary. I prefer to call such actions unfree. This difference in terminology is not important for the present discussion. For both Aristotle and I agree that a person may sometimes be in a situation such that it would be unreasonable to expect any rational man not to act so as to avoid certain consequences, for instance, in a storm a ship captain will always throw his cargo overboard if he believes it necessary in order to keep his ship from sinking. Both Aristotle and I agree that this kind of situation, in some sense, forces the person to act in a certain way, that he does not act freely (though I say that he acts voluntarily).[8] I do not think it accidental that Aristotle and all others who have discussed this issue always use examples of someone being forced to act in order to avoid some evil; they never use examples of someone being forced to act in order to gain some good.

This may seem simply another example of philosophical bias, of concentration on only one kind of example; but I do not think so. Consider a sea captain who comes upon a vessel which has been abandoned in a storm and which he knows to have an extremely valuable cargo. It is supposedly an acknowledged law of the sea that anyone who tows in an unmanned vessel can claim it and all cargo aboard. Suppose that this cargo has a value many many times

[8] Hobbes explicitly disagrees with this view. See *Leviathan*, Chapter 21, paragraph 3. However, Hobbes seems to have a different sense of freedom in mind; he calls it the "liberty of subjects," and it is closely related to what I call legally or morally free. See footnote 12 of this chapter.

larger than the cargo he is carrying, and that in order to tow this ship in it would be necessary to throw his cargo overboard. If the captain does this, is it correct that he is forced to do it? I think we would agree that to say this is incorrect. The mere gaining of a good, no matter how great, does not force one to do anything. What complicates the matter is that the gaining of a good is sometimes necessary for avoiding an evil. Thus we may say that a person was forced to accept a higher paying job if we believe that he needs the extra money in order to pay for an expensive operation for his wife or children. But when the gaining of a good, for example, more money, does not involve avoiding any evil, then it is incorrect to say that the person was forced to take the higher paying job, that he was not free to refuse.

I grant that the distinction between gaining a good and avoiding an evil is not perfectly precise. However, if we consider that a person was forced to do something, that the consequences facing him constituted an unreasonable incentive, then we invariably describe those consequences in such a way that they involve avoiding an evil. This does not mean I deny that there are situations involving the gaining of a good where that good is so great that we expect *most* rational men to act so as to gain it. But an unreasonable incentive is not merely one that it would be unreasonable to expect *most* rational men not to act on, it is an incentive that it would be unreasonable to expect *any* rational man not to act on. As there is no good which all rational men must seek, no matter how great the good it will never provide an unreasonable incentive.

We can now attempt to answer the questions that were raised in the first paragraph of this paper: "Does coercion necessarily limit freedom?" and "Does enticement necessarily limit freedom?" The latter question is easy to answer; not only does enticement not necessarily limit freedom, it does not limit freedom at all, for promises of good can never be unreasonable incentives. This means that there is no enticement in the narrow sense. I do not deny that there may be some promises of good so great that many, perhaps most, men would act so as to gain the good. Further, I do not deny that a person may sometimes seek to have a lesser punishment for his criminal act by claiming that he was enticed. But a person may also seek a lesser punishment by claiming that he was provoked. Although enticement, like provocation, may occasionally be a mitigating factor, this does nothing to show that it limits freedom at all. There are reasons for lessening punishment other than lack of freedom to do otherwise.

The relationship between coercion and freedom is more complex. If we understand coercion in the wide sense, simply as getting someone to do something by threatening him with an evil, then coercion does not necessarily limit freedom. Only when the evil is great enough to be an unreasonable incentive, that is, when it is coercion in the narrow sense, does it necessarily limit freedom. We can state our conclusions in the following paradoxical sounding way. Only in their narrow senses do coercion and enticement limit freedom, but there is no enticement in the narrow sense so that it is only coercion that sometimes limits freedom. Since my concern in this paper is with the relationship between coercion and freedom, unless I say otherwise, when I talk about coercion in the rest of this paper, I shall mean coercion in the narrow sense.

BEING FREE TO ACT VERSUS ACTING FREELY

There is a sense of freedom in which a person is free to do x if and only if he has the voluntary ability to do x, a reasonable opportunity to do it,[9] and there are no unreasonable incentives influencing his will either to do or not to do it. But this sense of freedom, though important in philosophical discussions of the problem of free will, collapses the distinction between liberty and power. Hobbes makes the contrast almost too clearly: "For whatsoever is so tied, or environed, as it cannot move but within a certain space, which space is determined by the opposition of some external body, we say that it hath not the liberty to go further. . . . But when the impediment of motion, is in the constitution of the thing itself, we use not to say; it wants the liberty; but the power to move; as when a stone lieth still, or a man is fastened to his bed by sickness."[10]

Since I want to keep the distinction between liberty and power, I shall not consider the voluntary ability to do x as necessary in order

[9] A has a reasonable opportunity to do x if and only if A is in a situation that a fully informed rational man would accept as one in which A's doing x, if he wills to do so, counts in favor of his having the ability to do x, and his not doing x, even though he wills to do so, counts against his having the ability to do x.

[10] *Leviathan*, Chapter 21, first paragraph.

to be free to do x. I shall say that a man is free to do x if and only if he has a reasonable opportunity to do x and there are no unreasonable incentives influencing his will either to do or not to do x. Thus I allow not only that a man may have the voluntary ability to do x but not be free to do it, but also that a man may be free to do x even though he does not have the voluntary ability to do it. However, freedom usually has value only to those who have the voluntary ability necessary to exercise that freedom. For present purposes I shall consider a voluntary ability to be composed of a physical ability and an ability to will. When we are concerned with physical abilities there is no difficulty in distinguishing between liberty and power. A man with no legs lacks the ability to dance, even though he may be free to do so. However, even this example shows the close relationship between freedom and ability, for it would be the sickest kind of humor to say to a person whom you know to be physically unable to dance, "You are free to dance."

It is not quite so easy to see that lack of the ability to will is also a lack of power and not a lack of liberty. It is common to talk of people who suffer from compulsions and phobias as not being free. Sometimes this is the result of using "free" in that sense which collapses the distinction between liberty and power. Other times, however, it is the result of regarding compulsions and phobias as a kind of coercion. It is easy to see how this happens. Coercion forces a person to act in a certain way by making him fearful of the consequences of not acting in that way. A compulsion or phobia also forces a person to act in a certain way because of fear. Since both coercion and phobias or compulsions force or prevent action through fear, it is most natural to group them together. But though fear is involved in both cases, the fear in coercion is a rational response to some real evil; the situation, not the person, is referred to in explaining the fear. The fear in phobias and compulsions is not a rational response to some real evil; the person, not the situation, is referred to in explaining the fear. The latter fear is the result of something about the person, the former is the result of the situation the person is in. Thus, only coercion is properly thought of as an external impediment and so only coercion limits freedom. To have a compulsion or a phobia is to lack an ability to will and not to be lacking in freedom.

We can now see that to force or prevent a person from acting, one need not deprive him of freedom; one can also disable him, either physically or by taking away his ability to will. When the latter is done by "brainwashing," that is, by causing him to have a compulsion or phobia, it may be impossible to distinguish clearly between disabling and depriving of freedom. But usually it is quite clear when we are disabling and when we are depriving of freedom. The two ways of depriving someone of freedom are (1) taking away all reasonable opportunity and (2) providing unreasonable incentives. The first is done most often by confining the person by some physical means, for example, chains or a cell. The second is usually done by means of threats. When we think a person is being deprived of his freedom in this latter way we say that he is being coerced, in the narrow sense.

To be deprived of freedom it is sufficient that one be threatened with unreasonable incentives. Whether one wants to do what one is being coerced to do is irrelevant to whether one's freedom is being taken away. Similarly, when one is put in jail one's freedom is being taken away regardless of whether or not one wants to stay in jail. Of course, if one wants to do what one is being coerced to do then one may not mind being coerced—just as if one wants to stay in jail one may not mind being put there. Loss of freedom often does not bother a person unless he wants to do what he is not free to do. That is why it is often difficult to get most people interested in defending the freedom of someone to do something contrary to social custom. Since most people have no desire to act contrary to social custom, they do not regard the loss of freedom to act in that way as important. Thus, most people do not object when their freedom is being curtailed by coercive laws because they have no desire to exercise that freedom. Only when they desire to exercise their freedom do they realize what they have lost. This explains, in part, both the necessity for organizations like the American Civil Liberties Union and the lack of universal support for such organizations.

A man does x freely if and only if he has the ability to will to do x, does it intentionally, and does not do it because of some unreasonable incentives. However, in the present discussion it would be useful if we considered both the ability to will to do x and doing x intentionally as presupposed before one can act either freely or not freely. This allows us to deny that a man who does x compulsively does x freely, but does not require us to call such an act unfree. Instead we can say that because his act was not voluntary, the question as to whether or not it was free does not even arise. Similarly, we can deny that a man who does x unintentionally does it freely, without saying that his act was unfree. Instead we can say that because his act was an accident, inadvertent, or a mistake, the question as to whether or not it was done freely does not arise. Only when a man does x because of some unreasonable incentives should we say straightforwardly that he did not act freely. If the unreasonable incentives were the result of threat by someone then he acted under coercion.

When a man is free to do x, (and the presuppositions discussed above are satisfied), then if he does x he acts freely. But a man can also act freely when he is not free to act, but is being coerced. This can be seen easily enough when he is being coerced to do x but does not do it, in spite of the coercing. Being coerced, though it deprives of freedom, does not necessarily prevent one from acting freely. However, it would be pointless to deprive people of freedom if no one were prevented from acting freely. The whole point of coercing is to affect conduct in a specific way; yet even when acting in that way one may be coerced and still act freely. This in fact is a quite common occurrence. People often obey various laws not because of the penalties attached to the laws, but simply because they do not want to act in the ways that the law prohibits. One of the most important functions of the law is to create a situation where people do not want to do what the law prohibits without even considering the penalties for violation. Thus coercive laws, though they deprive of freedom, often do not prevent people from acting freely and hence are not felt as any kind of burden.[11]

It is when laws fail to create this kind of situation that the deprivation of freedom is felt and resistance to the law becomes widespread. Laws enforcing the moral rules are generally not felt to be a burden, but laws enforcing social customs, especially when the customs are changing, are felt to be. Thus laws against marijuana, which

[11] Plamenatz neglects the distinction between being free to act and acting freely, as well as the one between being free to act and having the ability to will to act. His neglect of these distinctions explains, in part, why we arrive at different conclusions to a problem that we both state in the same way.

always deprived people of freedom, are only now being objected to because only now are they preventing many people from acting freely. Formerly very few wanted to violate these laws, now many do. Though we generally talk about freedom and claim to be against the deprivation of freedom, our primary concern is only with being prevented from acting freely. But as noted earlier, when we allow ourselves to be deprived of freedom we cannot help but increase the chances that we shall someday be prevented from acting freely. Thus no man of foresight will allow himself to be deprived of freedom without justification simply because it does not now prevent him from acting freely.[12]

EXCUSES AND COERCION

When a man acts freely then he is completely responsible for his actions. Nonetheless, even someone who is completely responsible for some crime may receive less than the standard punishment. This involves what are often called mitigating factors, for example, enticement and provocation; sometimes even being a first offender is a mitigating factor. Mitigating factors differ from excuses in that they allow for lesser punishments without lessening responsibility. To have an excuse is to be relieved of some responsibility for one's action. Thus, if one has some excuse for committing

[12] There is a sense of "freedom" in which being free to do x simply means that doing x is neither prohibited nor required but is permitted or allowed. When we talk of "being legally free to do x" we usually mean no more than that doing x is neither required nor prohibited by the law. Similarly, "being morally free to do x" means that doing x is morally permissible. I do not deny the importance of this sense of freedom, but I have not discussed it because it seems to me to have a very limited relationship to coercion. For example, many things that one is not legally free to do, one is also not free to do (in the sense I have defined) because the law imposes penalties that provide unreasonable incentives. There are many other senses of freedom, several of which are discussed by Felix E. Oppenheim, in *Dimensions of Freedom* (New York: St. Martin's Press, 1961), especially Chapters 6 and 7. I agree with much of what Oppenheim says, e.g., his account of acting freely is very close to mine. However, the sense of freedom which is central to his discussion, viz., "social freedom" (see Chapter 6) seems to me to be not very helpful as a basic category. I think Plamenatz correct in regarding freedom from constraint by others (which is close to "social freedom") to be a species of a wider sense (see pp. 122ff), though my definition of this wider sense is not the same as Plamenatz's.

a criminal act it is required, not merely allowed, that one receive less than the standard punishment. There is, of course, no sharp distinction between excuses and mitigating factors—coercion in the narrow sense is an excuse, otherwise it is a mitigating factor—but there are enough clear-out cases of each to make the distinction worthwhile. In what follows I shall be concerned primarily with coercion as an excuse.

When a person acts under coercion then he is not completely responsible for his action; he has an excuse. However, whether the threat of evil provides an unreasonable incentive, and so counts as coercive, depends upon the responsibility standards that are accepted.[13] Although one may be relieved of responsibility for good actions as well as bad ones, it is most important to determine responsibility for actions which deserve punishment. Thus all rational men will publicly advocate adopting those responsibility standards which combine maximum deterrence with minimum infliction of punishment. However, some may prefer greater deterrence even at the cost of greater infliction of punishment, others lesser infliction of punishment even at the risk of lesser deterrence. Further, stricter standards will generally be adopted for more serious crimes. This follows from the fact that rational men are more interested in preventing the greater harm that results from more serious crimes. Thus it may happen that the very same threat is regarded as coercive for one act and not coercive for another.

Though there are complicating factors, we usually allow that a man acted under coercion only if the harm he was threatened with was significantly greater than the harm he did under coercion. This means that coercion is not to be determined simply by looking at the seriousness of the threats, but that the act one does must also be taken into account. There should be nothing surprising about this. Unless we know what act he was supposed to perform, we cannot determine whether an incentive was such that it was unreasonable to expect any rational man not to act on it. A threat that provides an unreasonable incentive for telling a trivial lie will usually not provide an unreasonable incentive for killing a person. In determining whether one is in a coercive situation when being threatened

---

[13] For a fuller account of responsibility standards see Chapter 9 of *The Moral Rules*.

with some evil if one does not do x, the relevant factors are the amount of evil that will result from doing x, the amount of evil that will result from not doing x, and whether doing x involves violating a moral rule.

Suppose doing x consists of putting a pinball machine in your store. Suppose further that this is not illegal and does not violate any other moral rule. I would say that the threat of a severe beating would count as coercive. Suppose, however, that doing x involves a slot machine rather than a pinball machine, and that slot machines are illegal; suppose further that it is a crooked slot machine so people have very little chance to win. In this case I am not sure whether I would count a severe beating as coercive. Finally, suppose that you were to put the slot machine in someone else's store so that they would be arrested, imprisoned, and their business ruined. Here, I would say that a severe beating does not count as coercive. I do not claim that everyone must adopt the same responsibility standards that I have adopted in making my judgments on the previous examples. These examples were offered in order to show that what counts as coercive depends upon more than the nature of the threat involved.

With most excuses—for example, unavoidable lack of knowledge, lack of ability to will, or lack of the required physical or mental ability—the nature of the act committed is not relevant in deciding whether one had an excuse or not. In deciding whether one should be excused because of coercion, the nature of the act committed is important. However, coercion is not unique in this respect; whether lack of knowledge is accepted as an excuse also depends sometimes upon the nature of the act committed. For an act with serious harmful consequences we may hold that a person should have made a greater effort to find out the possible consequences than for an act with little or no serious harmful consequences. The nature and determination of excuses is a more complex matter than it is usually presented as being.

PRACTICAL REASONING

Coercion and enticement in the wide sense are not the only methods used to get someone to do something. There is also what is often called practical reasoning, persuasion, or pointing out the facts. This alternative method of getting someone to do something consists in pointing out the good and evil consequences of a given course of action which are not the result of an intentional action by the individual who points out those consequences. That is, in coercion and enticement the coercing or enticing party says that he will intentionally cause some evil or some good unless the person being coerced or enticed acts in a certain way. In practical reasoning, the reasoning party says that certain good or evils will result from the action of the person reasoned with, without any intentional action by the reasoning party.[14]

The distinction between coercion and enticement on the one side, and reasoning on the other, is not sharp. Suppose A points out to B that certain evils will result from B's doing x, when both A and B know that these evils could be avoided by A's intentional actions. It is not clear if A is reasoning with or coercing B. Sometimes it is clear that coercion is involved, for instance, when a kidnapper tells the parents of the kidnapped child that he will die if not rescued. It is a sick joke to say that the kidnapper is reasoning with the parents in order to get them to pay a ransom. There is absolutely no difference between this case and one in which the kidnapper threatens to kill the child if the ransom is not paid. Both are examples of coercion. A similar case is one in which the head of gang says that he is reasoning with a victim when he says that certain other parties will harm him unless the victim does what is wanted. All parties involved know that the gang leader can stop the harm from being done and that he will do so if the victim does what the gangster wants. Here again, this is a case of coercion and not reasoning. But the interesting point is that the travesty of reasoning provided by these examples shows that the formal distinction between reasoning and coercion is well understood. The gangster and kidnapper can claim to be reasoning because reasoning, unlike coercion or enticement, consists in pointing out the goods and evils that will result without an intentional action by the party doing the reasoning. The examples are travesties not only because the reasoning party has arranged the situation, but also because he is able by his intentional action to see that no evil is suffered.

[14] Assuming, of course that there are two parties involved. One can, however, engage in practical reasoning by oneself. For some reason, this is the kind of practical reasoning that most philosophers have concentrated on.

A clear case in which reasoning is distinguished from coercion is provided by various gangster movies. The leader of the gang is coercing the victim but is unable to move him. Then before he kills him, the gangster's girlfriend, who hates violence (but who is powerless to change the gangster's mind), pleads for a chance to reason with the victim. She then says exactly what the gangster himself said, only she is not coercing, but reasoning with the victim. She is simply pointing out what will happen to him if he doesn't do what is wanted of him, but it is made quite clear that none of this is what she herself would do to him and that indeed she is powerless to change it. Here is a clear case of what people mean when they talk about reasoning with coercion in the background. For the victim it matters little whether he is being reasoned with or coerced. The only thing that matters to him is that someone—and he does not care if it is the person he is talking to or a third party—is going to intentionally harm him if he does not act in the specified way.

Of course, reasoning does not always consist in pointing that some third party will intentionally do something if the second party does not do something. Sometimes there is reasoning which would not be coercion even if the speaker were different. Thus when we try to get a person to stop smoking we point out that he increases his chances of lung cancer, heart disease, etc. This might be called pure practical reasoning, for there is no coercive factor in the background. However, if we try to get someone to stop smoking marijuana, our reasoning may not be completely pure. We may first point out that marijuana sometimes leads to the taking of genuine habit forming drugs, that it is sometimes psychologically addictive, etc. All of this is pure practical reasoning. But the reasoning is not pure if we go on to say that there is a law against smoking marijuana, for then we are saying that certain penalties, say, twenty years in jail, may result from someone's intentional act. The reasoning is not pure because what is reasoning from us would be coercion if said by another, for example, a sheriff.

NEGOTIATION

In negotiating a treaty or a contract, the parties involved in the negotiation usually reason with, entice, or coerce (in the wide but not the narrow sense) each other. There is no coercion in the narrow sense because neither party is in a position effectively to threaten the other side with unreasonable incentives. This may be the result of both sides having the power to cause the other side such enormous evil that it would be pointless for either side to threaten to do so. This is the kind of situation in which the United States and the Soviet Union now find themselves. It is appropriately called a balance of terror, and the result is negotiation. For when coercion in the narrow sense is ruled out, only negotiation remains as a way to reach agreement.

Sometimes the negotiating parties do not have equivalent coercive power. Indeed, sometimes the stronger party has the power to coerce (in the narrow sense) the weaker one. In these situations negotiations are often only a cover for coercion, for example, Russia's negotiations with Czechoslovakia concerning the political liberalization of Czechoslovakia. But often, even when one party has the power to coerce the other in the narrow sense, it engages in genuine negotiation. Sometimes, though I imagine very seldom, this is done because the stronger party realizes that it would be morally wrong to use coercion. Most often it is due to third parties not formally involved in the negotiations. Thus a large company would be able to impose its will on a small union, or vice versa, except for the threat of government action or reprisals by other concerned unions or companies.

Negotiation generally takes place when each of the parties involved wants to reach an agreement and neither party is in a position to coerce (in a narrow sense) the other. Since both realize that an agreement cannot be reached unless the other party finds the agreement acceptable and knows that coercion in the narrow sense is ruled out, they realize that negotiation is the only alternative. Of course, both parties must prefer to have some agreement rather than no agreement; otherwise there will be no reason for one party to negotiate. Given these conditions negotiation will proceed with each party doing what it can to reason with, entice, or coerce the other party into accepting the agreement it wants. Naturally the stronger party, that which is able to entice or coerce more, will have the advantage. But there are other factors which are also important, for example, how important it is for each side to reach an agreement. Negotiation is a very complex process and its outcome will depend on many more factors than I have discussed. Nonetheless, analyzing it as a combination of practical reasoning, coercion, and enticement may be valuable in coming to understand it better.

COERCION, ENTICEMENT, AND PRACTICAL REASONING

In this final section I shall summarize and elaborate on what I have said about coercion, enticement, and practical reasoning by presenting brief accounts of each. However, I shall not distinguish between the wide and narrow senses of coercion as this already has been made clear enough.

I.   A is coercing B

(1) when he threatens to cause B or someone B cares for some evil unless B does or refrains from doing x.

(2) when he arranges a situation in which B or someone B cares for will suffer some evil unless A acts and threatens not to act unless B does or refrains from doing x.

(3) when he arranges a situation in which B or someone B cares for will suffer some evil unless B does or refrains from doing x.

(4) when he finds B in a situation in which B or someone B cares for will suffer some evil unless A acts and threatens not to act unless B does or refrains from doing x. (This last case is sometimes confused with enticement and there may be some borderline cases.)

B is being coerced by A if and only if A is coercing B.

B is acting under coercion if and only if B does or refrains from doing x because he is being coerced.

II.   A is enticing B

(1) when he promises to cause B or someone B has an interest in some good if B does or refrains from doing x.

(2) when he arranges a situation in which B or someone B has an interest in will gain some good if B does or refrains from doing x.

However, if A then goes on to threaten to prevent B from gaining that good unless B does or refrains from doing x, then A is also coercing B. Perhaps this situation is best regarded as a combination of coercion and enticement.

If A finds B in a situation in which B will gain some good unless A intentionally acts to prevent him and threatens to do so unless B does or refrains from doing x, A is coercing B. This is pure coercion, not a combination of enticement and coercion, for A is simply threatening to prevent B from gaining a good (which is equivalent to threatening to deprive B of some good) and this is identical to threatening him with some evil.

B is being enticed by A if and only if A is enticing B.

B is acting under enticement if and only if B does or refrains from doing some action because he is being enticed.

III. A is reasoning with B when A points out to B that he or someone else will suffer some evil or gain some good if B does or refrains from doing x; and A did not arrange this situation nor is he now in a position to affect whether B or the other person suffers the evil or gains the good.

A's reasoning is pure if he believes that there is no one other than B who is in a position to affect whether someone suffers the evil or gains the good.

A's reasoning has a coercive background if he believes that there is someone who in stating the same facts would be coercing B.

A's reasoning has an enticing background if he believes that there is someone who in stating the same facts would be enticing B.

A's reasoning has coercive elements if in addition to reasoning with B, A is also coercing B.

A's reasoning has enticing elements if in addition to reasoning with B, A is also enticing B.[15]

[15] I am grateful to my colleagues at Dartmouth College for their comments on an earlier version. I am also grateful to Professor Roland Pennock for his comments and for referring me to Benn and Plamenatz.

4

COERCION AND COERCIVE OFFERS

Virginia Held

POWER, FORCE, VIOLENCE, COERCION

Initially, we may distinguish coercion from such related concepts as power, force, and violence. One person may coerce another to do something, or he may use power, force, or violence to bring about a similar visible result. But the person who is being coerced to do something is not having the same experience and may perhaps not be performing the same action (if he is acting at all) as he is when power is being used to affect his action, or when force is being applied to determine his behavior, or when violence is being inflicted upon him.

Let us begin with power. We may say that power in this context is a capacity to cause someone to do something he would not otherwise do. What the person does or would do if power were employed may or may not be *against* his will. Power may be used simply to move him from a state of indifference or immobility to one of activity; power presupposes only the absence of a volition in accord with it. Power is exercised most frequently through the issuing of commands. Where commands are issued and obeyed without the use of force or coercion or violence, there may be little incentive to employ anything more than power. But when there is a will in opposition to that represented by the command, a test of strength is threatened and a temptation to use force arises.

There is no presumption that the term "power" refers to something physical; what form of power the term designates must be indicated, or remain vague. And power is usually a capacity as much as something used; we speak of a capacity to coerce but not of a capacity for power, because power is already that. Although power is not in all cases a dispositional term, we may perhaps take this meaning as primary.

Force does seem to presuppose a will in opposition to it. We may say, perhaps, that force is power to cause someone to do something against his will. It is usually power at the point of being used rather than held in reserve; in this it is closer to coercion or to violence than to power. Force may well employ nonphysical power, as when one person forces another to withdraw his candidacy or to vote for a measure of which he disapproves. But unless there is some indication suggesting otherwise, there may be a presumption that force is physical power, although more easily than in the case of violence the indication that it is not may be contextual rather than explicit.

Violence is the infliction of injury upon or damage harming a person. It has as its objective more than that of causing someone to do something, or of overpowering his will. The objective at least in part is to inflict injury or hurt. The injury may in turn cause the person suffering from it to do something; but if the resulting action takes place without injury, violence has not occurred, although coercion may well have.

Coercion is close to force, but it seems to be the activity term of which force is the dispositional term. Coercion can be effected through an exercise of power, of force, or of violence. The means used may be physical or nonphysical, but for coercion to occur the person coerced must in some sense be doing what he is doing against his will. He may be coerced by a threat, by being physically forced to do something, and perhaps in other ways.

Coercion is the activity of causing someone to do something

against his will, or of bringing about his doing what he does against his will. From what has been said before it follows that power may be used in noncoercive as well as coercive ways, but force can only be used coercively. However, force may be used coercively without coercion resulting from it if the person being forced to do something has sufficient power of his own to repel or overpower the force being exerted against him. A person has been coerced only if he has done something against his will. One person may attempt to coerce another and fail, but the failure does not mean he has failed to use force; it means, rather, that the force was insufficient.

Coercion may but need not involve a threat or a use of violence or injury—for example, one person may coerce another into remaining in a room by locking the only door, or coercion may have been used to transport a person from one location to another although no injury was inflicted or even threatened. If a person's will has been broken, so that it can no longer oppose a given directive, coercion is no longer necessary, although a given constraint may remain coercive in the sense that if the person willed to escape it, he would be prevented. But the outcome of a use of power or force or violence may be something beyond coercion: the person may be killed; his ability to will may be temporarily impaired, curtailed in some respect, or permanently destroyed.

Usually, one person coerces another for the purpose of causing him to do or not do something. Force is used to overcome a resisting will; if the force is sufficient, coercion occurs. But sometimes coercion is employed for the sake of the pleasure its use may provide to the person using it: de Jouvenel, for instance, writes that "a man feels himself more of a man when he is imposing himself and making others the instruments of his will"; this causes him "incomparable pleasure."[1]

ACTION, THREATS, OFFERS

What else can be said to delineate instances of coercion from surrounding activities? Recommendations for deciding what is and what is not an instance of coercion range from the terse

---

[1] Bertrand de Jouvenel, *On Power. Its Nature and the History of its Growth* (New York: Viking Press, 1949), 121.

formula of Harold Lasswell and Abraham Kaplan—"coercion is a high degree of constraint and/or inducement"[2]—to the multiplication of statements compounded by Robert Nozick in an examination of what he takes to be some of the necessary conditions contained in the "core" of the notion:

Person P coerces person Q into not doing act A if and only if . . .

(1) P threatens to bring about or have brought about some consequence if Q does A (and knows he's threatening to do this).

(2) A with this threatened consequence is rendered substantially less eligible as a course of conduct for Q than A was without this threatened consequence.

(3) (Part of) P's reason for deciding to bring about the consequence or have it brought about, if Q does A, is that P believes this consequence worsens Q's alternative of doing A (i.e. that P believes that this consequence worsens Q's alternative of doing A, or that Q would believe it does).

(4) Q does not do A.

(5) Part of Q's reason for not doing A is to avoid (or lessen the likelihood of) the consequence which P has threatened to bring about or have brought about.

(6) Q knows that P has threatened to do the something mentioned in (1), if he, Q, does A.

(7) Q believes that, and P believes that Q believes that, P's threatened consequence would leave Q worse off, having done A, than if Q didn't do A and P didn't bring about the consequence.[3]

Intermediate to these suggestions are those of Bernard Gert, who holds that "only voluntary actions are done freely or under coercion. . . . A man who acts voluntarily, but only because of some unreasonable incentives, does not act freely. If the unreason-

---

[2] Harold D. Lasswell and Abraham Kaplan, *Power and Society. A Framework for Political Inquiry* (New Haven: Yale University Press, 1950), 97.

[3] Robert Nozick, "Coercion," in Sidney Morgenbesser, Patrick Suppes and Morton White, eds., *Philosophy, Science, and Method. Essays in Honor of Ernest Nagel* (New York: St. Martin's Press, 1969), 440-472. The statements cited are directly quoted from 441-443, but the identifying numbers have been slightly altered, and intervening arguments not indicated.

able incentives were the result of a threat of evil by someone, then he acted under coercion. If the unreasonable incentives were the result of a promise of good by someone then he acted under enticement."[4]

Clearly, there seem to be obvious cases of coercion (although Nozick and Gert are not concerned with them) in which a person literally has no choice in doing what he does because of external physical compulsion (e.g., "his body hit the floor as he was thrown into the cell"). According to some writers the concept of action implies that the agent has some choice in doing what he does, and hence such happenings are events or items of behavior but not actions.[5] The distinction, however, between actions *defined* as voluntary, and involuntary behavior, can often be drawn only after an inquiry into coercive circumstances (e.g., "he knocked down the barricade as the crowd surged forward"); and, for a discussion of coercion at least, it seems reasonable to be able to raise the question of whether an action or something a person does is or is not voluntary rather than specifying that, by definition, if A is an action then A is voluntary, which might at least mean that it was not the result of outright external compulsion.

Without even beginning to discuss the concept of action or the requirements for voluntary or involuntary action, let me simply state that as used here, that which we will consider as being either coerced or not coerced will be something that some person or some social entity such as a state does, or refrains from doing. Whether

[4] Bernard Gert, "Coercion and Freedom," this volume, Chap. 3.

[5] Felix Oppenheim considers actions a subclass of behavior, but defines actions in terms of choice and decision, specifying that "all actions are by definition voluntary." Felix Oppenheim, *Dimensions of Freedom* (New York: St. Martin's Press, 1961), 15-17. John Plamenatz had earlier overstated this position as follows: "It is, of course, quite clear that all action is necessarily voluntary, since it is never possible for a man to do what he does not wish. Indeed, to do what one wishes is the same thing as to act, for an action which has no motive is inconceivable." John Plamenatz, *Consent, Freedom and Political Obligation* (London: Oxford University Press, 1968), 110. For a more judicious discussion of these concepts, see Norman S. Care and Charles Landesman, eds., *Readings in the Theory of Action* (Bloomington: Indiana University Press, 1968). In their introduction, the editors consider handing over one's money to a thief threatening one's life a "paradigm case" of something done under duress and hence not voluntary, and yet still "an action."

that person or social entity is responsible for the action or behavior or event will be taken to be a separate question.[6] And it will be assumed that some acts or items of behavior[7] are coerced and some are not coerced, that persons and social entities are more coerced in some cases than in others, and that they may be coerced in different ways. Coercion will not be restricted to the bringing about of actions that are in some sense or by definition voluntary or chosen, for as J. R. Lucas points out, "imprisonment is the paradigm form of coercion."[8] To restrict the applicability of the concept of coercion either to the use of threats only, or to voluntary actions only, would be to exempt the practitioners of other forms of coercion from a wide range of appropriate judgments. To approve such an exemption would be both serious and dangerous.

Let us consider carefully the question of whether making an offer that it would be costly for a person to turn down can ever constitute coercion. If so, then selling someone a bargain or offering someone a better job than he now has might seem to be coercive; if not, a government offering personal security only to the politically obsequious might seem not to be coercive. Nozick tends to find threats coercive and offers noncoercive; on Gert's analysis no offer of good, however enticing, can be coercive. Lasswell and Kaplan base their answer on the degree of inducement.

Nozick suggests that in general we welcome offers and shun threats. But, it would seem, this depends. The legal system threatens that if a person commits murder he will be subject to a very high penalty. If he has no desire or intention to commit murder this threat may be quite welcome to him, and in a moment of passion he may even hail the restraint it provides. The editors of a volume of

    [6] For discussion, see Virginia Held, "Can a Random Collection of Individuals Be Morally Responsible?" *Journal of Philosophy,* LXVII (July 23, 1970), 471-481.
    [7] For discussion, see P. J. Fitzgerald, "Voluntary and Involuntary Acts," in A. G. Guest, ed., *Oxford Essays in Jurisprudence,* reprinted in Alan R. White, ed., *The Philosophy of Action* (New York: Oxford University Press, 1968). As Fitzgerald acknowledges, "the most difficult distinction . . . is that between acts over which a man has control, and happenings over which he has no control" (p. 122).
    [8] J. R. Lucas, *The Principles of Politics* (New York: Oxford University Press, 1966), 60. Lucas' definition of coercion is: "A man is being *coerced* when either force is being used against him or his behaviour is being determined by the threat of force."

papers threaten that if authors do not submit their work by a certain date, it will not be considered for inclusion; some authors appreciate a deadline as a spur to effort. On the other hand, a person may be surrounded by offers—to buy this or that product, to try this or that service, to support such and such candidates, to go here or there—all of which he may shun. So, in establishing when coercion is taking place, we may be led back to considering the degree of constraint or inducement involved rather than considering merely which of the two is present.

Nozick might say of much law that it is not coercive, and that a person is not threatened by a law if he has no desire or intention to violate it. But there is something problematic about this. Surely one of the primary characteristics of much law is its coercive nature; we would find it difficult to say that a given law relative to a given individual is constantly in flux, that it is coercive at the moment that it operates as a psychological factor restraining the person from performing an act, but the rest of the time it is noncoercive. What seems more reasonable to assume is that within the web of social realities surrounding an individual, various laws provide permanent threats that *if* the individual does A, B is likely to happen, or that *if* the individual wanted and intended to do A, among the reasons that *would* restrain him would be B. (This is not all that laws do, but we are concerned here with threats.) What changes is not the coercive character of such laws, but the individual's interest in risking or not risking the consequences of violation. Similarly with offers: some are persistently there in the background (unemployment insurance, welfare, the public library, an uncle to whom one could appeal), and some bombard the individual with noisy insistence. Among both threats and offers, some are welcome and some are not. Offers, as well as threats, have their price.

And there seems to be a way in which threats and offers can be translated into one another: the law that threatens punishment may offer liberty ("just stay out of trouble, and we'll leave you alone," quoth the policeman, after Locke[9]), and the offer that could please may conceal a venom ("you can turn me down, girl, but go home

---

[9] ". . . the end of law is not to abolish or restrain, but to preserve and enlarge freedom . . . for liberty is to be free from restraint and violence from others, which cannot be where there is no law." Locke, *Second Treatise on Civil Government,* § 57.

and think about it"). Other things being equal, an arrangement is
not substantially more, or less, coercive if it is described as "If you
don't join the union, you cannot get the job," rather than as "If you
join the union, you can get the job."

Gert makes a deep distinction, fundamental to much of his work,
between seeking a good and avoiding an evil. Coercion occurs only
when a person acts because of unreasonable incentives which are
the result of a threat of evil. But the world we inhabit does not
seem to lend itself to the precise descriptions he presupposes. Using
his own examples, it would seem that avoiding the evil of sinking
could be easily redescribed as seeking the good of staying afloat,
gaining the good of possessing more money could as well be described as avoiding the evil of having too little, and so on.

One way that is sometimes suggested to escape this difficulty is to
hold that an arrangement is not coercive as long as it does not
threaten a person with being worse off than he is already. But this
assumes a satisfactory status quo, and serves conceptually to justify
its preservation. Another suggestion is to establish what are taken to
be basic needs, and then to hold that to threaten to deprive someone of their satisfaction is to be coercive, but to offer someone anything above what might be called a "deprivation line" is not coercive. Again, this seems to assume absolute standards of need and
deprivation that may underlie but are only dimly reflected in the
multiple arrangements of political and social reality.

Consider the following case: Suppose a law is passed requiring
that anyone who wishes to apply for a job with the Federal government must sign a loyalty oath and a pledge to cooperate with any
and all efforts of the F.B.I. to "root out subversion." To deny anyone a job with the Federal government is not exactly to "deprive"
that person of a basic need or to threaten him with an "evil." An
applicant might not even suffer pain at being denied a job with a
government that would require such a pledge. Yet surely we would
consider such a requirement coercive.

Or suppose an offer would be made to citizens that all recipients
of Social Security benefits who would submit to investigations of
their political beliefs could continue to receive benefits. For all others the program would terminate, as, in the normal course of things,
many programs terminate, for instance, mental health services, job
training programs, programs to combat poverty. Persons who did
not accept this offer, and for whom Social Security benefits thereby

ended, would not thus be denied the basic necessities of life—they would still be eligible for welfare, let us say. Could we then conclude (with, presumably, those who accept the analyses of Nozick and Gert) that such an "offer" would not be coercive?

Or perhaps welfare itself would be seen as something offered. A majority opinion of the Supreme Court on January 12, 1971 declared welfare to be like "charity," and asserted that the supplier of both rightly "expects to know how his charitable funds are utilized." Presumably, those who concur with this view think of charity as something that is offered, not something whose denial is threatened. Until recently, a welfare mother could be subject to the regulation that if a male was discovered to be sharing her bed she was no longer entitled to benefits. Suppose such a woman had denied herself the pleasure of male companionship for five years in order to have the funds to care for her children, which she may well have been coerced by the law to give birth to through being denied legal means to terminate accidental pregnancies. Would we then say that such a regulation was not coercive at this later point in time because it did not take away from her anything which she had not already, for five years, been doing without? Would we agree that since the city offered the goods of welfare payments to all those who met the minimal requirements for them, and since offers are not coercive, the welfare mother's sexual abstinence was uncoerced?

What Nozick and Gert seem to be describing in their discussions of noncoercive offers are not offers, but rather gifts. Gifts, we may say, are at least sometimes not expected to be repaid, and gifts do not ordinarily have a price attached to them. Offers, on the other hand, ordinarily do. It seems fair to say that gifts are among the rarest of entities in the political and public realms. And I think it reasonable to conclude that as an inducement to accept an offer approaches a high level, it approaches coercion proportionately.

KINDS OF COERCION

There is an important distinction underlying the discussions of Nozick, Gert, and others of threats and offers. But it is perhaps more significantly a distinction between kinds of coercion than between coercion and noncoercion.

Nozick says that "when a person does something because of threats he does it unwillingly, whereas this is normally not the case when someone does something because of offers."[10] This does not seem quite right, for the reasons suggested. A person unable to spurn an offer may act as unwillingly as a person unable to resist a threat. Consider the distinction between rape and seduction. In one case constraint and threat are operative, in the other inducement and offer. If the degree of inducement is set high enough in the case of seduction, there may seem to be little difference in the extent of coercion involved. In both cases, persons may act against their own wills. Contrary to Nozick's suggestion, it seems clear that persons are very frequently seduced, in various senses, involuntarily and against their wills, by offers of innumerable kinds. Social, political, and economic reality is replete with evidence.

On Gert's analysis, coercion can occur only when a person has "the ability to will to do what he does."[11] Coercion then only takes place when evil is threatened rather than when good is offered; enticement and coercion are mutually exclusive. But this does not seem right, also for reasons suggested. An unreasonable incentive to accept a good might be no less coercive than an unreasonable incentive to avoid an evil.

And yet there is a difference here. It is not only a feminine bias that finds seduction morally superior to rape, in various senses. The difference may not be that in the one case the act is done willingly and in the other not. The difference seems more importantly to be that in the one case the person performing the act *might* (whether "if his character had been different," or "through a creative act," or in some other way, need not be explored here) himself have supplied the deficiency of will, in the other case this was impossible. This is not a function of whether the person was subject to a threat or an offer, since a person may yield to a threat he *might* have resisted as well as accept an offer he *might* have turned down. Whether the coercion is through threat or offer is independent of the distinction I am suggesting here. There are forms of coercion, however, where the person coerced did what he did against his will,

[10] Robert Nozick, *op. cit.*, 459.
[11] Bernard Gert, *op. cit.*, 32.

but might himself have supplied the deficiency of will, and there are forms of coercion where the person coerced did what he did against his will, but might in no way himself have summoned the courage to resist.

In fact it may be the case that offers, when coercive, are more frequently coercive in the first way and that threats, when coercive, in the second. We might conclude, then, that when the degree of coercion is equal, inducement is better than constraint. However, a higher degree of coercion through inducement may be worse than a lower degree of coercion through constraint. Sometimes a social arrangement that smothers the citizen with irresistible offers with regard to a wide range of actions is worse than a law that enforces his submission with regard to a limited and particular kind of action, and a parent whose offers repeatedly put a child into emotional debt may be more reproachably coercive than one who sometimes threatens physical restraint.

Thus the more fundamental distinction seems to be between coercion that is subject to resistance, and coercion that is not. That this is not simply a matter of "degree"—whatever "degree" here may mean—may be shown by the following example: If a subject is threatened with death if he fails to salute his "leader," we might say that the degree of coercion involved in his saluting is "greater than" the degree involved in his not entering the grounds of a government building because a fence prevents him from doing so. Yet the act of saluting is such that he could have resisted; the act of not entering may not be. Degree of coercion seems to be a function of the undesirability of the outcome and the probability of its occurring; it is a measure of the risk involved in resisting a threat or an offer.[12] The *kinds* of coercion I am here distinguishing depend upon the possibility or impossibility of choosing that risk.[13]

---

[12] For a related account, see Felix Oppenheim, *op. cit.*, Chapter 8, "Degrees of Power and Freedom."

[13] See also Oppenheim's distinction in Chapter 2 between the two forms of control: influencing and restraining. On Oppenheim's analysis, "by influencing X not to do x (whether by means of dissuasion or deterrence or conditioning), Y controls X's not doing x but does not limit his freedom to do x, while on the other hand, by restraining X from doing x (either in the strict or in the broad sense), Y not only controls X's not doing x but also makes him unfree to do x" (p. 38).

THE JUSTIFIABILITY OF COERCION

Let us agree to use the term "initial coercion" for that kind of coercion in which the person coerced might in some sense himself have supplied the deficiency of will, and to use the term "final coercion" for that kind of coercion in which such a possibility is precluded. And let us assume that an adequate way can be found of establishing the truth of the claims "C is an instance of initial coercion in degree x" and "D is an instance of final coercion in degree y." I use the term "instance," vague as it is, so as to include cases of coercion in which one person coerces another to do something and also cases in which one nation coerces another, or one government or institution or social entity coerces another or coerces a person, or vice versa, and so forth. We can then go on from these claims to consider some possible grounds according to which coercion may or may not be justifiable, and according to which some instances of coercion may be more justifiable than others.[14]

If we can establish a distinction between kinds of coercion, I think we can then agree that as between two instances of coercion which are equal in degree, that one which is an instance of final coercion is less justifiable than that one which is an instance of initial coercion, for initial coercion is vulnerable to courage and to the decision of the coerced to mount resistance. Explicitly, we seem to be able to conclude that when x and y are equal, as between

(a) "C is an instance of initial coercion in degree x"
    and
(b) "D is an instance of final coercion in degree y,"

a lower level of justifiability is to be given to (b). The conclusion remains whether the coercion is of or by persons, governments, nations, or other social entities. Employing one of our earlier examples, we could say, for instance, that while it would be coercive to deny Social Security benefits to those refusing to submit to an investigation of their political beliefs, this would be less unjustifiable than

---

[14] That coercion is more nearly a descriptive than a moral concept is adequately argued by Gerald B. Dworkin in "Compulsion and Moral Concepts," *Ethics,* 78 (April, 1968), 227-233, and I am assuming that we can separate the claims "C is an instance of coercion," and "C is unjustifiable."

to imprison such persons for a period of time which would constitute a degree of discomfort and coercive pressure equal to that resulting from lost benefits.

What has not yet been discussed but can I think rather easily be agreed to, is that although coercion is not *always* wrong (quite obviously: one coerces the small child not to run across the highway, or the murderer to drop his weapon), there is a presumption against it. Other things being equal, a noncoercive rule, policy, or action is better than a coercive one. This has the standing of a fundamental moral principle. It need not be considered self-evident in the traditional sense, or part of a single, immutable, order of Values or of Nature. It is a principle that morally responsible persons may commit themselves to as a persuasive and reasonable assumption; the moral standing traditionally ascribed to autonomy and to freedom are obviously reflected in it.

That the principle must be a deontological rather than a teleological one can be shown by the following argument: Let us suppose that proposal A and proposal B are similar with regard to all other relevant moral principles (telling the truth, for instance, or keeping one's promises, etc.), that proposal A embodies a lesser measure of coercion than proposal B, but that in the given circumstances we can make *no* prediction that the consequences of A will be better than the consequences of B. If noncoercion were a teleological value, we would have no basis for judging proposal A to be morally deserving of being given the benefit of the doubt. Because a presumption against coercion is a deontological principle, however, we would judge a proposal embodying less coercion to be morally superior to one embodying more coercion (if the coercion was of the same kind in both cases, and if the cases were otherwise equal on deontological grounds), *unless* we could predict and judge that the consequences of the latter proposal would be better than the consequences of the former. Then, if we could make such a prediction and judgment, we would have to decide which consideration—the principle that coercion is to be avoided or the good consequences to be achieved—should be given priority in this case.[15]

[15] A useful, brief account of the deontological-teleological distinction and its implications for ethical judgment is provided by William Frankena in his *Ethics* (Englewood Cliffs, N.J.: Prentice-Hall, 1963), although Frankena's account of freedom, with implications for coercion, does not seem to me altogether satisfactory.

Of course, in trying to consider whether coercion is or is not justifiable, other things are rarely equal. Other principles cross the path of the presumption against coercion. Familiar conflicts arise when, for instance, a principle of justice requiring an equitable distribution among persons of the benefits and burdens of a society cannot be fulfilled without the use of coercion. If justice demands a rule which must also be coercive such as the enforcement of requirements that tax the rich more heavily than the poor, such a rule may well be justifiable. And considerations of consequences intervene. We can, for instance, decrease pollution by imposing controls on the use of automobiles, or reduce deaths by enforcing regulations on medicines and food products; coercion in such cases may be justifiable if the teleological factors in favor of such measures supercede the deontological presumption against coercion.

What can be concluded at the moral level is that we have a *prima facie* obligation not to employ coercion. This may sometimes be everridden by other deontological considerations, or by an estimate that the consequences of the instance of coercion in question will be more beneficial than burdensome. But the principle is nevertheless of fundamental importance.

It allows us to say that as between two acts or rules fulfilling some other principle, such as a principle of justice or of human rights, that one which involves the lesser degree of coercion is *prima facie* more justifiable. And it allows us to say that as between two acts or policies whose good consequences relative to bad are thought to be equal, or unpredictable, the less coercive of the two is more justifiable.

Once a decision has been reached that a given degree of coercion would be justifiable to fulfill certain moral requirements or to bring about certain good consequences, then a judgment can be made that we ought to favor initial coercion over final coercion. Coercion that allows for the rise of resistance, and in fact does not encounter it, is more justifiable than coercion against which the courage to resist would be to no avail whatever.

5

COERCION, SPACE, AND THE MODES OF HUMAN DOMINATION

Michael A. Weinstein

Coercion is an experience that is primarily associated with the human condition of being-in-space. As such, the discussion of coercion as it appears in political and social affairs may be conducted best in the context of the polarity between restraint and release that forms the background of human activities in their spatial aspect. At any moment of human existence neither restraint nor release is absent, though attention may be fixed more on one of the conditions than on the other. It is perhaps impossible even to conceive of a situation in which restraint played no part. A situation of complete release might be described fancifully as the condition of having all of one's plans fulfilled in action immediately as they appeared. No conflicts between plans, precipitating the pain of deliberation, would be possible in this case; and there would certainly be no tragedies in which one had to sacrifice a cherished value so that he could attain another. The situation of complete release would nullify the problematic character of human existence, of which the polarity between release and restraint is merely an expression. Equally, a situation of total restraint does not accord with the character of human existence. Total restraint implies that none of one's plans are fulfilled in action; that one is, in other words, dead. The Latin word *arca,* from which coercion is derived, denotes a coffin, and it has come into English as a word denoting a reliquary. While the limiting case of restraint is death, as long as one exists there is release. Thus, the problematic character of human existence is described, from the spatial point of view, as a polarity between release and restraint. Upon every action, however satisfying, there are limits that give it a determinate meaning, and thereby save it from being experienced immediately as absurd. Alongside any restriction, however onerous, there is vitality that renders the situation somewhat indeterminate, and thereby saves it from being experienced as hopeless. Having his existence in space structured by this polarity, the human being may experience varying proportions of release and restraint at different times. When restraint with respect to any planned action is experienced as the result of the efforts of another person or a group of people, and no more satisfactory alternative action has replaced the original planned action, coercion has appeared.

COERCION DEFINED

Coercion is one of a number of English words that is derived from the Latin words *arca* (box or coffin) and *arcere* (to shut in). Coercion itself is most directly derived from the Latin verb *coercere* (to surround). The family of English words derived from *arca* all pertain to the characteristics of human existence in space. *Arca* refers to a reliquary, ark may refer to a place of refuge, as well as a holy chest or a boat, and arcanum denotes hidden knowledge. Arctation means the contraction of a natural opening and coarctation means restraint upon liberty or confinement to a narrow place. To coarct means to crowd in upon or restrain someone. Coercion, of course, has taken on a much wider meaning than these related terms through its use as a term in the discourse of political and legal theory. However, coercion still may refer to the condition of being controlled by force. In all cases, the English words derived from *arca* cluster about the pole of restraint in human affairs. Either the restraint is exercised in the interest of security, as when a person takes refuge in an ark, places relics in an arca, experiences arctation, or protects arcane knowledge; or the restraint is exercised directly by an outside agent, as when a person is coarcted or submits to coarctation. Of course, restraint exercised in the interest of security is usually the result of anxiety or fear that someone or something may invade one's space and deprive him of the means to the realization of his plans. Thus, the ark, the *arca,* and arcana are cultural objects that have been devised to protect persons and their possessions from being coarcted. Coercion may appear in human affairs as restraint exercised in the interest of security or restraint exercised directly by an outside agent. Often coercion is initiated by an agent who believes that his security is in jeopardy, upon an individual who constitutes a supposed threat. In this case one attempts to master danger rather than hide in an ark.

Coercion characterizes a situation when one or more persons are restrained by one or more others from using a space in some way, providing that the coerced person planned to use the space in the manner that is being prevented, and the coercer expressly intended to prevent that use. In this case, the coerced must not have substituted a more satisfactory plan for his original plan of action. Coercion may also characterize a situation in which one or more persons are compelled by one or more others to use a space in some way, providing that the coerced did not plan to use the space in the manner that is being compelled. In this case, the actions that are being compelled must not be judged as more satisfactory by the coerced person than his original plan of action. Essentially, the second situation is not very different from the first, since being compelled to use a space in a certain way restrains one from using that space or another in an alternative manner. However, there is a difference in difficulty between restraining an action and compelling one. If one wishes to restrain another's action, he need only move the other to a space in which the action is no longer possible, or transform the space in such a way that the action is no longer possible. If one wishes to compel a specific action, he must retain enough release in the situation so that the coerced person will not believe that performing the action leaves him hopeless. Coercion as restraint produces the condition of coarctation, in which the coerced is deprived of his liberty or "confined to a narrow place." Coercion as compulsion produces the condition of slavery, in which the actions of the coerced become means to the realization of another's plan. It is necessary to note, however, that coercion as compulsion presupposes coercion as restraint. One cannot begin to compel another to use a space in a certain way unless he has already restrained the other from using spaces in alternative ways. At the center of coercion is effective control of space. This is the point of Kelsen's remark that coercion is a technique of "indirect" rather than a means of "direct" motivation.[1] One is coerced through another's control of the available spaces for action, or release. In fact, one can frequently be compelled to perform a series of actions that are means to the realization of another's plan merely because the other can exclude him from certain spaces or confine him to a narrow space at will.

COERCION AND SPACE

Coercion is defined in terms of controlling spaces rather than in terms of controlling actions in order to prepare a ground for distinguishing among significantly different processes through which human actions are controlled. Once the control of spaces has been described, this mode of domination will be contrasted with the control of imagination, the control of will, and the control of opportunity. Given the definition of coercion as the restraint or compulsion of human beings by others with respect to the utilization of space, types of coercion can be identified in a three-dimensional classification system. First, kinds of coercion can be defined according to the types of spaces that are being controlled. Second, kinds of coercion can be defined according to the types of actions that are being restrained or compelled. Finally, types of coercion can be defined according to the means that may be employed to coerce.

With regard to the kinds of spaces in which coercion may be exercised, we can identify five general categories: private spaces, communal spaces, group spaces, organizational spaces, and cultural spaces. This classification is not necessarily exhaustive, and the cat-

---

[1] Hans Kelsen, *General Theory of Law and the State* (New York: Russell and Russell, 1961), 19.

egories are not completely exclusive. The types are defined according to the uses to which the space is normally put, and who controls it. Private spaces are controlled by individuals and they are used for contemplation, recuperation from bruising social contacts, creation of novel products, amusement, solitary work, and planning for future social activity. In this case control does not mean so much a legal right to use the space without interference by others as it denotes a present ability to undertake such utilization. Perhaps the paradigm for a private space is the study or workshop that an outsider enters only after he has gained permission to do so. Any space, however, may become private if it has been preempted for personal uses, and it may be private for different people at different times. Private spaces are of great importance in the good life because they are the places in which human beings define their individualities and perfect the plans of action to which they commit themselves. Communal spaces are controlled by the government and they are used as places in which the members of a community can orient themselves to the affairs of the entire community. The halls of Congress may be used for lobbying, the streets may be used for political demonstrations and parks may be used for political rallies, when they become communal spaces. The ready availability of communal spaces that may be used to orient the individual to the issues pertaining to his entire community is also a condition of the good life, even in an era of mass media. The opportunity for unmediated public experiences must be present if individuals are to have the means to understand their age and to act upon that understanding. Group spaces are controlled by primary groups and they are used for camaraderie, discussion, planning, creation, and intimate relations. Paradigms for group spaces are the club house or club room, and the bedroom. Group spaces are quite similar to private spaces, and they are necessary to the fulfillment of the good life because they provide the setting for the perfection of social relations, the development of the personality through criticism and support, and the transformation of relationships between human beings. Private and group spaces have been the traditional sites for cultural innovation, both for good and evil. Organizational spaces are controlled by the government, corporations, groups or individuals, and they are used for the promotion of the parts of the controller's plans that require specific actions from other people. When he is in an organizational space, the individual is usually a worker or a client who is expected to conform to the system of rights and duties that are defined by the organizational rules. Organizational spaces are, of course, necessary to the realization of the good life, because their efficient utilization often results in the creation of desired products or the performance of desired services. Cultural spaces may be controlled by individuals, the community and its agents, primary groups or corporations, and they are used for the exhibition of symbolic and dramatic productions. In cultural spaces the individual experiences intellectual constructions that fuse "concept and emotion into an image."[2] Theaters, libraries, and TV rooms are cultural spaces, and their availability is necessary to the fulfillment of the good life because they provide the setting for the enrichment of consciousness and the integration of the individual into his civilization.

Actions that may be compelled or restrained vary according to the kind of space through which coercion is exercised. In the case of private spaces, contemplation, recuperation, creation, amusement, and planning are restrained by abolishing the space through intrusion or removing the person from the space. It is a peculiarity of private spaces that actions cannot be compelled within them. This fact illustrates the principle that compulsion presupposes restraint, and also illustrates why privacy and voluntariness are so often associated with one another. In communal spaces, the entire range of acts of protest, expression of opinions, and exchange of information can be restrained. In addition, people may be compelled to utilize communal spaces for particular demonstrations and may even be compelled to express certain opinions. As in the case of private spaces, typical activities in group spaces (camaraderie, discussion, planning, creation, and acts of intimacy) can be restrained by invasion of the space or removal of the group members from the space. However, in group spaces typical actions can also be restrained by members of the group who gain dominance over others. Further, dominant members may be able to compel others to perform actions that do not accord with their plans. Outsiders, of course, cannot coerce activities in group spaces until they have intruded into them and have thereby transformed them. In organizational spaces, activities that are involved in fulfilling the controller's

---

[2] Henry Nash Smith, *Virgin Land* (New York: Random House, 1950), v.

purpose can be restrained, as well as actions pertaining to primary relations, political expression, symbolic exhibitions, and private pursuits. Such actions can also be compelled so long as the physical structure of the space permits. In cultural spaces, exhibition of particular symbols can be restrained and the exhibition of other symbols can be compelled. Further, the behavioral responses of participants and observers can be restrained or compelled.

The means of coercion vary according to the kind of space in which coercion is being exercised, the types of actions that are being coerced, and whether coercion as restraint or coercion as compulsion is being exercised. In its general form, coercion consists in transforming private, communal, group, and cultural spaces into organizational spaces in which people perform actions directed towards the fulfillment of another's plan, or refrain from performing actions subversive of the realization of another's plan. Coercion may also involve restructuring of organizational spaces so that actions are performed or restrained in the service of a new plan. Coercion may also be exercised, in a secondary sense, to protect spaces from transformation or restructuring by others. In the case of private spaces, in which only coercion as restraint is possible, the basic means of coercion is simply intrusion into the space. Any restraints or compulsions that are exercised over and above intrusion are instances of coercion in a space newly organized by the intruder. With respect to communal spaces, both coercion as restraint and coercion as compulsion are possible. The activities that dominate communal spaces, such as acts of protest, expression of opinions, exchange of information and mobilization of political power, may be restrained by the application of force on persons or property, the threat of force, and intimidation through the presence of police or military officers. Attendance at rallies and the expression of opinions may be compelled by threats of force and threats that nonattendance will be followed by deprivation of employment, position, property, liberty, or health. Groups of private citizens may attempt to control communal spaces through the exercise of force or the threat of force. Like private spaces, in group spaces the basic means of coercion is intrusion by outsiders. However, part of a group may convert the group space into an organizational space through the use or threat of force, or the threat of deprivation of valuables. In organizational spaces, coercion may restrain the exercise of rights, compel the exercise of duties, or restrain or compel other activities through force, the threat of force, or the threat of deprivations of valuables. In cultural spaces, the exhibition of symbolic productions may be prevented by censorship or compelled by force or threats. Audiences may be compelled to respond outwardly to exhibitions in specified ways by force or threats.

Wherever coercion is exercised, spaces become organizational. In other words, the actions of one or more individuals are made into means to the realization of the plans of others. This does not mean that all of the actions that are performed by subordinates in "organizations" have been compelled by decision-makers. Many of the actions that take place in organizational settings form a part of the client's or worker's plans and are satisfying in themselves, reasonable because they will effect a desired end, or motivated by the desire for benefits. However, whenever the person is in an organizational space he is open to the realization that his acts can be described as parts of another's design, even if other descriptions of his acts are possible. This is why coercion is essentially destructive of the good life, particularly when it is exercised in private, communal, group, and cultural spaces. Organizational roles are means to the creation of products or the performance of services, and, more important, means to the enhancement of power, wealth, and status of decision-makers. When private spaces become organized, the free activities of contemplation, relaxation, and solitary experimentation are no longer part of life. When communal spaces are organized, the unmediated relation of people to their community becomes impossible. When group spaces become organized, the free activities related to intimacy and the spontaneous exploration of satisfying interchange disappear from human existence. When cultural spaces become organized, genuine symbolic expression and authentic aesthetic experience become impossible, leaving barbarism. Coercion, as the imposition of restraint in the spatial dimension of human existence, banishes from life all of those situations in which human beings find release. In the polarity between release and restraint, restraint is a means and never an end. That it is a necessary means is unquestionable. In fact, preparation for the good life might be described as the perfection of methods of self-discipline that, when employed, will obviate many of the restraints that are externally imposed and will leave the person free to experience maximum release of his potentialities. Coercion, except when exercised very carefully as a secondary means of teaching children the methods of self-restraint, is the very opposite of self-restraint. Instead of freeing the person to experience release, it abolishes the conditions through which the person finds release. Instead of developing the person's autonomy, it destroys independence. Coercion may be justified when it is exercised to protect access to private, communal, group, and cultural spaces that have been set aside under a system of just laws. Depending on the degree of injustice and the availability of alternative means to realize justice, coercion may also be justified when it is exercised to gain a system of just laws in which access to private, communal, group, and cultural spaces is possible. Coercion is also justified when it is exercised to maintain organizations that provide goods and services necessary for the fulfillment of the good life and, under certain conditions, to gain such goods and services when they are unjustly withheld.

EXTENSIONS OF COERCION

The meaning of coercion has been extended far beyond its traditional reference to being-in-space by many contemporary political theorists and legal philosophers. Writers like Yves Simon, Carl Friedrich, and Karl De Schweinitz have defined coercion in such a way that it becomes any mode of human domination, in the sense that Santayana discussed dominations. For Santayana, the dichtomy between powers and dominations was an expression of a far more fundamental condition than being-in-space. It was the basic duality arising from the human condition of being-in-the-world: "The distinction therefore arises from the point of view of a given person or society having initial interests of their own, but surrounded by uncontrollable circumstances: circumstances that will at once be divided, by that person or society, into two classes: one, things favourable or neutral, the other, things fatal, frustrating, or inconvenient: and all of the latter, when they cannot be escaped, will become Dominations."[3] If a domination is something "fatal, frustrating, or inconvenient" that cannot be escaped, we may say that a human

[3] George Santayana, *Dominations and Powers* (New York: Charles Scribner's Sons, 1952), 1.

domination is a person, group, or social organization that destroys, frustrates or inconveniences another person, group, or social organization. Human dominations refer to the human condition of being-among-others. Among the states occurring as a result of human dominations are coercion, coarctation, repression, oppression, and suppression. When the significant context in which a human domination appears is the human condition of being-in-space, we speak of coercion or coarctation. When the significant context in which a human domination appears is some other condition than being-in-space, we may speak of repression, suppression, oppression, among other states of being-among-others. A review of some of the arguments for extending the use of coercion beyond its core meaning of domination in space will reveal that such extensions confuse coercion with phenomenologically distinct experiences such as restraint of thought (repression), restraint of will (suppression), and restraint of opportunity (oppression). Failure to distinguish among the various types of human domination destroys the basis upon which people come to understand their social experience and gain the means to change it intelligently. We are concerned not so much with a satisfactory political lexicon, as we are interested in identifying the significant distinctions between political phenomena. Three types of extensions of the meaning of coercion can be identified. Yves Simon, Carl Friedrich, Hans Kelsen, and John W. Meaney confuse coercion and repression, or restraint in space and restraint of thought and imagination. Harold Lasswell and Abraham Kaplan confound coercion and suppression, or restraint in space and restraint of will. Karl De Schweinitz confounds coercion and oppression, or restraint in space and restraint of opportunity. While instances of coercion overlap with instances of the other three modes of human domination, each mode of human domination has a distinct core. When the meaning of coercion is extended to include the meanings of repression, suppression and oppression, important theoretical and practical distinctions are lost.

In extending coercion beyond its core meaning of domination in space, Yves Simon has discussed the concept in terms of its opposition to the state of voluntariness and the process of persuasion. First, he distinguishes coercion from voluntariness, in that voluntariness "constitutes the most distinguished kind of spontaneity," and coercion denotes the absence of spontaneity.[4] With this distinction in mind he classifies the processes through which people's attitudes and actions are changed by others on a continuum between the poles of coercion and persuasion. Coercion is always exercised externally upon an individual and reduces the person to an object of scientific control. Persuasion, though it is exercised in an interpersonal relationship, is marked by the fact that the new attitudes and principles of action are "actively interiorized by the subject."[5] Between actual coercion and persuasion unsullied by fear and coercion are "persuasion motivated only by fear of actual coercion" and "persuasion born of the fear of coercion (combined) with persuasion born of some other motive, such as veracity and justice."[6] Coercion, as the denial of voluntariness, always implies a scientific view of the human being: "When the means of influence operate determinately, there is necessitation from without, i.e., coercion, regardless of whether the means are physical or psychical."[7]

Carl Friedrich has developed a similar analysis, in which coercion and consent are opposed to each other. Both coercion and consent are means to attaining power, and in most power situations both means are utilized. Coercion characterizes involuntary changes of attitudes and actions, while consent is voluntary. As for Simon, coercion can be physical, economic, or psychical. However, Friedrich recognizes a difficulty in the notion of psychic coercion: " . . . it is apparent that the phenomenon of psychic coercion and the power generated by it raise some of the most difficult questions of politics and power. For it is at this point that the distinction between coercive and consensual power becomes most elusive."[8] Similar to the discussions of Simon and Friedrich is the analysis of Hans Kelsen. For Kelsen, coercion is a technique of indirectly motivating behavior that should be opposed to techniques of direct motivation. Coercion is the technique for gaining obedience in which punishments are threatened and meted out in cases of refractory be-

---

[4] Yves R. Simon, *Freedom and Community* (New York: Fordham University Press, 1968), 117.

[5] *Ibid.*

[6] *Ibid.*, 118.

[7] Yves R. Simon, *Philosophy of Democratic Government* (Chicago: University of Chicago Press, 1951), 125.

[8] Carl J. Friedrich, *Man and his Government* (New York: McGraw-Hill Book Company, 1963), 168.

havior. Another technique of indirect motivation is inducement or persuasion, in which rewards are given for compliant behavior. Both coercion and persuasion or inducement differ significantly from voluntary obedience, the technique of direct motivation. However, voluntary obedience, as a form of motivation, is a form of coercion, "and hence is not freedom, but is coercion in the psychological sense."[9] In Kelsen's view, if we have an idea of a norm that makes us behave in accordance with it, we are being coerced: " . . . moral and religious norms, too, are coercive insofar as our ideas of them make us behave in accordance to them"[10] John W. Meaney, who defines the essence of coercion as exteriority and opposes it to the interiority of voluntary actions, as well as the spontaneity of natural processes, also argues for a psychic dimension to coercion. He identifies psychic coercion as preying upon an individual's weaknesses, dividing him against himself and thereby dominating his will.[11] In each of these discussions, the concept of coercion has been extended to operate in other human conditions than merely being-in-space. Specifically, it has been extended to characterize all of the various types of human domination.

An even further extension of coercion has been proposed by Harold Lasswell and Abraham Kaplan. Lasswell and Kaplan oppose coercion to choice and identify the exercise of power with the exercise of coercion. Coercion is defined as a "high degree of constraint and/or inducement": "We say that coercion is involved in an influence situation if the alternative courses of action are associated with severe deprivations or indulgences, and choice if they are mild."[12] Thus, for Lasswell and Kaplan, promises as well as threats, and benefits as well as harm, may be associated with coercion. Christian Bay explicitly follows Lasswell and Kaplan in defining coercion as the exercise of physical violence or *"the application of sanctions sufficiently strong to make the individual abandon a course of action or inaction dictated by his own strong and endur-*

[9] Kelsen, *op. cit.,* 19.
[10] *Ibid.,* 23.
[11] John W. Meaney, "Propaganda as Psychical Coercion," *Review of Politics,* 13 (January, 1951), 66.
[12] Harold D. Lasswell and Abraham Kaplan, *Power and Society* (New Haven: Yale University Press, 1950), 98.

ing motives and wishes."[13] Bay argues that while it may seem counter to common sense to call a high degree of inducements coercion, "it is in the interest of clear thinking to admit that (it) can be, if strong enough."[14] He offers the example of a poor and principled man who is offered money to perform an illegal act. The inducement creates "a new perspective of the future, and from that moment on the necessity of either performing the deed or letting go of the new perspective may be psychologically equivalent to a high degree of constraint."[15] In the cases of Lasswell and Kaplan, and Bay, coercion is no longer necessarily a type of human domination, but may even be a power.

Finally, Karl De Schweinitz has extended the application of coercion to include cases in which social systems can be termed coercive. De Schweinitz defines coercion as "the act by which one individual (or group) compels another individual (or group) to behave in a way that conflicts with his (or its) preferences or conscience."[16] He proceeds to argue that coercion has a quantitative and a qualitative dimension. With respect to the quantitative dimension, coercive acts may be scaled according to the number of people who are coerced. With regard to the qualitative dimension, coercive acts may be classified according to the degree of frustration they cause. Judgments on the quality of coercive acts depend upon the values and norms of the individuals who are subject to the acts. Having defined coercion and its dimensions, De Schweinitz distinguishes between explicit and implicit coercion: "Coercion is explicit where specific and easily identifiable organs of society compel people to behave in some particular way. . . . On the other hand, coercion is implicit when the structure of and the values symbolized by, social institutions restrain the behavior of individuals."[17] Explicit coercion is usually personalized, while implicit coercion is normally impersonal, and the coerced may not be

[13] Christian Bay, *The Structure of Freedom* (New York: Atheneum, 1965), 93.
[14] *Ibid.*
[15] *Ibid.*
[16] Karl De Schweinitz, Jr., "Economic Growth, Coercion and Freedom," *World Politics*, IX, 2 (January, 1957), 167.
[17] *Ibid.*, 168.

keenly aware of his situation. As an example of implicit coercion, De Schweinitz cites a situation in which an individual wishes to make a purchase for which he has insufficient money. Since he cannot consummate the transaction, "he is being coerced by the whole economic organization rather than by a particular element within it."[18] De Schweinitz argues that explicit and implicit coercion are polar types that form the limits of a continuum. He contrasts a person who conforms to traffic regulations out of fear that he will be arrested to a person who conforms to such regulations because they are the "law," and who may, in fact, not even be fully aware of his compliance. He claims that one would "hardly call" such a person coerced, but, like Kelsen, he must treat him as coerced.[19] While Simon, Friedrich, Kelsen, and Meaney extended the meaning of coercion to include cases of psychic manipulation and deprivation, and Lasswell and Kaplan, and Bay broadened it further to include certain instances of reward, De Schweinitz stretches the meaning of coercion even farther to include situations in which actions are restrained by social structures, even when a plan including these actions is not in the victim's consciousness.

COERCION AS ONE MODE OF HUMAN DOMINATION

Rather than having identified experiences that are phenomenologically distinct from coercion, the writers who have extended the meaning of coercion have confounded coercion with other phenomena. In the cases of Simon, Friedrich, Kelsen, and Meaney instances of coercion are classified with instances of repression. When Simon uses the term "psychic coercion" he refers to situations of hypnotic control, control through intensive propaganda, and, at times, any human action that has a determinate effect on another human being. When Friedrich uses the term "psychic coercion" he refers to the control that a charismatic leader exerts over his constituents, as well as control through intensive propaganda. For Kelsen, the term coercion seems to cover every form of control—even the control that an idea may exert over a

[18] *Ibid.*
[19] *Ibid.,* 169.

person, whether or not the person is conscious of the source of that idea. Meaney confines his discussion of "psychic coercion" to control of attitudes and actions through intensive propaganda. With respect to Kelsen, it would seem that the only noncoerced actions are those that are performed unreflectively and spontaneously. Thus, most of human existence is reduced to coercive situations, thereby denying the distinctions between release and restraint that most people draw in their experience. With regard to Simon, the only noncoerced actions are those that are not done as a necessary effect of another's initiative. It is likely that Friedrich and Meaney would adopt the same definition. If acts of coercion are those that have a determinate effect on other human beings, where the victim is not aware of the effects of the act before it is performed and has not consented to the performance of the act, a large portion of social existence is coercive. In itself, this is not an objection. However, a listing of the kinds of situations that are included in this definition will show that significantly different phenomena are brought together. Every society has a system of socialization that is somewhat determinate in its effects. Every society has an ideational culture, through which expression is limited by determinate symbols, and every society has a material culture that limits the fulfillment of certain interests. Most important, every society is stratified according to class, status and power, and thereby builds in limitations to the aspirations of most of its members. Further, the wealthy, the esteemed, and the powerful generally resort to propaganda to justify their social positions and convince subordinates that they should be satisfied with their lots. Often this propaganda is successful in realizing the disseminator's aim, particularly when rationalization of one's position is more comfortable than rebellion against it. In other words, all societies are repressive in that they prevent, to some degree, the appearance of attitudes and actions that are inconsistent with widely accepted norms. Some of the attitudes, actions, and experiences that are repressed may be prerequisites to the full development of the human being. However, many instances of repression are quite different from coercive situations, which also have determinate effects. In general, the way to overcome repression is self-knowledge and imagination. In general, the way to overcome coercion is counter-coercion or persuasion, if either tactic is possible. Of course, there are cases in which repression and coercion overlap, as when a person is forcibly prevented from gaining access to the means necessary to self-development. This combination of repression and coercion is an instance of control of space, and its widespread occurrence may have led writers to confound coercion and repression. Behavior and even mental events can be repressed through actions that have a determinate effect on human beings, where the victim is not aware of the effects of the act before it is performed and has not consented to the performance of the act. Behavior, not mental events, can be coerced through actions that restrain human beings from using spaces in certain ways or compel human beings to use spaces in certain ways. Propaganda, charismatic leadership, and social engineering may repress. Restraint of access to the means to expression coerces. Repression and coercion are distinct modes of domination.

In the cases of Lasswell and Kaplan, and Bay, instances of coercion are confounded with instances of suppression and seduction. For these writers the term coercion seems to cover all of the situations in which human beings make serious attempts to control the behavior of others. One can be coerced when he is rewarded for abandoning a course of action, or when he is given the benefits for adhering to a new plan of action. The only noncoercive situations would be those in which nobody cared about a person's behavior enough to make serious efforts to change it or to reinforce it. The offering of strong inducements is never a characteristic of coercion. Rather, it is one of either of two techniques of indirect motivation that we may term moral education and seduction. In some methods of moral education, individuals are given rewards if they conform to the norms that are being taught. If punishments are not meted out in cases of nonconformity, coercion does not characterize moral education. With regard to seduction, individuals are given rewards if they perform an action that they believe is wrong or bad, or refrain from performing an action that they believe is right or good. When either moral education or seduction is exercised with the intent of convincing a person to refrain from performing an action, we may speak of a condition of suppression. Of course, instances in which suppression and coercion overlap are very common in social life. The combination of suppression and coercion is merely what we previously designated coercion as restraint. Behavior can be suppressed through offering people strong inducements or threatening people with severe deprivations. Behavior can be coerced through threatening people with severe deprivations. The distinction between suppression and coercion is not merely a matter of the correct usage of words. Suppressive seduction is generally overcome through moral strength, rather than threat or persuasion.

In the case of De Schweinitz, instances of coercion are confounded with instances of oppression. While De Schweinitz begins his discussion of coercion by defining coercion as the act by which a person or group gains dominance over another person or group and thereby compels the subordinates to perform actions at variance with their preferences or moral standards, he goes on to argue that coercion can be exercised through the mere existence of social institutions, as well as through the agencies of determinate individuals. For De Schweinitz, coercion seems to cover all of the situations in which human beings are restrained from performing actions that are consistent either with their preferences or their moral standards. The only noncoercive situations would be those in which a person acted in accordance with his preference or his conscience. Thus, such an analysis of coercion would include cases in which individuals are restrained from performing certain actions due to lack of social opportunity, as well as cases in which people are restrained from performing actions due to force or threat. However, lack of social opportunity, while it bears many resemblances to coercion, is more aptly defined as oppression. Oppression appears when people are systematically excluded from social opportunities by force, lack of wealth, status deprivation, or the mere allocation of services in the society. Of course, coercion and oppression overlap, and coercive denials of social opportunity are widespread. Differential enforcement of the law, gang rule, and industrial violence are all types of coercive oppression. However, while the ultimate strategy against oppression is the type of coercion termed revolution, there are many other strategies for overcoming oppression, such as community organization, boycotts, and demonstrations in communal spaces. People can be oppressed by the allocation of goods and services in a society. Behavior can be coerced through the exercise of police and military force and gang rule. Thus, the distinction between coercion and oppression is not merely a matter of usage. Like the other distinctions, it leads one to an understanding of the various means to social development and the proper contexts for their use.

Coercion, repression, suppression, and oppression may all characterize social situations. At times, two or more of them can be used to describe the same situation. However, their core meanings are quite different, and when they are preserved the student of human affairs gains a much more acute awareness of social phenomena than he would have by confusing them. The core of coercion is restraint in space, the core of repression is restraint of thought, the core of suppression is restraint of will, and the core of oppression is restraint of opportunity. Each one of these terms describes a restriction on human development and a possible domination. The advantages of keeping clearly in mind the distinctions between the various modes of human domination are both theoretical and practical. From a theoretical viewpoint, the differentiation of human domination into four modes aids in comprehending the pluralism of social experience. An awareness of the qualitative differences among social processes is one of the important contributions of a phenomenological approach. From a practical standpoint, the ability to identify significantly different processes of domination, and to describe their dynamics, may aid in the rational effort to overcome domination.

The wide use of the terms coercion, repression, suppression, and oppression in contemporary political discourse gives testimony to a world in which restraint is judged too often as an end rather than a means, and release is too often separated from any restraint.

6

SPONTANEITY, JUSTICE, AND COERCION: ON *NICOMACHEAN ETHICS,* BOOKS III AND V

Robert K. Faulkner

Doubts as to the use of coercion are heard ever more frequently these days, both on the campuses and from less sheltered platforms. Some of these are perfectly understandable. The application of force to control men never can be regarded as very desirable in itself, especially by the more humanitarian and democratic citizens of a liberal democracy.

Still, what might not be desirable may nonetheless be necessary. Prisons, police, and judges have in one form or another generally been with men, and also the more subtle disciplines of parent, school, religion, job and media. Nevertheless, there grows a visible doubt as to the legitimacy of such institutions of coercion, discipline, and education. Even more moderate citizens who admit the

81

need for governance in some circumstances now tend to restrict the circumstances. Within home, school, church, and other American institutions appears a pervasive if gradual reduction of requirements and restraints.

The cutting edge of this movement attacks everything "authoritarian," the bounds between this and legitimate authority being unclear. What *is* clear is the impulse to avoid anything fostering "specialization" and "conformity", or anything "repressive" (to come nearer the core). The new doubt follows from a new certainty: that men are to be left free "to develop their true self", to be creative with special attention to their peculiar gifts, and thus to develop their *own* potential or, in the most popular version, to "do their own thing."

Coercion's place turns on the place of spontaneity—untrammeled human action. To clarify the former one must clarify the latter. That is the task of this paper, to a modest extent. It seeks to clarify that place as presented by Aristotle in the *Nicomachean Ethics* (agreed to be his authoritative statement on this subject). It concentrates upon only the two chief discussions in the *Ethics,* that in Book III treating conduct voluntary and involuntary from the point of view of individual choice, and that in Book V discussing the same questions under the horizon of law and justice. By contrasting these two, we can illuminate the fundamental relations between spontaneity and governance, as Aristotle understood them. Since these fundamentals can most safely be grasped in the very manner and order in which Aristotle brings them to light, the paper takes the form of a commentary. This procedure allows us to recover the very perspective in which spontaneity, now so puzzling to us, was understood by Aristotle.

The common translation "voluntary" and "involuntary" does not suffice for the *hekousion* and *akousion* of Aristotle, as commentators such as Joachim and especially Hardie have rightly observed.[1] "Voluntary" connotes an act of will, especially of reason over passion, and the post-Rousseauan or post-Kantian discussions have tended to revolve about the "problem of free will." Yet Aristotle applies the term to the unforced acts of animals and children, and

---

[1] H. H. Joachim, *Aristotle, The Nicomachean Ethics* (Oxford, Oxford University Press, 1951), 97. W. F. R. Hardie, *Aristotle's Ethical Theory* (Oxford, Oxford University Press, 1968), 152-3.

to human acts motivated by desire and anger, nobility and baseness, as well as deliberation. The substitution or addition of "willing" and "unwilling" by Joachim, and to some extent by Hardie, manages to avoid the clear implication of conscious determination. Yet the connection with "will" is retained and thereby some such connotation. One still finds difficulty in so describing acts of animals, or acts from anger and desire, or even acts from habit, the crucial case in Book III. Perhaps these substitutions fail to get outside the Kantian orientation of the influential scholar, Sir W. D. Ross, who unhesitatingly translated "voluntary" and "involuntary." As Ross concludes his valuable survey, he charges that Aristotle "shared the plain man's belief in free will," but failed to "examine the problem thoroughly," perhaps because "he had no clear conception of a universal law of causation."[2] The criticism begs all the interesting questions. Hardie rightly wonders at "those commentators who tell us that Aristotle has no notion of will or of free will . . . He did not do so badly without it." Aristotle does not presuppose a mechanical or providential theory of nature's operation, and hence he need not have the Kantian preoccupation with accounting for human "free will" outside a determined system of causes. Instead he takes his bearings from the opinions and judgments involved in the practical activities we all know (if not merely of the "plain" man), as Leo Strauss has explained.[3] Aristotle considers whether such actions are those to which men tend by their own inclination (be that from nature, choice, habit, or whatever). Thus *hekousion* and *akousion* refer to acting readily, in an unforced manner, and its opposite: let us say spontaneously and unspontaneously.

"Spontaneous" action, however, does not simply mean that based upon feeling, genuine and authentic or otherwise. Today the word has this connotation, or at the least immediacy of response, whereas acts from choice (involving deliberation that may be slow while action is quick) are clearly counted as spontaneous by Aristotle. Also, choice may be moved by external factors that prevent in practice what is best in principle, a further check on "spontaneity" of the "self" as now understood. Clear in Book III, the point is more evident in Book V on justice. Any country's laws prescribe

[2] *Aristotle* (New York, Meridian Books, 1959), 196-97.
[3] "On Aristotle's Politics," *The City and Man* (Chicago, Rand McNally, 1964), 11-12, 19-29. Hardie, *Aristotle's Ethical Theory*, 163.

many things that perhaps no one would do spontaneously (in the
current sense). Besides, the judgment of most citizens overcomes
selfish desires for pleasure and gain only with difficulty and pain,
and through a certain compulsion of the law. Even a nobly disposed
man must contend occasionally with the attraction of low
pleasure, and with aversion to pain. Hence some of the connotations
of "voluntary," implying the governance of reason over desire,
are present as Aristotle talks of practical action, and these no
doubt explain in part the term's acceptance to this day. We will
adopt it occasionally.

Still, "spontaneity" conveys Aristotle's essential meaning. The
fine man's deeds and "self-control" occur with a view to the noble.
Loving the noble—which connotes the beautiful as well as the
good, somewhat like our "fine" but with a more manly and less aesthetic connotation—he loves noble deeds as expressions of his own
activity and of his own nobility, and accordingly hates the ignoble
and base. Noble deeds are rooted in self-love. It is significant, however, that we learn this late in Book IX.[4] Aristotle has reached the
level of the higher forms of friendship, comprising the mutual admi-
ration of one another's fine actions (which are as a friend's in a way
one's own) and conversation about them. Here at the border-line
between friendship and philosophy pleasure can be praised as a
good, if not *the* good. Aristotle is nearly to the discussion of philosophy, in which the good is defined as unimpeded activity of the best
in man, his intelligence. The connotations of "spontaneity" are most
appropriate, for the activity is natural in the best sense, the pleasures most pure, and the happiness least flawed. Still, noble actions
also possess a basic spontaneity even if diluted by the need to govern body and lower desires, and to take account of various external
forces. Perhaps Ross's Kantian emphasis upon duty for its own sake
(not action for the noble things desired) explains his unhesitating
use of "voluntary."[5]

[4] *Nicomachean Ethics* 1168ᵃ 28 - 1169ᵃ 18.

[5] *Aristotle,* 184-5, 191-2, 196-7, 200, 203, 227. Note that Ross is surprised
to find "two whole books" devoted to friendship. He accounts for this only
as a "valuable," "altruistic", "corrective" to the "decidedly self-centered"
remainder of "Aristotle's moral system." 223. In a later sketch of the *Ethics*
Ross omits entirely any treatment of VIII and IX, since they have "no vital
relation to the rest of the work." Introduction to *The Nicomachean Ethics
of Aristotle* (Oxford, The World's Classics, 1959), xx-xxi. Hardie's comments are instructive. *Aristotle's Ethical Theory,* 317-335.

It is clear, then, that Aristotle treats spontaneity in action within a more fundamental discussion of noble action and of happiness in general. As his consideration of the goods that comprise human happiness progresses from level to level, from moral virtue to judgment, friendship, and philosophy, so too his account of spontaneity.[6] Let us begin by considering the broad outlines revealed by the context and tenor of Books III and V.

Book III concludes the discussion of moral virtue in general by considering choice. The discussion is expected, for Book II had defined and discussed moral virtue as a disposition to choose the mean. Somewhat unexpected is the introduction at the beginning of Book III of *hekousion* and *akousion* in acting, with choice treated as a subspecies in the sequel. Why this interruption in the account of moral virtue? Apparently the intervention introduces conditions other than virtue that impinge upon its sphere. Here Aristotle starts to treat the circumscribing forces external to character and action, yet affecting the prospects and possibilities of both. The subject is said to be necessary to the student of ethics (to help him know when to praise and blame, and how to encourage praiseworthy acts and discourage the opposite) and, Aristotle notes already in Book III, to the legislator in assigning rewards and punishments.

Book V's discussion also concerns the intrusion into virtue's sphere of things other than the agent's virtue, and yet it is more complicated because the virtue justice is itself conditioned by law, polity, and other such things. Justice is first identified with what the law prescribes, and law at its best is said to command all

---

[6] This paper involves the thesis that the argument of the *Ethics* itself "develops." Somewhat like a living organism growing to adulthood, earlier stages of discussion can be understood with greater clarity only in light of the final and developed perspective. This is not to say that the earlier remarks can be simply deduced from the later, which would involve the absurdity that the life of political action might be deduced from that of philosophic contemplation. It is to say that greater clarity and light is shed gradually but regularly upon earlier levels, as the dimnesses appropriate to these levels need no longer go unquestioned. Consider the reservations as to moral virtue expressed only in X, if prefigured to an extent in VIII and IX on friendship, and the basis of noble action in self-love, brought to the surface only when the understanding appropriate to noble action has been surpassed (in IX). We cannot argue this thesis here, except as particular remarks in the text confirm the general point. For a fine argument, see Chapter IV of Harry V. Jaffa's *Thomism and Aristotelianism* (Chicago, University of Chicago Press, 1952).

virtuous actions (so far as other men are concerned). This preliminary equation of justice with law, and both with perfect virtue in
action, is soon qualified, however. Law attends less to my good as
such than to the common good, and thus to what serves the community rather than to what is noble in itself, to the lower expedien-
cies like trade and punishment that common life requires, and to
what people generally (especially those in power) wish. Excellence
is shaded by what is common and necessary. Also, justice consists
most obviously in the specific acts prescribed by law. Only as more
deeply considered is justice an equitable disposition. The law-maker
attends first to instituting good actions, or what men insist upon and
their needs require. External to the agent and yet governing his action, law by its very character provokes a question as to the agent's
"responsibility" for his conduct, especially where guilt and punishment must be determined.

Nevertheless, Books III and V both treat external influences as
qualifications of a fundamental spontaneity of action, in contrast to
the insistent determinism of some modern discussions. Book III
even exaggerates considerably the scope of human effort. At one
point Aristotle contends that a man can control his very dispositions, a view contrary to remarks in Books II and X, and substantially retracted late in III itself. Why this perspective?

Aristotle starts with the practical viewpoint appropriate to the
practical dispositions, not a detached determinism originating in a
theory about sub-human particles. In practice a man looks at the
forces about him as his "opportunity," the circumstances favorable
or unfavorable for doing what he wishes. So does Aristotle. Such a
point of view has its limitations, however. Attuned to what is open
to choice and accomplishment, the agent fails to see as clearly the
limits upon choice, especially the deeper factors in his own nature
and character. Aristotle's procedure is faithful to this outlook, while
gently indicating its limits. Beginning with the most obvious barriers
—compulsion and inadvertance through ignorance of the circumstances—he takes us back only gradually and quietly into the whole
web of conditions circumscribing choice. He often presents these in
the course of rebutting more prominent arguments upholding the
power of effort. His procedure may also reflect the practical character of moral science itself, concerned less with knowing what is

good and more with encouraging its practice.[7] Some exaggeration of human powers is salutary. To say that effort doesn't matter deters effort that could matter, and some exaggeration of the power of effort encourages effort. Besides, the noble man should try to act nobly whatever the obstacles.

The argument in Book III then moves visibly from the environment of particular acts to more subtle conditions of acting, including our desires and intelligence that condition what we can do and even what we wish to do. An initial mention of obvious and external forces—a man swept up by a storm—is succeeded by attention to influences upon the agent's own wishes—the last example concerns the natural origin of a man's moral "vision." The discussion passes in turn from external forces compelling the agent's action, to his inadvertent ignorance of important circumstances, to choice and the things unsuitable for deliberation because beyond the agent's control, to a final reconsideration of spontaneity in the face of ends somehow by nature.

This unfolding of noble action's context alludes inevitably to goods beyond practical action, and hence to the limited worth of noble action. The clearest indication occurs just prior to the discussion of choice, as that of spontaneity concludes. Acts from desire must be called spontaneous, writes Aristotle, since acts for good things must be deemed spontaneous, and we act to obtain health and learning out of desire.[8] There are things desirable apart from the moral excellences, and of course this becomes an explicit concern of Aristotle's teaching about happiness when friendship and philosophy come to be discussed. Choice is principally of actions, of means to ends, of things only equivocally desirable in themselves. Friendship and philosophy have more to do with ends, are desired more for their own sake, and are more directly connected with desire. Book III's attention to human desire calls forth a foreshadowing allusion. Its preeminent concern with conduct and moral excellence, however, limits the remark to an undeveloped allusion.

Book V differs remarkably in its general tenor. It puts the quietus on Book III's exaggeration of individual powers, while observing its own surface exaggeration. The argument proceeds from celebration of justice as law providing for perfect virtue (and hence perfect spontaneity, in a way), to law as only accidentally just at best and usually worse, to the exploration of a grave tension between political life and human spontaneity, to a flat statement that doing a truly just act is not in our power. In acting we must know the particular things we are to do, definite means to the ends to which Book III had vaguely alluded. Book III had already intimated that law (including custom) is the primary source of these more particular opinions. To this extent human action is not free, but decisively subject to the law and the community that forms the law. Aristotle goes so far as to call the citizen in his deeds a mere instrument of the law. Such is the massive and inevitable impact upon man's freedom of his peculiar natural dependance upon his fellows, of his inevitable status as a part within the political whole.[9]

That impact is complicated. A noble *polis* comprises the stage or opportunity for noble deeds. Even the best of laws must also provide for the necessities of political life: for exchange, punishment, the customs that bind citizens into a country. Besides, laws are seldom the best laws. Their quality varies with those who frame and preserve them, rarely the best men. The intervention of political life between man's natural end and his efforts to reach it again beclouds the whole question of voluntary conduct. Aristotle renews in Book V his account of the compulsion and ignorance that make for involuntary acts. Yet he acknowledges the "indefiniteness" of his discussion:[10] little is said as to precisely which actions and dispositions are truly just. Book V's discussion lacks Book III's constant if vague overtones of the natural limits of desire, anger, wish, intellect, even vision.

A hard passage indicates why: men can be unjustly treated only against their wish.[11] An act of x to y, harmful to y, is nevertheless not unjust treatment if y wished it. In matters of justice the wish of the one acted upon, rather than what is truly to be wished for, is decisive if the laws permit. So with respect to laws and those subject to them; convention governs in accord with the wishes of the citizens, or whoever shapes the laws. Book III's occasional reminders

[9] Consider *EN* 1136[b] 29-32 in its context. See Strauss, *City and Man,* 16-17.
[10] *EN* 1136[a] 10-1136[b] 15.
[11] *EN* 1136[b] 2-5.

of nature are replaced by Book V's attention to the various regimes that yield various kinds of laws—aristocratic, democratic, and so on. There is a natural limit implicit in some basic conventions: the very necessities of men in getting along with one another dictate a natural floor, so to speak, that any polity must provide.[12] Citizens such as prisoners of war should be rescued from undeserved suffering in their country's service, founders and other patriotic heroes should be revered, and opportunity for trade of goods and punishment of evils must be given. Apart from these necessities common to all regimes, however, there is a disparity between the natural and the just in all except the naturally best regime. Thus the discussion of just acts and dispositions lacks "definiteness." Aristotle attends in Book V to the just actions necessary in any polity, and the equity needed to justly apply any law, but not to the just actions that vary according to the regime. It is not accidental that Aristotle alludes, as Book V concludes, to the distinctions between law and act and between act and disposition, to the several kinds of acts injurious whatever the motive, to the fact that an unjust act does not necessarily mean an unjust or base disposition, and to acts "incidentally just" (done out of a motive, like fear or vengeance or righteous indignation, other than justice). He finally calls the acts prescribed by law only "accidentally" just.[13]

ACTION UNDER COMPULSION

We turn from context and tenor to specifics. Book III considers the two ways men act, but not in the full sense: under compulsion from a force, and in ignorance of an important circumstance. Some forces compel the body willy-nilly: the sailor swept away by a storm, the prisoner transported by his captors. Aristotle attends mostly to "mixed" cases: actions done through fear of a worse alternative (jettisoning cargo during a storm) or for a noble object. He calls these actions in general or in themselves compulsory, but in the circumstances spontaneous. "For the end of an action is relative to the occasion." As a rule, no sensible man throws away his property, and yet sailors occasionally do so to survive.

---

[12] See the author's "Reason and Revelation in Hooker's Ethics," *American Political Science Review,* Vol. LIX, No. 3, September, 1965, pp. 680-88.
[13] *EN* 1135^a 6-1136^a 5, 1136^b 33-1137^a 17.

Similarly, for enduring the painful or even the base for the sake of the noble men are praised, a sure sign of conduct not compelled. Yet a deeper problem arises: are not some threats and pains beyond endurance? Sometimes "pardon is bestowed when one does a wrongful act under pressure which overstrains human nature and which no one would withstand." Nevertheless, "some acts, perhaps, we cannot be forced to do, but ought rather to face death after the most fearful sufferings:" it seems absurd that certain threats forced a character of Euripides to matricide.

The high posture adopted as the discussion moves through forces simply external to the pain they may cause, is maintained as Aristotle turns to the force exercised by pleasure and the noble. To call acts done for these motives "compulsory" is to make all acts compulsory; these are the motives of all acts. Besides, compulsory acts are regarded as painful, whereas those motivated by nobility or pleasure are pleasureable. The question recurs at a deeper level—is it not pleasure and thus desire that compels our action? As if in reply Aristotle concludes with the viewpoint of a noble disposition: "it is absurd to blame external things, instead of ourselves for falling an easy prey to their attractions; or to take the credit for our noble acts ourselves, while blaming pleasant things for base acts." One is reminded of Nietzsche, who so passionately desired a rebirth or new birth of nobility, and who said that only weak souls think men at the mercy of pleasure and pain.[14]

This discussion of the obstacles confronting nobility is itself characterized by an austere nobility, rising to heroism. The perspective is more manly than the deterministic hedonism now decaying. Yet it is more balanced and compassionate than the Kantian moralism that rebelled against liberal hedonism, and the nearly fanatical Nietzschean and existential "will" or "commitment" of the "self" that rebelled against both. What is fitting and right is to prevail, and in a crucial case perhaps to predominate over the worse racking of the body. This marks the high point of the claims of morality. We are prepared by the "perhaps" for qualifications. Hardie with reason calls "Aristotle's opinion on this point questionable."[15] It is also true, however, that the opinion is subsequently questioned by Aris-

---

[14] *Beyond Good and Evil,* 225.
[15] *Aristotle's Ethical Theory,* 155.

totle himself. While discussing courage Aristotle says without qualification that some terrors are thought to be beyond human endurance. Later he remarks that pain can upset and even destroy the
sufferer's nature, later still that passions like sexual desire can alter
the body's state and even cause madness, and that there is nothing
wondrous if a man is defeated by violent pleasures and pains; we
are ready to pardon if only he has resisted.[16] There is a bodily
limit to the claims of excellence. Nevertheless, those claims are allowed at first to appear unqualified, according to their own self-ap-
praisal. The truth in Kant's insistence on moral obligation is present
and salutary, but without Kant's unqualified and unsupportable insistence.

We may also observe that the external constraints mentioned in
Book III are only the tips of some very interesting icebergs. There
is climate or natural necessity (with a subtle indication of the need
for property), and the impact of other men (here the extreme, almost apolitical case of a mere captor). More oblique is a reference,
through the "threats" of Alcmaeon's father as presented in Euripides, to the father's authority (which can shelter slavery of the
children, we are later told)[17] and perhaps even to the authority of
God as men mistake it: the threats aimed at Alcmaeon appeared as
curses. All these are expanded later in the *Ethics* and in the *Politics*
as well.

Book V differs in crucial respects. Since a man's deeds are
acknowledged to be largely controlled by law, the excuse of compulsion is now appropriately limited. In defining a voluntary act, pri-
macy in even the order of treatment shifts from absence of compulsion to the requirement that the act be done knowingly. Further, the
compulsion excluded is limited to that involving particular circumstances of the act—and the act's character, and its object or effect,
are not listed here as relevant circumstances (as they had been in
Book III). From the point of view of justice, the proper posture is
that of citizen, and spontaneity takes place within the definitions of
just action ordered by the political whole.

Book V shows this in another way. A third possible cause of involuntary action is emphasized: an action may be involuntary be-

[16] *EN* 1115^b 6-7, 1119^a 23-4, 1147^a 15-20, 1150^b 5.
[17] *EN* 1160^b 28-29.

cause of compulsion, or ignorance, or, third, because "not in the agent's control" even if neither compelled nor inadvertent. Strictly speaking, compulsion is not at work. There is a kind of mixed act that may be motivated by some necessity like imperfect law or justice, and for which men cannot be blamed. Aristotle's example is curiously apolitical: "There are many natural processes that we perform or undergo knowingly, although not voluntarily or involuntarily, for example, growing old and dying." Our opportunities for acting seem to exist in a context of necessity, political and (more basic and somehow related) natural. Man is by nature a political animal.

It is fitting that Book V no longer affirms the unequivocal ability to master the pleasures and pains. The painful passion of vengeance "or any other unavoidable or natural passion" excuses where an external "provocation" justifies "retaliation."[18] Sexual desire is mentioned in this context. These remarks are not restricted to most men, and the distinction between (occasional) unjust actions and an unjust or ignoble disposition is clearly drawn if its implications left undrawn. Also, the higher forms of justice (distributive and commutative) are shown here to depend upon the necessary and lower relations (trade and revenge).

Book V then lacks the almost heroic tenor of Book III. The demands of justice cannot be higher than what the general citizenry will bear. Countries vary enormously in the quality of this common life. Without a scrupulousness amounting to fanaticism, however, law can never as an everyday matter demand of all men an heroic denial of their lower nature. Also, the particular virtue of justice (having to do with gaining and losing from others) is not directly but only proportionately attuned to noble action or character. Commutative justice has to do with *exchanging* goods and correcting evils, distributive with *apportioning* money, office, and honor in accord with nobility or some such standard, and not with nobility as such. Book V points to VI's elevation of judgment above noble deeds. Besides, goods that can be exchanged and apportioned are common and generally good (noble actions and the excellences of soul can't be exchanged or distributed). Book V attributes nobility to an act of justice only in the case of an equitable man *refraining*

[18] *EN* 1135^b 21-2.

from pressing his claims to the limit.[19] From the *Ethics'* beginning Aristotle allows the distinction between the just and the noble to stand, and no doubt this points up the chief cause for the absence from Book V of a heroic posture.

ACTION THROUGH IGNORANCE

The treatment of inadvertence in Book III also starts with the obvious case. Only particular ignorance, "ignorance of the circumstances of the act and of the things affected by it," renders an act involuntary and thus to be "pitied and forgiven." Indeed, a third class of "nonvoluntary" actions is added to those voluntary and involuntary. One might act through ignorance and yet approve the action inadvertently done. Aristotle reserves "involuntary" for actions through ignorance that are accompanied by the pain and regret of compunction.[20] Thus understood, an involuntary action is done in ignorance of particular circumstances. However, the ignorance must be the cause of the act. A man drunk or in a rage may act inadvertently, but the cause of his ignorance is his own fault in getting drunk or angry. Aristotle expands the point in a manner that leads very far. "Now it is true that all wicked men are ignorant of what they ought to do and refrain from doing, and this error is the cause of injustice and the whole of vice."[21] General ignorance of correct choice is vice; only particular ignorance is excused.

As the various circumstances of which the agent might be ignorant are distinguished, however, the discussion points beyond these simple certainties. The most important circumstances are the character of the act and its effect or object, although Aristotle mentions also the agent, the thing affected by the act, the instrument used, and the manner of doing. Only as to the act's character does he give

[19] *EN* 1136^b 23.

[20] Ross denies without argument any "real difference" between the two. *Aristotle*, 193-4. Is there not a great difference in "voluntariness" or spontaneity between a choice fortuitously acceptable in its results, and one fortuitously horrible in result? The first might not be spontaneous (since inadvertent); the second is decidedly unwished for, as the subsequent pain (a mark of unwilling action) shows. Is it Ross's Kantianism, in which intention alone is moral, that leads him to disregard the awkward connection between intention and result?

[21] *EN* 1110^b 27-30.

several examples. All the examples are allegations of mistake used
as excuses by men on trial: the political whole is foreshadowed.
The first example comprises speech "slipping out" contrary to intention; the second, a speech of Aeschylus contrary to a supposedly
unknown intention of others (a "secret" evidently of the Athenian
mysteries); the third, the firing of a weapon when the agent "only
meant to show how it worked." One might paraphrase: To control
one's speech judiciously is hard; one has to know the laws and customs of one's country in order to know what is illegal or harmful or
irreligious; when merely trying to instruct, one may set off a dangerous weapon if one doesn't know its works. Similar complications
follow from the illustration of an action's effect or object. "One
might kill a man by giving him medicine with the intention of sav-
ing his life." A need is implied for unusual knowledge of cause and
effect, like the doctor's art, and a natural end is taken for granted.

    We have touched what is implied: Book III presupposes that
knowledge of things, arts, and ends taken for granted by the gentleman, at once Aristotle's subject and his chief addressee, like all
men is dependent for much knowledge upon his upbringing and
country. He is aware implicitly of what is customary, lawful, and
sacred, acquainted with his country's arms, machines, and arts,
guided by the horizon of objects that the country shelters and encourages. "Voluntariness" in the ordinary sense (and Aristotle's
discussion is permeated here by explicit adoption of ordinary usage
and by such phrases as "it seems") does not turn on deep knowledge, but on the citizen's common knowledge of what to do and on
the arts of doing. Consider the ensuing discussion on "taking counsel" or "deliberation."

    As the ignorance that excuses implied the knowledge that is ex-
pected, the discussion of deliberation shows how such knowledge is
obtained. We move from environment of acting to choice of appropriate action. The perspective remains that of the individual's action. We don't investigate all his sources of knowledge, but the way
he himself obtains it as he chooses: by deliberating. Deliberation
draws deeply on other knowledge that it presupposes. Many limits
circumscribing spontaneity appear here as the factors (nature, necessity, chance) about which a sensible man does not deliberate
(because he can't do anything about them). Choice selects means
to ends, moreover, and this discussion of choosing appropriate

means prepares the subsequent account of wishing and the final re-consideration of spontaneity in the light of ends somehow natural. Deliberation is an investigation of things within our power, attainable by action, to select the means to our ends. The qualification "within our power" marks the rising prominence of unchosen things that circumscribe choice. Aristotle excludes matters about which an intelligent man does not deliberate, such as things that don't change, or that change regularly, or things that change inevitably but irregularly (climate), or things that happen by chance. Nor do we even deliberate about all human affairs, only those (unlike grammar or spelling) not pretty much reduced to a science, and those attainable by our own actions. "No Lacedaemonian deliberates about the best form of government for Scythia" (which was "a long way from them," Thomas commented wryly). The last examples indicate the circumscription of choice by knowledge, and by men beyond one's power, but are silent as to (1) choices that ignore knowledge and (2) the way one's country controls one's choice.

As to (1), Aristotle's very definitions indicate the problematic relation of choice to knowledge. His first definition is indefinite as to whether knowledge guides choice: choice is voluntary action preceded by deliberation.[22] In the ensuing treatment of deliberation, he takes the perspective of a man of intelligence, however, and a firmer definition is given: "choice will be a deliberate desire of things in our power; for we first take counsel, then select, and finally fix our desire according to the result of our deliberations." Choosing thus understood requires a rare strength of soul. Aristotle shows the point politically: "This may be illustrated by the ancient regimes represented in Homer: the kings used to proclaim to the people the measures they had chosen to adopt."[23] Monarchy is but one of many regimes, however. Besides, Aristotle intimates in the *Politics* that this form of unlimited monarchy presupposes but one superior man or family and is hardly possible or suitable outside of countries just emerging from barbarism. In civilized polities, justice and expediency dictate sharing of rule among even the best, and the best never rule unchecked. They rarely predominate, in fact. When Aristotle speaks of choice in the context of justice, he reverts to the

[22] *EN* 1112ᵃ 15-16.
[23] *EN* 1113ᵃ 5-14.

first and vaguer definition: voluntary action preceded by deliberation.[24] We will return to this and the related problem (2) when we return to Book V.

Within the sphere of actions within our power, and not obvious through settled knowledge, deliberation attends to means. That choice is of means is shown first by three examples, all from the arts; the orator and statesman being added to the doctor in this section on choice (the distinctively human form of voluntary acting). The doctor does not deliberate whether to heal, the orator to persuade, the statesman to secure good laws. Again the common arts guide men in their deeds; implicitly they supply the objects or some objects of acting. The central example of the orator indicates the difficulty: a dependence upon opinion, and hence upon the variety of priorities even as to the arts that is present in different countries, according to the views urged and what the rulers will accept. Later there is a deeper argument than these mere examples: "all actions aim at ends other than themselves," and thus are in themselves means. Action occurs in the light of some opinion or inkling not itself action, a point considered with "wish."

Deliberation takes for granted some end and investigates how to achieve it. The first step in producing the thing is the last step in the order of discovery. Here, as elsewhere, Aristotle uses the analogy of geometrical investigation. One sees in the mind's eye the "figure" in question, the kind of action desired, but then has to analyze or determine its necessary conditions. In Book VI this step is expounded, with the prerequisites of experience (for "sizing up" the situation) and moral virtue (for seeing the kind of act "called for" by the situation) made explicit. The agent molds his opportunity in accord with the shape he wishes, as the craftsman does his material. This viewpoint so favorable to human power is only partial, however. Like the craftsman, the agent is limited by his material and his tools. To radicalize the point: the capacities internal (body, soul, intellect) and external (property, friends, country) must influence the actions we can take and hence seek. In choosing we are hardly aware of this, and in considering choice Aristotle hardly alludes to it. Yet the awareness permeates all particular actions, and permeates Aristotle's discussion in Books III, IV, and V of actions

[24] *EN* 1135[b] 8-11.

appropriate to the particular moral virtues. It is implied as the discussion of deliberation concludes by setting human spontaneity between two perceptions: we don't deliberate about particular perceptions—is this object a loaf? is it properly baked?—any more than about the ends of our acting. Yet our perception of bread and consistency surely reflects our appetite for food and our desire for food suitable and tasty. One doesn't note as naturally bread's sound when struck, for example. We have to consider the ends that guide our deliberations, and the desires that affect our ends.

Let us first recapitulate Book V's account of the matters just discussed: the ignorance and knowledge involved in voluntary action in general and in choice in particular. We have seen that Book III's dimness as to the things sought is replaced by Book V's reliance on law (including custom). Book III had tacitly abstracted from the point: that the Spartan can't control the Scythian is said, that his own regime makes him a Spartan is not. Book V's attention to *nomos,* opinion, common demand, political necessity, and political regime replaces Book III's concentration upon individual knowledge, the arts, and deliberation. Still, this is not the last word. The questionable relation between law and virtue has consequences for practical knowledge: to know the law is not enough.

Law's prescriptions are appropriately followed only in appropriate circumstances and in the proper manner; this calls for judgment and a fair disposition. How to act or to distribute is harder to know than the medical art, and this for many reasons.[25] Law governs all goods more or less, not just a single or partial good. Also, justice deals with not merely the agent's good, but the apportionment of goods according to an appraisal of others' deserts. Acting justly is complicated, calling for the judiciousness of judges treated in Book V, and the more comprehensive judgment of statesmen touched in Book VI. The tender relation of the expedient to the good adds to the complication. Besides, a country's laws may need to be renewed, or improved, or ignored, or even founded or refounded. The legislator's art is also touched on in Book VI. In addition, however good its prescriptions, law is inherently faulty in its generality due to the variable material of conduct. Hence the need to rectify law's inherent doctrinarism through equitable judgment as

[25] *EN* 1137ª 13-15.

to particulars. Finally, an equitable man takes less than law allows when the pettiness of a stickler would cost him glory or would be ignoble or (points not developed until Books VIII, IX and X) would detract from friendship or from philosophic taste and activity. Justice in the deeper senses requires knowledge, not merely of how to apply law or to improve and form law, nor even of the fairness by which one rectifies a law, but also of goods other than justice in the light of which the demands of justice are put in their place. If to act spontaneously is to act without ignorance, then practical wisdom is required, and even a wisdom as to what is truly good. Book VI's discussion of practical judgment points toward the higher wisdom of the philosopher: in matters of pleasure and pain "the architect of the end whereby we pronounce things good or bad simply."[26]

SPONTANEITY AND HUMAN ENDS

By the conclusion of Book III's discussion, the knowledge needed for voluntary action is said to encompass relevant circumstances, suitable means, and finally our end, perhaps some end intimated by nature above and apart from moral virtue. The subordination of virtue and action implied, however, is not clarified. The end is presented as it appears to an agent choosing; it is presented as what is wished for.

This perspective of appearance or opinion (rather than the later philosophic perspective pronouncing good and bad simply) accounts no doubt for the hesitancy and inconclusiveness of treatment. Book III never discusses what ends are to be pursued. The gentleman "knows" that. The gentleman takes for granted an orientation by the noble and just; and his awareness comes in good part from his virtues and his country's laws. The time for reconsidering that awareness, from a perspective outside and above it, arrives only with the reconsideration of pleasure in Book VII. By their wishes, nevertheless, fine men show some inkling of an end above virtue and law, whose impact upon spontaneity must be considered.

We must digress briefly, however. Even Book III abounds with indications that its somewhat moralistic account of choice and wish

[26] *EN* 1152[b] 1-4.

should be complemented by considering the various things desired apart from the end of virtue.

Choice is destinguished from desire, anger, wish, and opinion.[27] Yet Aristotle takes up its relation to wish alone. That its connection with desire and anger should be considered as well had already been intimated. It is probably not noble to say that "acts caused by anger or desire are not spontaneous."[28] The reasons proceed through (1) the acting from such motives by children and animals, to (2) the doing of noble or good acts out of anger and desire, to (3) the fact that acts from desire are pleasurable, one sign of spontaneous acting, to the fourth and dual reason: (a) acts if wrong are to be avoided whatever their motive and (b) "the irrational passions are thought no less human and so (naturally) the actions of a man from anger and desire." The last duality points up the natural dualism in conduct: the need for control of desire by virtue and choice, and the naturalness of even uncontrolled desire. Reason (2) speaks to this and will repay a little attention.

It seems strange "to call involuntary the noble things one needs to desire, and one needs to feel anger at some things and to desire some things, such as health and learning."[29] Book III's antithesis between desire and the noble does not exhaust their relation. Some noble acts are moved by desire or anger. There is now intimated even a cooperation between virtue and desire, moral virtue being after all a disposition of desire.

From Book II through the discussion of continence in Book VII, Aristotle tends to deprecate desire and pleasure as dubious forces that call for a strong master. Only allusions indicate in Book III what becomes explicit in Book X's criticism of the practical life.[30] The virtues shape the lower desires and are not concerned with the desire to know, which is characteristic of man's distinctive intelligence. "Gentleness is the mean with respect to anger," moderation with respect to the cruder bodily desires, and so on. Still, mastery of

---

[27] *EN* 1111^b 7 - 112^a 13.

[28] *EN* 1111^a 24-26.

[29] *EN* 1111^a 30-32. I have varied the common translations (Rackham, Ross, Litzinger) from the moralistic "ought" to the more equivocal "need". I seek to convey the connotations of necessity and want, as well as being obliged or bound, in Aristotle's *dei*. Rackham's "it is right to" is at the moralistic extreme.

[30] *EN* 1178^a 9-1178^b 7.

these desires is necessary for noble action, high friendship, and philosophy itself, and hence the necessity of moral virtue. Only as Book VIII treats of friendship does Aristotle take his bearings from the things liked and loved, and only with the discussion of higher friendships are noble deeds themselves derived from the noble soul's self-love: It loves the noble and its own life of activity, and noble activities as the true self, the self in action.[31] These clarifications occur after the "fresh start" of Book VII no longer presupposing the supremacy of moral virtue, and after the "legitimation" of pleasure at Book VII's conclusion, which marks the end of an orientation by right reason and opinion. Yet an orientation by pleasure and desire is inappropriate to the perspective of moral virtue, itself needful for the proper disposition of the lower desires and thus one's taste in pleasure.

To return: Book III attends to wishing, and only to whether we wish for what seems good or for what is truly good. If the latter, many do not wish; if the former, there is nothing by nature for which to wish. Aristotle reconciles appearance and nature, but according to appearance, especially the appearance to the good man. Men wish for what appears good, although wishing in the full sense is for the truly good. To only the good man does the truly good appear good, and on this appearance Aristotle elaborates in a passage of almost haunting pregnancy. Each character has its own idea or divination of what is noble and pleasant. What distinguishes the good man is that "he sees the truth in each class of things, being himself as the standard and measure."[32] As Aristotle turns from action and choice to that in light of which we choose, he exchanges the language of good and ends and effort for that of vision and truth and nature. To choose the mean one must see the true, as the eye of a man of taste lights up at the sight of a noble statue, or man, or horse. The term "noble" connotes beauty as well as goodness, we have noted. Perhaps one could say that a noble disposition sees in a particular thing its approach to the truest example of that kind of thing, which itself would appear as a noble specimen.[33] A nobly disposed man might simply admire such a specimen, as one's

[31] *EN* 1168ᵃ 28-1169ᵃ 18, 1155ᵇ 17.
[32] *EN* 1113ᵃ 33-34.
[33] Consider Jacob Klein, "Aristotle, An Introduction," in Joseph Cropsey, ed., *Ancients and Moderns* (New York, Basic Books, 1964), 61-68.

eye or ear lingers lovingly upon something beautiful. That is not the perspective of action, however, with which we are here concerned, but that of recreation from action, or perhaps leisure. The true kind divined appears to the practical man only as the kind of thing wished for through action. There is a disparity between the divination of the true outside of action and the end of action, and more generally between the divination of intellect and practical action.

The motives for actions are as many as the necessities and desires of a man, and all are different from the mere seeing of the true or noble. The noble enters only into the *manner* in which a man acts, as a disposition is the proper *form* of a particular desire or passion. One doesn't do the noble as such. If the noble be the end of the virtues (as Aristotle will finally say in Book III), it is not so simply the end of our acting. One acts "in the light" of the noble, rather than with it as (strictly speaking) the end, the purpose sought in one's actions. A noble or decent disposition of the various passions is far more important for action than a divination of the noble as such. There is a second cause for the disparity. Not only are various motives intrinsic to action; various actions are called for by the necessities of life. After all, the virtues are inculcated by the repeated performance of particular acts, of which the laws are the most massive source. The appropriate dispositions are evoked especially by authoritative opinions as to appropriate acts. In turning from knowledge of ends to their effect upon spontaneity, let us take up in turn the bearing of the need for (first) proper dispositions and (second) proper laws.

The final treatment of spontaneity in Book III appears the most optimistic as to human power of the whole *Ethics*. Our actions follow from our choices, and our virtues are formed by repeated actions. In choosing our actions we form our dispositions: virtue and vice are within our power, and we are responsible for them. The view is somehow extreme. The exaggeration of Book II, whereby upbringing in good habits is said to make "a very great difference, or rather all the difference"[34] is replaced by that salutary in Book III. By his efforts to realize the end he sees, a man can even form his character. Carelessness and slackness are blamed here, and impossible short-cuts of the drunk or dissolute (which promise the

[34] *EN* 1103ᵇ 24-25.

end without the pain of effort, or blot out the end and the need for effort), are mentioned. Yet this optimism is finally modified (as Hardie has rightly noted): "we are somehow partly the cause of our dispositions."[35] Even the early argument is hedged about with qualifying "ifs" that remind of intruding forces. The discussion reveals dialectically, if unobtrusively, the chief external influences upon one's vision of the end.

The voluntariness of action and disposition is said to be proved by the honors and punishments given by private men and legislators to encourage noble acts and to discourage base. Whatever the truth in this, it doesn't prove the whole point. If I read the implications correctly, optimism as to self-control somehow underlies the expectations of the law, and of men from one another. The expectations presuppose too much, most obviously the agent's knowledge of what is expected of him. Aristotle next observes that the law holds men responsible for blotting out what they know (as by drunkenness); the knowledge is that of the law. Ignorance of the law is then remarked to be no excuse, and even blameworthy. The extreme argument for human spontaneity is presupposed by the law, and ignores all the authoritative directions coming from the law. Perhaps the law presupposes itself to be in accord with nature, to prescribe the acts of perfect virtue (the supposition with which Book V begins). Such arguments ignore also the lower and selfish desires with which the law must deal. Note the noble light of moral instruction in which punishment and redress are cast; the passion for vengeance shown in Book V does not appear here. Even here Aristotle remarks that "we can't be persuaded not to feel heat or pain or hunger or the like, because we shall feel them all the same."[36]

Motives other than the noble come to the fore shortly, as Aristotle considers a man's negligence in pursuing the good he sees. Such a fellow is responsible by his careless acts for his careless disposition. The man "in training" for some contest or pursuit shows that one's acts can form one's disposition. There is truth in this, and also intimations of the unexplored context. No account is given of the many motives (like honor, custom, and natural powers) that occasion the variety of contests and pursuits. Aristotle is explicit as to other difficulties. A disposition once formed cannot be varied at

[35] *EN* 1114[b] 23-24.
[36] *EN* 1113[b] 27-30.

wish, even if one might determine as one wishes its inception. The example is again suggestive: a man sick because of intemperance and disregard of his doctor's advice. A training regimen supposes awareness of what may not be obvious: the connection between act practiced and disposition sought. Besides, those in training may well be those naturally fit, and only a few diseases follow from moral faults. We are reminded of the influence of nature. Book VI tells us that virtue involves natural as well as acquired dispositions.[37] Even Book III throws out a sudden spate of allusions to nature, especially to bodily beauty and disease. The most important says that no one would blame a man blind by nature, or disease, or a blow, although one would blame someone blind from drink or debauchery. The moral analogies to thoese blinding diseases and blows are not spelled out. Does Aristotle allude to the pervasive temptations of pleasure and pain, or to the "unnatural passions" of the "bestial" treated in Book VII, or to bad parents, rulers, and laws? Book III limits itself to a man "blind" by nature.

Suppose a man's view of his end were a kind of "moral vision." Such a natural endowment would seem to constitute a good disposition in the full sense, and cannot be voluntary or reflect our own effort. Does Aristotle think here of differences in intelligence enabling some to grasp qualities of things more easily? Or does he allude to differences in desire and spirit that differentiate the daring from the cautions, the exuberant from the quiet?

Whatever his question, Aristotle's reply is characteristic. It cannot be true that nature determines one's view of the end, because virtue as well as vice is thus made involuntary. Such a view is contrary to the gentleman's awareness and must be rejected, it seems, along with the proposition from which it follows. Then Aristotle explains, to an extent.

He treats equivocally and gingerly the argument for "moral vision" by nature, as if the naturalness of the vision varies with the character, as if practical action depends in any event more on sound character than on a vision of the end as such, and finally as if the practical ends of the base man might be more natural (arising from the desires, passions, and necessities) than the gentleman's ends (product of much practice, restraint, and parental care).[38]

---

[37] *EN* 1144^b 1-1145^a 7.
[38] *EN* 1109^b 2-12.

Without clarifying any such inferences we might make, Aristotle concludes that the actions of both good and bad men remain voluntary, whether because a man's end is natural but his actions to obtain it are voluntary, or because the end is not set by nature but partly by himself. Because we can affect either our end or our actions, our actions are voluntary.

Nevertheless, the old premise that we control our dispositions has suffered grievously in this exchange. The formative acts are chosen in light of our end—and the end may be either by nature or itself the product of a disposition already formed. Just visible is the dependence of excellence upon parents and the community as well as upon the individual's nature. Aristotle repeats the old premise that we control our dispositions, but almost immediately qualifies it to say only that we are partly the cause. The importance of our efforts is upheld to the last, with only muted intimations of the context of desire, opinion, and parental and political upbringing.

To consider the bearing of justice as an end upon spontaneity, we need only deepen what has already been said. We have remarked that justice appears at first in the guise of presumably fine laws, commanding actions according to the moral virtues so far as they affect others. There seems a perfect harmony between acts required and dispositions to be cultivated. Practicing toward others is especially perfect, Aristotle argues, and many of the virtues, such as liberality, or gentleness, or magnanimity, cannot be practiced at all by oneself. "In justice is all virtue found in sum," as the poet Euripides wrote, and its acts seem perfect spontaneity. Think of Churchill's exuberance in the powers of Prime Minister, the office to which he aspired from youth.

The identification of just deeds with happiness, however, proves to have elements of poetic license. "Office may show a man," but the opportunity to rule is rare, hard to seize, subject to chance. Usually one is a followed, with the ensuing restraints. Besides, it is a rare regime that elevates the best men. The oligarchies and democracies that predominate are preoccupied with wealth or equality. They elevate the rich or the majority. The chances for harmony of office and law with the best activities decline accordingly. Also, the common goods and evils apportioned by particular justice are neither the best things nor good for all (not for the incurably vicious). Book V concludes that justice has only a metaphorical relation with the ordering of the soul.

Justice is then some way from the exercise of perfect virtue that is perfect spontaneity. Even high office involves immense time and effort in activities of little intrinsic grandeur or reward. Rulers need be repaid with honor and dignity (if they don't strive for tyranny). Aristotle later mentions graft.[39] The particular acts required by law are truly just only if done with the proper manner and understanding; law-abidingness is not itself noble and to be a stickler for ones rights is even ignoble. In short, given the deference to lower tastes characteristic of justice and its overriding concern for certain needful acts, the individual lacks strong natural motives to restrain the strong natural desire for his own good and gain. The *Politics* says at an early point that habit alone makes men obey the law.[40] Just deeds are related only distantly to that intrinsically attractive vision moving in any event only the nobler souls. Desire is for one's own pleasure and cooperates hardly at all with virtue here,[41] being too likely to hasten by what is owing to others. Hence the need for rule, discipline, and education, and thus coercion to sustain the others.

Sophisticated Americans often sympathize today with a revulsion against contemporary society in the name of spontaneity, or "liberation" from a narrow system. A vociferous movement is passionately eager to throw off the enlightenment's systems in politics, economics, and even in the mind itself. Like its intellectual forbears Heidegger, Nietzsche, and Marx, the movement identifies thought and philosophy with the calculating, deterministic, and systematic models emerging from the enlightenment's passion for useful and certain science. The movement thus revolts irrationally against everything "established," and even and especially against every restraint by the reason and laws common to men, which now seem so utilitarian, ignoble, and conforming.

If Aristotle is correct, however, the road of "do your own thing" is an alley not only blind but dark and terrible. It is a path away from beauty, nobility, and justice, back into the dim recesses of a self deprived of such aspirations. These seem to arise somehow from the intellect's inklings as to what men and other things are at their best, and hence as to the fine possibilities shared and delighted in by the promising of all generations. The inklings seem

---

[39] *EN* 1163^b 10-12 - 1134^b 7.

[40] *Politics* 1269^a 20.

[41] See the comments of Strauss, *City and Man,* 22, and also 37-38, 40.

to be embraced in the civilized opinions, customs, and laws to which civilized men look up, and which noble and just men seek to improve. To turn from these is to turn from noble and just conduct toward its opposite. There results the diversity now so often praised. On the closer scrutiny that experience allows, however, this appears a diversity of lives fundamentally the same in shallow mixtures of dulled passivity and impulsive activism. Those caught in the "counterculture" find themselves too often in a mindless titillation and degradation, a mindless turning on of the imagination to obtain artificial excitement by graceless and dangerous stimulants, and a mindless politics that vacillates between unlimited democracy and unmoderated tyranny. All this disguises only barely a dependent, profoundly lonely, and darkly corrosive aimlessness. Such a movement falls below what an enlightened country of even moderate justice stands for. It is constitutionally incapable of considering the laws, customs, and governance that nourish independent human action at its best.

7

COERCION AND SOCIAL CHANGE

Samuel DuBois Cook

FOUNDATIONS AND MEANING: HUMAN
ENCOUNTERS

Coercion is not a pretty word. Unlike such honorific terms
as freedom, liberty, order, democracy, and justice, coercion does
not evoke pleasant thoughts, beautiful images, celebrated memories,
or cheerful anticipations. On the contrary, the idea of coercion creates symbols and images of fear and terror, arbitrary and irresponsible naked power, violence and the threat of physical brutality, the
negation of freedom and individuality, or radical infringement of
the rights of personality and the sacred domain of the human spirit.
In particular, coercion is often viewed as the simple and direct antithesis of freedom. The very thought of it offends the sensibilities
and embarrasses the conscience and rationality of libertarians and
many others who have a heightened view and appreciation of what
it means to be truly human, an authentic self.

But is not an alternative approach to coercion possible, meaning-ful, and significant? Is coercion, regardless of its nature, source, form, condition, and consequences necessarily the archenemy of human freedom? Can it be a servant of moral and rational goals and processes? May it not be an effective instrument of social change, justice, liberation, and other worthy objects of human striv-ing? Does not our association of coercion with negative qualities serve to benefit the *status quo*? The established social order is al-ways supported and sustained by a multiplicity of built-in coercive forms and imperatives which are all the more perilous because they are sanctified by institutions, customs, and habits of obedience and conformity and are hence beyond the requirement of moral and ra-tional justification. Masked coercion is no less coercion; indeed, it may be even more offensive and deadly.

Perspective is crucial. Coercion must be understood in terms of a larger framework of analysis and structure of meaning. To isolate it from wider issues is not only to insure its misunderstanding; it is also to falsify its nature, possibilities, significance, and relationships. Coercion must be perceived and judged on the ground of its connections with broader human concerns. In a profound sense, the problem of coercion is a part of the larger problem of human power —power in terms of legitimacy, forms, uses or purposes, abuses, and control. Involved, of course, is the question of the relation of human power to human values. As such, the problem of coercion is crucial to the perennial and complex task of the reconciliation of liberty and authority, freedom and order, individuality and com-munity, change and stability, justice and the tyranny of man over man. That the problem of coercion vitally touches the nerve center of the fundamentals of the public order is a truism.

We tend to identify coercion with the sovereign power, majesty, and prerogatives of the state and its government and legal appara-tus, but it is difficult to find any institution, social force, or signifi-cant sector of human existence entirely free of some coercive power. Social interaction has its own way of generating sanctions and imperatives and various degrees of conformity with centers of vitality outside the isolated and lonely self. Human encounters—es-pecially on the level of institutional life and public experience—are honeycombed with coercive constituents. In a variety of subtle and complex ways, forms, and degrees, elements of compulsion pervade and influence the interstices and landscape of human encounters. As life interacts with life, self-restraint or self-propulsion is only one facet of the toal web of the vast network of human regulation, control, and direction. External regulation does not, by any means, exhaust the realm of social control. Self-legislation is equally significant. Both the individual self and other selves are crucial in the prevention of the domination of human life by human life and hence the subordination of some men to other men. This entails a process and structure of power—including coercive power.

There is nothing mysterious about the virtually universal character of coercion as a property of human interaction and public life. Political, social, economic, legal, governmental, and other institutional relations and phenomena are, at heart and in varying degrees, power relations and phenomena. They are primarily collective interests, vitalities, desires, habits, attitudes, configurations, and wills. Social conflict and competition, no less than social harmony and cooperation, are an ineradicable feature of the human enterprise. "The ultimate and inescapable fact of politics," said Harold J. Laski, "is the final variety of human wills. There is no continuum which makes all of them one. Experience suggests common objects of desire, but each will that wills these common objects is a different will in every sense, not purely metaphorical."[1]

Involved is the ultimate problem of the nature of man, how that nature expresses itself in collective relationships, and the nature of man's world. Experience and reason suggest that collective encounters entail, among other things, endless conflict, tension, strife, pressure and counter-pressure, and competitive pursuits born of, and sustained by, human egoism, intelligence, aspiration, pride, the will-to-power, the will-to-meaning, and desire for fulfillment in the context of the scarcity of "goods," "services," and other values of the human economy.

Human life aspires to dominate and control human life and hence to use men merely as means of self-satisfaction and self-realization. The strong are inclined to oppress and degrade the weak, and the privileged—never bothered by doubt of their own virtue and merit—are often insensitive to the miseries and woes of their

---

[1] Laski, *Liberty in the Modern States* (Paulton and London: Penguin Books, Ltd., 1937), 59. Also see S. I. Benn and R. S. Peters, *The Principles of Political Thought* (New York: The Free Press, 1965), 308.

fellows. The powerless, unless protected by institutional and other safeguards, are invariably victims of the exploitation of the powerful. Man, no doubt, is an ambiguous and contradictory creature in terms of social conscience, sympathetic imagination, and civic responsibility. He is not without a sense of justice, but that sense of justice, without special cultivation and strong support, is feeble in comparison to the inclination to self-serving conduct and hence to the subordination of the interest and claims of others to his own. Progress toward more inclusive structures of justice is impossible unless it recognizes and builds on man's tendency toward narrow and exclusive principles and institutions of justice.

The history of social injustice, tyranny, and oppression is not kind to optimistic and sentimental views of man. Ironically, because of their failure to come to grips with the depths and persistence of individual and collective self-interest, pride, and self-love, shallow romantic conceptions of man militate against the achievement and maintenance of a more universal and progressive justice. In the very nature of the case, such blindness to realities produces misconception of the problem and hence misconception of the solution.

The sordid record of man's degradation and oppression of man tells us a great deal about the limits and possibilities of man's ethical, rational, and moral resources and sense of, and will to, justice and injustice. It is instructive of the necessary and sufficient conditions of a just social order and political system. As Morgenthau asserts, "man living in chains not only wants to be free but also wants to be master."[2] "This lust for power and this fact of political domination are universal experiences of man."[3] History demonstrates both the tyranny of power and the power of tyranny.

Why is coercion necessary? The answer, as already suggested, is not to be found in tyrannical institutions, authoritarian structures, oppressive systems, or anachronistic habits and customs—although these are, of course, a profound affront to the human mind and spirit. Nor is the answer to be discovered in human ignorance—though an excess of which is an integral component of the human condition. Embarrassing evidence and sober reflection suggest that the necessity of coercion is rooted in the very nature of man—pride, greed, ambition, self-love, and the will-to-power.

[2] Hans J. Morgenthau, *The Decline of Democratic Politics* (Chicago and London: The University of Chicago Press, 1962), 311-12.
[3] *Ibid.,* 314.

In the drama and flow of collective life, the infinite desires of men collide with finite means of satisfaction and self-realization. The desire for power and its benefits is self-feeding; the escalator of *hubris* is in a state of perpetual motion. Insatiable ambition and longing beat ceaselessly against the cold, stubborn, and brute rock of restricted experiential opportunities and fulfillments in life's continuum. Men clash. Conflicts rage. Groups seek self-advantage and management and direction of institutions and processes that will insure, or so they think, the protection and advancement of their special interest. They seek to dominate and control the authoritative allocation of public values—the benefits and rewards of the political system and social order.

There are, however, limits to the unmitigated and uncontrolled struggle for power and its rewards. Power has to be tamed somehow and to some degree. At some point, it has to be "civilized," if excessive destruction, anarchy, or tyranny is to be averted. Adjustment and accommodation of interests, the regulation of the struggle, and the peaceful resolution of conflict are necessary to prevent common disaster or, at least, constant warfare and indeterminate destruction. The means, content, principles, institutions, and goals of "conflict resolution" tell us much about the quality of a culture as well as the character and viability of the political system and social order.

Men are, therefore, always engaged in the competitive pursuit of objects of desire and interest, and they are aggressive and imperialistic in their encounters and claims. The will-to-power and the aspiration to domination are never absent from the estate of man. While consensus and cooperation are necessary to the maintenance of some degree of order and harmony, conflict is also necessary, even among men of reason, good will, and tolerance. Participants in the struggle for power and its benefits seek not simply justice, their reasonable "due," but victory, domination, mastery over their rivals. "Every man would like to be God," observed Russell, "if it were possible; some men find it difficult to admit the impossibility."[4]

Accordingly, the moral and rational resources of man, for all their power and creative possibilities, are insufficient to restrain and

---

[4] Bertrand Russell, *Power: A New Social Analysis* (London: George Allen & Unwin, Ltd., 1938), 9.

regulate human ambition, arrogance, pride, and behavior, and to insure an orderly and peaceful environment and process. Indeed, rationality and morality inspire, inform, and command the invocation of coercive factors of restraint and regulation. Coercion is introduced in the form of institutionalized norms, laws, courts, customs, regulations, and constitutions. Ideally, coercion becomes so much a part of ways, habits, feeling, thinking, and acting that men tend to assume its nonexistence.

When necessary and appropriate, however, coercion is invoked. The coercive element in the electoral dimension of democracy, for example, is generally so concealed that the limits of democracy's substitution of "ballots for bullets" are forgotten until something of a constitutional crisis develops. The majority in a democracy is not a symbol of reason, justice, or virtue but, in the final analysis, a symbol of coercive power. The sheer weight of numbers is a chief restraint on the will of minorities to attempt to seize power and the inclination of a defeated party to cling to office.

If men were angels, it has been well said, no government would be necessary. Coercion is necessary to the final regulation of social conduct, the peaceful management and adjustment of complex interests, and the resolution of human conflict. It is often disguised in terms of rationality, loyalty to the rules of the game, fair play, custom, habit, practicality or convenience, consensus, a certain way of life, cooperation, and "ordered liberty," but it surfaces when deemed by authorities as necessary and desirable.

The antisocial inclinations and acts of men, if unchecked by coercive power, would transform civilized communities into anarchy and barbarism.[5] Men, at times, have to be compelled to limit their wills, actions, and desires and to recognize the rights and claims of others. Above all, they must be restrained from oppressing, demeaning, and exploiting their fellow human beings. This means, among other things, that the advantage of man over man must be minimized, hemmed in, checked, controlled, and robbed of its arbitrary and irresponsible features. The community or "common good" must be safeguarded against the selfish ambitions and barbaric proclivities of its members. In both positive and negative forms, coercion is essential to freedom, order, justice, and public welfare. Compulsion is necessary both to prevent certain actions

[5] *Ibid.,* 227.

and to require specific forms of conduct.

Anarchism insists that the coercive character of the state makes it undesirable and unnecessary. For coercion means the domination of man over man. There is a staggering amount of evidence to indicate that all too often states and governments have meant precisely the exercise of tyranny by some men over other men, and usually the few over the many. The crucial mistake of the anarchist is the identification of the principle of coercive political authority and power with the behavior of a variety of states and governments. Coercion does not necessarily mean—though it does often mean in fact—the domination or enslavement of some men by their fellows.

On the contrary, it can mean—as democracy seeks to institutionalize—the liberation of the many from the few, the release of the masses from chains. It can be a decisive instrument of the abolition of the domination of man by man. This is the democratic philosophy of coercion—that through the principle of consent as the source of legitimate power and by means of the institutionalization of certain rights and liberties, coercion is made the servant, not the master, of human justice, equality, dignity, and freedom.

Coercion, therefore, is a double-edged blade: it cuts both ways. Illegitimately lodged and used, it is a deadly weapon of human enslavement, oppression, and exploitation. Legitimately institutionalized and utilized, it is a unique agent of human freedom and the enlargement and enrichment of human experience. It can be a tool for the exploitation of the weak by the strong, but it can equally serve both for the protection of the weak against the strong and for the humbling and weakening of the strong and the strengthening and elevation of the weak. Creatively used, coercion can be a great equalizer and liberator in the affairs of men. Perhaps what is needed is this: enlistment of coercion in service not of an insensitive, oppressive, and socially and morally blind *status quo* but of the weak, poor, oppressed, disinherited, and despised.

Anarchism identifies coercion with the state. It is surely a major attribute of the state, and the state does possess a final monopoly of legitimate coercive power and authority. "The state is an organization exercising coercive power for social good."[6] But it is disastrously false to assume either that coercion is the essence of the

---

[6] Harold J. Laski, *The State in Theory and Practice* (New York: The Viking Press, 1935), 53.

114   SAMUEL DUBOIS COOK

state,[7] or that the state is the only institution that exercises coercive power and authority.[8] The coercion of the state can be used to restrain the coercive oppression of private individuals and groups—economic, social, religious, educational, and civic—and thereby extend, strengthen, and protect the realm of human freedom and social justice. Some theorists argue that the use of force by government is chiefly justified because of its function in the prevention, minimization, and suppression of coercion by private governing powers.[9]

According to Bertrand Russell,

> Liberty demands self-government, but not the right to interfere with others. The greatest degree of liberty is not secured by anarchy. The reconciliation of liberty with government is a difficult problem, but it is one which any political theory must face.
>
> The essence of government is the use of force in accordance with law to secure certain ends which the holders of power consider desirable. The coercion of an individual or a group by force is always in itself more or less harmful. But if there were no government, the result would not be an absence of force in men's relations to each other; it would merely be the exercise of force by those who had strong predatory instincts, necessitating either slavery or perpetual readiness to repel force with force on the part of those whose instincts were less violent.[10]

[7] See, for example, David Spitz, *Patterns of Anti-Democratic Thought* (New York: The Macmillan Company, 1949), 82-88; Robert M. MacIver, *The Modern State* (London: Oxford University Press, 1926), 14-15, 221-38, and the same author's *Power Transformed* (New York: The Macmillan Company, 1964), 83-88, and *The Web of Government* (New York: The Free Press, 1965), 12-13, 65-71.

[8] William Ernest Hocking, *Man and the State* (New Haven: Yale University Press, 1926), 54-55, and John Dewey, *Liberalism and Social Action* (New York: Capricorn Books, 1963), 64. "It is foolish," remarked Dewey, "to regard the political state as the only agency now endowed with coercive power. Its exercise of this power is pale in contrast to that exercised by concentrated and organized property interests." *Ibid.*

[9] Frank H. Knight, "The Meaning of Democracy: Its Politico-Economic Structure and Ideals," in *Freedom and Reform* (New York: Harper and Brothers, 1947), 193-94. "The *primary* function of government is to *prevent coercion* and so guarantee to every man the right to live his own life on terms of *free* association with his fellows." *Ibid.*

[10] Bertrand Russell, *Political Ideals* (New York: Barnes and Noble, 1963), 21-22.

The foregoing raises a number of issues about the meaning, dimensions, and forms of coercion. In concept, dimensions, and the realities of phenomena, coercion is indeed laden with ambiguity, complexity, and elusive ingredients. To begin with, it involves the human will which, itself, has been the source of endless controversy in philosophy, theology, psychology, and other universes of discourse. Consider, for example, the issues of determinism and indeterminism, the role of the will in the determination of human conduct and objects of value, and the relation of will to conscience, intelligence, and "ultimate reality" or "the nature of the universe."

Will involves the organization and direction of human desires, impulses, interests, and habits. "Will means the conscious and purposive activity of a self."[11] The concept of coercion is meaningful and significant only in the context of its polar opposite: freedom, voluntary behavior, self-determination, unrestrained choice. In the very nature of the case, coercion is an interruption or blockage of, an interference with, the flow of the volitional life of a particular agent of action. But, as we shall see, this antithetical arrangement does not exhaust the relation of coercion and freedom. On another level of analysis and meaning, the relation of coercion and freedom is not one of mutual exclusion but of mutual implication, interaction, and interdependence.

Coercion exists wherever and whenever human conduct is prohibited or required by a center of power, meaning, or action external to, or independent of, the human self—individual or collective. To coerce is to compel or restrain the human will by an outside agent. "Roughly, a man is subjected to coercion when power originating outside himself causes him to act or be acted upon against his inclination."[12] Christian Bay argues that coercion means "(a) *the application of actual physical violence,* or (b) *the application of sanctions sufficiently strong to make an individual abandon a course of action or inaction dictated by his own strong and enduring motives and wishes.* A man who conforms willingly, abandoning his earlier desires, is no longer coerced."[13]

[11] Joseph A. Leighton, *The Individual and the Social Order* (New York: D. Appleton and Company, 1930), 289.

[12] Yves R. Simon, *Philosophy of Democratic Government* (Chicago: The University of Chicago Press, 1951) 109.

[13] Bay, *The Structure of Freedom,* Atheneum ed. (New York: Stanford University Press, 1968), 93. Also see 132, 259, and 274.

Coercion takes a variety of forms. The tendency to identify it with purely physical force—violence and the threat of violence, physical sanctions and rewards—is not only misleading but profoundly dangerous. Nonphysical forms are as significant and far-reaching as physical manifestations. In fact, because of their subtle and insidious character, they may be, in some situations, of greater significance and consequence. With the increasing complexity of modern industrial, technological, and "mass" culture, the mechanization, impersonalization, and bureaucratization of life, centralization of the modern state, and the revolution in communication, electronic media, and the art of human manipulation and control —advertising, indoctrination, propaganda, brainwashing, and managed information (or misinformation)—nonphysical forms of coercion assume deeper and enlarged importance. How can the individual human will maintain autonomy and self-direction?

Coercion may be physical or nonphysical (psychological, spiritual, intellectual, aesthetic), violent or nonviolent, public (official) or private, individual or collective, overt or covert, legitimate or illegitimate, positive (rewards or promise of benefits) or negative (punishment, threat of deprivation), formal or informal, etc.

Coercion is often contrasted with persuasion. Unlike coercion, said Simon, persuasion is "a moral process. To persuade a man is to awaken in him voluntary inclination toward a certain course of action. Coercion conflicts with free choice; persuasion implies the operation of free choice."[14] As a matter of principle, the distinction is valid and necessary. But when the context shifts from the level of abstraction and principle to that of operational reality and application, we are confronted with complexity, ambiguity, and vagueness. In the realm of actual choice and conduct, it is difficult—and sometimes impossible—to distinguish and separate coercive and persuasive factors.[15] These features are often mixed and the situation blurred. Only close and exhaustive empirical analysis of conditions and consequences is capable of yielding anything approximating sufficient answers. Can we always know or generally know with cer-

---

[14] Simon, *op. cit.,* 109.
[15] Reinhold Niebuhr, *Moral Man and Immoral Society* (New York and London: Charles Scribner's Sons, 1932), xxiii and 211.

tainty when a course of action is taken in response to persuasion rather than elements of coercion or a combination thereof? Is the difference between coercion and persuasion always a matter of kind rather than of degree?

In comparison with its generic alternatives, democracy is often described as government by persuasion instead of force. There is, of course, a profound and compelling element of truth in the description. But is the process by which democracy institutionalizes the principle of the responsibility of power—elections—purely a method of persuasion or does it contain an element of coercion for both aspirants for public office and the electorate? Are the management and manipulation of public opinion and consent a form of coercion or are they, at least, constitutive of a coercive component? Acceptance of the results of the democratic political process is generally a mixture of consensus, tradition, habit, and coercion. If acquiescence in the decision of the majority is not secured by voluntary action, the threat of coercion and the use of coercion will be the course of action.

If a public official votes against his own will and deep wishes in order to please his constituents and thereby insure his own re-election, is he really coerced or persuaded by his constituency? Or shall we evade the issue by asserting that the "real" will of the public official is to remain in office? Is a filibuster in the Senate an example of persuasion in action by the "world's greatest deliberative body" or is it a form of minority coercion of the majority? Or perhaps both? Are serious inducements or incentives—promises of benefits —appeals of persuasion or refined forms of coercion? Say, for example, the promise, for a heavy price, of favored legislation for the rich or for the poor.

What is generally peddled and accepted as pure persuasion is not infrequently constitutive of covert ingredients of compulsion. Coercion can be subtle. It has a way of masking itself behind niceties, rituals, conventions, habits, routine, and group or community "spirit of cooperation." "It is not altogether true," said Russell, "that persuasion is one thing and force is another. Many forms of persuasion—even many of which everybody approves—are really a kind of force."[16] Knight, in fact, not only insists that persuasion is

---

[16] Russell, *Power: A New Social Analysis, op. cit.,* 280-81.

a form of force, but, because it is, in his view, deception, it is the worst and most dangerous kind of coercion.[17] "It is, perhaps, legitimate," Neumann asserted, "to consider persuasion, as a rule, to be merely a form of violence, 'violence committed against the soul'. . . ."[18]

Beyond the most intimate orbit of relations, coercion appears to be, in varying forms and degrees, a property of human existence. Men as different as Tillich,[19] Hocking,[20] Cohen,[21] Jaspers,[22] and Whitehead[23] find coercion a vital feature of social control and the human predicament. "Coercion," said Hartz, "is a law of life."[24] It has been well said that a "coercionless society is inconceivable. Coercion takes place whenever two or more living organisms different from one another live together."[25]

Inherent in the social system itself are coercive constituents related to social control.[26] They express themselves in terms of socialization, customs, habits, institutions, and pressures for conformity. "Free" societies, as Tocqueville, John Stuart Mill, and Bryce noted, tend to subject the human will to "the tyranny of public opinion" or popular sentiment. "The multitude," observed Tocqueville, "require no laws to coerce those who do not think like them-

[17] "(Please note that coercion includes all persuasion, of which the essence is deception, and because the victim is not conscious of it, persuasion is the most dangerous form)." Knight, op. cit., 185. Also see 183, 185, 191, 208, 244, and 304.

[18] Franz Neumann, "Approaches to the Study of Political Power," in The Democratic and the Authoritarian State (Glencoe: The Free Press, 1957), edited and with a Preface by Herbert Marcuse, 9.

[19] Paul Tillich, Love, Power, and Justice, Galaxy ed. (New York: Oxford University Press, Inc., 1960), 47-48, and 51.

[20] Hocking, op. cit., 66.

[21] Morris R. Cohen, Reason and Nature, 2nd ed. (Glencoe: The Free Press, 1953), 342-43. Also see his Reason and Law (Glencoe: The Free Press, 1950), 83 and 199.

[22] Karl Jaspers, "The Goal: Liberty," in Charles M. Sherover, ed., The Development of the Democratic Idea (New York: Washington Square Press, Inc., 1968), 572 and 587.

[23] Alfred North Whitehead, Adventures of Ideas, Mentor ed. (New York: The New American Library, 1955), 63-64.

[24] Louis Hartz, The Liberal Tradition in America (New York: Harcourt Brace & World, Inc., 1955), 164.

[25] Horace M. Kallen, "Coercion," Encyclopaedia of Social Sciences, 617.

[26] Robert M. MacIver, "Social Pressures," in Robert M. MacIver: Politics and Society, ed. David Spitz (New York: Atherton Press, 1969).

selves: public disapprobation is enough; a sense of their loneliness and impotence overtakes them and drives them to despair."[27]

Coercion is a component of economic life, even under systems of free enterprise.[28] "Force," said Cohen, "is an element in all government or legal systems."[29] Coercion is so much a part of law that many have made the mistake of assuming that the whole province of law is exhausted in it. Coercion is not entirely absent from educational institutions. Nor is religion always devoid of coercive elements.[30]

Coercive factors are an integral part of political life, including the structures and processes of democracy. "The coercive factor," observed Niebuhr, "is . . . always present in politics."[31] Belief in the genuine possibility of the elimination of coercion from the political system and process is perhaps rooted in illusions about human nature and collective relationships. While insufficient, coercion is a necessary component of the stability, cohesion, continuity, and operational efficiency of the political system and culture. "Politics will, to the end of history, be an area where conscience and power meet, where the ethical and coercive factors of human life will interpenetrate and work out their tentative and uneasy compromises."[32] Coercion in politics takes many forms—ranging from a system of rewards and punishment to revolution, various forms of bargaining, compromise, and pressure and counterpressure, to insurrections, rebellions, sundry kinds of protests and threats, aspects of diplomacy, war, boycotts, strikes, civil disobedience, minority or majority tyranny, legislation, administration, and adjudication.

Is the realm of coercion coterminous with the realm of power? Does not power mean the capacity to control and direct the will, desires, choices, and course of action of others? In the final analysis, the estate of power and that of coercion come perilously close

[27] Alexis de Tocqueville, *Democracy in America,* Vintage ed., II, 275.

[28] See, for example, Robert L. Hale, *Freedom Through Law: Public Control of Private Governing* (New York: Columbia University Press, 1952), 3-12. "Economic monopolies are a form of coercion." See Knight, "Ethics and Economic Reform," *op. cit.,* 63.

[29] Cohen, *Reason and Law, op. cit.,* 83.

[30] Niebuhr, *op. cit.,* 6.

[31] *Ibid.*

[32] *Ibid.,* 4.

to being identical—depending, of course, on the matter of one's definition and criteria. David Easton, for example, says that power is a relationship

> in which one person is able to determine the actions of another in the direction of the former's own ends. Furthermore, and this is the aspect that distinguishes power from broad influence, this person or group must also be able to impose some sanction for the failure of the influenced person to act in the desired way. Power, therefore, is present to the extent to which one person controls by sanction the decisions and actions of another.[33]

Or is coercion, as C. Wright Mills asserted, merely "the 'final' form of power"?[34]

VALUE, COERCION, AND FREEDOM

What about the ethics or value of coercion? Anarchists through the centuries have affirmed the proposition that political and legal coercion is evil because it involves the domination of some men by others or the enslavement of one group by another. Informed by a vision of the virtually absolute freedom of the individual, they have argued that coercion is incompatible with human liberties and rights and that man's rational and moral resources are sufficient to secure liberty, justice, and the common good. Voluntary efforts and cooperative impulses are, in their view, adequate to the achievement of the Good Life.

Christian Bay asserts that coercion "is the supreme political evil."[35] He goes on to say that coercion "can be justified only if it serves to reduce the occurrence of worse kinds of coercion."[36] Knight argues that "the principle of democracy as an ideal means that freedom is ethically good and coercion, evil. . . ."[37] Others insist that, even while necessary, coercion violates unique human

---

[33] Easton, *The Political System* (New York: Alfred A. Knopf, 1964), 143-44.

[34] C. Wright Mills, *Power, Politics and People,* ed. Irving Louis Horowitz (New York: Ballantine Books, 1963), 23.

[35] Bay, *op. cit.,* 92; also see 93-93.

[36] *Ibid.,* 94; also see 133.

[37] Knight, "The Meaning of Democracy: Its Politico-Economic Structure and Ideals," *op. cit.,* 192.

relationships and the essence of civilization. According to Hocking, "when force is used, human relations in their distinctive character are at an end. To use force on a person is *ipso facto* to cease to move him by reason."[38] And Whitehead argues that

> The creation of the world—said Plato—is the victory of persuasion over force. The worth of men consists in their liability to persuasion. They can persuade and can be persuaded by the disclosure of alternatives, the better and the worse. Civilization is the maintenance of social order, by its own inherent persuasiveness as embodying the nobler alternative. The recourse to force, however unavoidable, is disclosure of the failure of civilization, either in the general society or in a remnant of individuals.[39]

In the first place, the foregoing thinkers generally affirm a narrow view of coercion—identifying it with physical force. It is neither necessary nor desirable to deny that the resort to physical force is a negation of rational human relations. Perhaps the destruction or rupture of rational relations is precisely what explains—and maybe justifies—the invocation of physical force. If the choice and conduct of individuals and groups disrupt and corrupt rational and moral relations, physical coercion may be necessary to restrain the offenders, correct the situation, and restore proper and unique human dimensions, experiences, and relationships.

Rational and moral persuasion is always preferable in the management of human affairs, but it is sometimes ineffective. The failure of reason and morality in the affairs of men is a sad but common occurrence. No matter how much we regret it, it is an obvious fact of human life. Force may be essential to the prevention of greater evils in the world. It may, indeed, be a necessary instrument in the preservation of civilization itself—as the policies and actions of the modern Caesars of the Left and Right are a grim reminder.

When force is used, it should be minimized, and it should take those forms most compatible with man's rational capacity and moral resources and his vision of a more just and humane social order. But even assuming that coercion is evil, it can hardly be denied that there are greater evils: slavery, oppression, and tyranny. Or, rather, since these evils are themselves bolstered and largely

[38] Hocking, *op. cit.*, 58.
[39] Whitehead, *op. cit.*, 90.

sustained by coercion, the real issue is the alternative use of coercive power—by whom, how, and to what end. The creative and wise use of coercion to eliminate the destructive forms of institutionalized coercion would be beneficient in diminishing the total amount of coercion in the world.

Second, the assumption that coercion is intrinsically evil must not go unchallenged. Is coercion evil in itself—regardless of the context, form, source, purpose, and consequence? Is its value to be judged independent of the specific freedom and restraint entailed? What are the grounds of the claim that coercion is intrinsically evil and hence coercive acts are always wrong?

The argument in favor of the intrinsically evil character of coercion is *a priori* and based on the assumption of self-evident validity. It is more than a kind of Kantian formalism. It involves circular argumentation, assuming the very point at issue. But whether or not coercion of the will is good, bad, neutral, or merely inconvenient and irritating depends on a number of considerations—including what the specific will wills specifically. Coercion of and by whom, from and for what, and how? What are the genuine alternatives? What are the specific conditions and probable consequences? What are the form and degree? Coercion must be approached and dealt with not in terms of *a priori* formalism but in specific, empirical terms.

It is, of course, desirable to maximize freedom—at least certain freedoms. And coercion, like all forms of power and influence, can be evil and destructive—just as the exercise of certain freedoms. Apart from the logical difficulties, it is dangerous to absolutize and universalize freedom as such, freedom in general. Freedom "at large" is too full of ambiguity to be intelligently discussed and managed. Wisdom dictates that we seek to deal with specific freedoms and restraints and their conditions, context, and probable consequences, not vague and general "freedom." What and whose freedom? Freedom from and for what? All freedom is not good and all limitation is not bad, either intrinsically or extrinsically. Some restraints are simply inconveniences and minor irritations, others are good, and still others, evil. It all depends on which freedoms are at stake.[40]

[40] See, for example, Harold J. Laski, *A Grammar of Politics,* 4th ed. London: George Allen & Unwin, Ltd., 1938), 142-43.

A fundamental problem of freedom is that of selection from among the infinite number and variety of freedoms. Freedom as choice also means the choice of freedoms. Freedoms have to be selected, structured, and harmonized in a pattern of significance and coherence. There is a hierarchy, an order of priority in the dominion of freedom. All freedoms (or possible freedoms) are neither consistent nor on the same plane of meaning, relevance, and significance; some are contradictory, and some are infinitely more important than others. Those freedoms essential to equality of citizenship and humanity and the enrichment of human personality, for example, are infinitely more precious than those relating to membership in a private club or association, traffic in firearms, automotive speed on highways, of the employment policies of sectarian schools.

The real problem is that of evaluation, discrimination, the balancing of competing claims, and choice—the deciding on which freedoms are deserving of expression and which worthy of repression. "To protect certain kinds of freedom and suppress other kinds," observed Cohen, "is one of the principal functions of a legal system. . . ."[41]

It is not evil—though the agent might think otherwise—to coerce the will that seeks to murder, steal, rape, tyrannize, engage in arson, or mindless acts of violence and terror. It is not evil to use compulsion to prevent oppression and to restrain the strong from the exploitation and dehumanization of the weak or to restrain a street gang from bullying and terrorizing the community. Such coercive restraint protects and expands the total amount of freedom enjoyed by the population. The locus of evil in the foregoing illustrations is not in the coercion exercised but in the will that makes the use of coercion necessary. If it is asserted that in such situations both the will and the resort to coercion are evil (coercion being a necessary evil), a rejoinder is that this introduces the thorny problem of a comparative analysis and evaluation of evils and their consequences and balancing. And clearly, the greater evil lies not in the application of compulsory sanctions but in the exercise of unrestrained "individual liberty." But, again, except on the premise of absolute freedom, which is logically and socially impossible, there is no rational basis for the assumption that the coercive act is intrinsically evil.

[41] Morris R. Cohen, "Freedom: Its Meaning," in *The Faith of a Liberal* (New York: Henry Holt and Company, 1946), 163.

From another angle of vision, the coercive requirement of necessary public order and safety, public school attendance, sanitation, minimum wage, traffic regulation, improvement in the lot of the poor and hungry, housing standards to insure decent habitation, protection of the environment against unnecessary pollution, pure food and drugs and other consumer safeguards, social service, and civil rights for oppressed minorities is not evil but good. It makes for a better life for the total community. The price paid in the loss of certain freedoms by the previous order of power and institutional arrangement is insignificant in terms of the freedoms gained. The significance of coercion is not to be found in its alleged abstract metaphysical character but in terms of concrete and specific conditions and consequences—the difference it makes in the totality of human experience, particularly in the organization and distribution of power, human rights and liberties, and related benefits.

An element of coercion is inherent in all law and legal systems, but that does not make them intrinsically evil. Law, *qua* law, is morally neutral. It must be evaluated not on *a priori* grounds but in terms of its total context—operations, social utility, and consequences for justice. It is not necessarily true that the more law, the less freedom, any more than *vice versa*. It all depends upon what the laws do in terms of the distribution of liberties and restraints. The net result may be either an increase or a decrease in the total amount of freedom.

A priori conceptions, while necessary and significant, do not always help in the understanding and treatment of the brute realities of life. The framework which finds coercion intrinsically evil does not help in dealing realistically, sensitively, and creatively with the problems, dimensions, perils, and possibilities of coercion. It is suggestive but too formal and abstract, too divorced from the phenomena of social conflict, justice, and power. As Cohen remarked, "to trust rigid principles regardless of specific consequences makes for inhumane absolutism. . . ."[42]

It appears that the condemnation, on *a priori* grounds, of coercion is as unwarranted as its glorification. We mean, it should be remembered, coercion not in the narrow sense of physical force but in its fullest and broadest sense of external, whatever the form, control

[42] Cohen, *Reason and Law, op. cit.,* 5.

or compulsion of an individual or collective will. There is nothing sacred, indeed, nothing valuable in itself, about the human will completely independent of what it wills. Some tragic things are freely willed—including injustice and the denial of self-autonomy to others. Volitional actions, saturated with ignorance, hate, and ill-will, can—and often do—produce massive destruction and other evils.

Presumption, it is true, favors freedom of the will, the play of initiative, spontaneity, and individuality, the value of personal responsibility and choice. It is based on the pragmatic ground of the career, psychology, and perils of power. Power is always tempted to perversion and corruption. Coercion or any other kind of restraint is not self-justifying; it does not carry its own credentials. It must bear the burden of justification in moral and social terms. This is the only way, in principle, to prevent the tyranny of coercion. The inclination of man to the domination of man is much too great to place the burden of justification on the coercee rather than the coercer. This is vital to the strategy as well as the principle of freedom. Presumption in favor of compulsion would give the state and government, with their unique claim to the legitimate use of coercive power and authority, a dangerous built-in justification and sanctification and freedom of action.

Before coercion is used, both the wisdom of history and the method of intelligence command that persuasive evidence be presented that moral and rational resources are inadequate to the task, that voluntary impulses, at strategic points, are on the side of recalcitrance. Because of the terrible destructive possibilities of coercion —and all forms of power—resulting from the same egoism and pride that make coercion—and resistance to it—necessary, its advocates must have the responsibility of showing that the issue is really important, that recalcitrance is deep and strong, that the cost has been counted, and that the alternatives and probable consequences have been carefully weighed.

But the presumption against the use of coercion and the correlative requirement of social and moral justification also apply to the use of noncoercive power by an individual or group against another. The problem is protection against human egoism and the consequent use by some men of others as mere means to their selfish ends. Noncoercive forms of power contain no self-justification.

A major assumption of this paper is the proposition that coercive power in itself is ethically neutral, and that its *a priori* rejection is perilous and may well be self-defeating. Inherent in coercion are certain dangers but also certain positive opportunities and creative possibilities. It is a means, not an end, and must always be the servant, never the master. Its major danger, like that of all power, is corruption or perversion so that it becomes the master, not the servant, of moral, rational, and social ideals.

Rejection of coercion on *a priori* grounds would preclude, in principle, the experience of certain qualities and objects precious to human life—values whose realization and protection are dependent upon the exercise of coercive power. Coercion of the human will is intrinsically neither good nor evil. It may be either—or perhaps a mixture of both—depending on a variety of other considerations such as how and why, and the form, process, and results of its use. And this is essentially a matter of empirical analysis, not of formal declaration.

The consequences of coercive action may be good or bad (or ethically indifferent), creative or destructive, desirable or undesirable, or a combination of these qualities. Part of the evaluation will be a function of how it affects different individuals and groups. The moral quality of coercion issues from its purposes, forms, processes, consequences, and alternative possibilities inherent in the objective situation. Noncoercive power may be evil and destructive. It, too, must be evaluated in terms of a number of considerations.

The ideal home of creative coercion is, of course, the firmament of the legal order and political system—preferably of the democratic variety. But law and politics themselves, in no small measure, reflect broader social forces and private centers of power, including coercive impulses and structures.

Another assumption that must be examined is that which views freedom and coercion as a simple and direct antithesis, as a relation of mutual exclusion.[43] There is a crucial element of truth in the contention. In a sense, freedom and coercion are antithetical relations or realities: freedom entails the absence of coercion, and coercion involves the absence of freedom. But the relation of freedom

---

[43] See, for example, Knight, "The Meaning of Democracy: Its Politico-Economic Structure and Ideals," *op. cit.*, "For coercion, the antithesis of freedom, is of the essence of government" 184.

and coercion is much more complex; the simple antithesis does not exhaust their significant relation. In one sense, they are foes; in another, they are friends and allies. It is necessary to distinguish levels of analysis and meaning.

Restraints, including coercive ones, are a cornerstone of freedom. Freedom is not an isolated, self-contained but a relational phenomenon. It is not self-sufficient but depends for its security on a context and continuum of restraint, an order of limitations. The social order is always a system of liberties and restraints. Independent of restrictions on others, freedom is defenseless and empty. Freedom and order go hand-in-hand to prevent tyranny and oppression, on the one hand, and anarchy and chaos, on the other. Freedom and order

> are not only opposed to each other, they also presuppose each other. For there cannot be individual liberty if there is no order in society, and there cannot be a durable order without a minimum of liberty. In this sense everything depends on balancing the two against each other and redefining this balance ever anew under changing circumstances.[44]

And ultimately, the kind of order which restrains individuals and groups from interfering with the freedom of and imposing their arbitrary will on others contains a significant component of coercion. Law, with its coercive restraints and sanctions, is a necessary condition of freedom. The freedom of X ultimately depends upon the law's restraint of Y. "Laws may be tyrannous," said MacIver, "but only under laws are we free."[45] Freedom presupposes restraint. As Cohen asserted, "our liberty or freedom within the law to do what we want would be null if it were not effectively protected by prohibiting everyone else from interfering with such liberty."[46] Dewey observed that

> wherever there is liberty at one place there is restraint at some other place. The system of liberties that exists at any time is always the system of restraints or controls that exists

[44] Eduard Heimann, *Freedom and Order* (New York: Charles Scribner's Sons, 1947), 9.
[45] Robert M. MacIver, "Liberty and Authority," in *Robert M. MacIver: Politics and Society, op. cit.,* 260.
[46] Cohen, *Reason and Law, op. cit.,* 5.

at that time. No one can do anything except in relation to what others can do and cannot do.[47]

Freedom is as much a social as an individual category, if not more so.

Another dimension of the complex and interactive character of the relation of freedom and coercion is that coercion can expand as well as curtail the realm of individual freedoms. As an instrument of social control, law, for example, can enlarge freedoms. The critical questions are: whose freedom and what freedom? Freedom from what? Freedom to do what? Curtailment of the freedom of some may mean enlargement of the freedom of others. The object may be (1) government, (2) private powers sanctioned and supported by government, or (3) nongovernmental institutions exercising coercive powers.

To limit the freedom of the strong to exploit and oppress the weak is, at least, to expand the freedom of the weak and perhaps the total freedom of the community. Conservatives are in the habit of opposing social legislation ("welfarism," "statism," "collectivism," "social planners") largely on the ground that it involves compulsion and hence interference with individual freedom or liberty.[48] Charity is their approach to problems of social welfare.

But whose freedom or liberty is curbed by social legislation? And what freedom? Surely not the liberty of those who benefit from social security, unemployment compensation, medicare, medicaid, and poverty measures. The liberty of some is doubtless restricted by such legislation, but that of the mass of men is expanded. Minimum wage laws restrict the liberty of employers to pay certain wages, but they extend that of workers. Social and economic reform legislation strengthens and multiplies the significant liberties of the mass of human beings. We must deal not with metaphysical and ethical abstractions but with concrete and specific situations and human encounters.

[47] John Dewey, "Liberty and Social Control," in *Problems of Men* (New York: Philosophical Library, 1946), 113.

[48] See, for example, William F. Buckley, Jr., *Up From Liberalism* (New York: Hillman Books, Hillman Periodicals, Inc., 1961). "I conclude," said Buckley, "that the most serious argument against the federal social security laws of the United States has to do with its compulsory character" 195; also see 194. And see Barry Goldwater, *The Conscience of a Conservative* (New York: Hillman Books, Bartholomew House, Inc.).

Civil rights legislation, no doubt, restricts the liberty (putting aside the question of legitimacy or right) of certain racists but extends the liberty of blacks and insures that liberty guaranteed by the Constitution and the promise of American life. The Voting Rights Acts of 1965 and 1970 interfere with the liberty (again bypassing the issue of legitimacy or right) of racial discrimination, but they protect and enlarge the liberty of blacks to participate in the political process and thus to exercise their liberty under the Constitution.

The easy assumption, therefore, that coercion automatically and inevitably decreases freedom is false. The issue is whose freedom and the degree, kind, and sum of freedom. Whether coercion in the form of legislation, administration, adjudication, or other methods involves a net gain or loss of freedom is not to be answered by an appeal to abstractions and vague *a priori* generalities about "individual liberty" but by an analysis of the consequences in terms of various segments of the community.

Essential, too, is a comparative evaluation of priorities and competitive claims and conflicts in the realm of liberty. As previously stated, some liberties are infinitely more precious than others; the liberty of equal participation in the political process is infinitely more precious than the liberty of registrars to maintain lily-white voting rolls. The former is essential to democracy and humanism; the latter is their nullification. The liberty of dissent is much more vital than that of officialdom to hear only agreement and praise. In considering the impact of coercion on liberty, the total consequences and their quality are crucial. It is a sheer *non sequitur* to assume that every increase in coercion means a decrease in freedom. Once more, we must deal with not freedom in general but specific freedoms, specific consequences, and specific individuals and groups.

Finally, it is important to realize that in the complex and interactive relation of freedom and coercion, the value and utility of coercion are not limited to negative functions of restraint. As already suggested, coercion in the form of law and other institutions and processes of social control can, through the conferment of power and opportunity, enlarge and enrich the dominion of freedom. Such is the general case with social reform legislation of the welfare state. Freedom is more than the absence of restraint or external compulsion and the presence of formal, abstract choice. It also means the presence of certain conditions of *effective* choice and action, the reality of power. Liberty, said Dewey, "is power, effective power to do specific things." It involves what people *"can* do and what they *cannot* do."[49] Coercion can alter the material as well as the formal conditions and the positive as well as the negative circumstances of freedom. It can modify—indeed revolutionize—the institutions involving the distribution of power, the system of opportunities, benefits, and rewards in a given society. It can be a vital agency of social change in the direction of a freer, more just, and more humane society. It can supplement and complement—and indeed stimulate, enlarge, and bolster—voluntary forms of action and be made the instrument of rational, moral, and social imperatives and forms of human existence.

In summary, instead of coercion being "the supreme political evil," it may be or can be, under oppressive, tyrannical, or anarchic circumstances, a supreme instrument of the highest political and social goods, and thus a supreme historical causal or utilitarian agency of creative processes. There are political evils infinitely worse than coercion. Political goods and evils must be grasped and evaluated in the light of concrete and specific conditions of human experience, the context of action.

SOCIAL CHANGE AND CREATIVE COERCION

Continuity and discontinuity, permanence and change, stability and innovation, growth and decay, and the static and the dynamic are all aspects of human life and community. In varying degrees and kinds, change and stability are attributes of all societies. All societies are a symbolic contest between, and an embodiment of, both Parmenides and Heraclitus. If the former was the symbolic model of the Middle Ages, the latter is the symbolic patron saint of modern and contemporary culture.

"Advance or Decadence," said Whitehead, "are the only choices offered to mankind. The pure conservative is fighting against the essence of the universe."[50] Social change entails a basic alteration of the structure of institutions, laws, habits, attitudes, and life styles of a given society. It affects and re-orders, in various ways and de-

[49] John Dewey, *op. cit.,* 111.
[50] Whitehead, *op. cit.,* 273.

grees, the distribution of power and its benefits, the allocation of community resources, the foundations of public policy, and the agenda of priorities. From our perspective, the heart of social change is a fundamental modification of the power relations of society, what John Dewey called the "institutional set-up." The only way to make social change possible, meaningful, effective, and enduring is to build it into the structure of the institutional life of culture. Institutional reform is the essence of social change. There is no persuasive evidence for—and much against—the conservative assumption that institutions, over a long period of time, necessarily grow wiser and better. There is no logical connection between the order of time and the order of reason, wisdom, moral excellence, and social virtue, and justice.

There are, of course, many approaches to social change—economic, ideological, demographic, technological, scientific, geographic, political, and biographical, and there are numerous instruments or historic agents. Generally speaking, social change requires a combination of impersonal forces, men, and sympathetic conditions. It is never easy. It always has a regular army of diverse opponents. Customs, habits, fears, conventions, inertia, prevailing ideas, and indifference, as well as organized and unorganized resistance, militate against social change. There are always differences on the method, direction, rate, conditions, and specific agenda of social change.

Conscious social change is difficult and complex. Because it threatens the foundations of the value of the prevailing structure of social control, social change requires sustained deliberate effort, intelligence, skill, organization, leadership, and a variety of vast resources and powerful forces. For social change involves the human will—the will for change and the will for continuity. Will is a key factor in the affairs of men, the direction of history, and the structure and quality of culture. At the juncture of will, coercion enters the picture and becomes a strategic factor in the equation of social change. The relation of coercion to social change is fraught with ambiguities and complexities. The coercive features of the *status quo* are a decisive consideration.

Coercion has been a central element in historical and social change and progress—just as it has been in historical continuity, oppression, and stagnation. Virtually all significant social reforms have been a product of the exercise of, among other things, coercive power and authority. In general, privileged individuals and groups—those who benefit from existing social arrangements—do not voluntarily surrender their advantages, which they identify with merit, the common good, and the peace and harmony of the community. They equate their partial interest with the general interest and universal good. Various forms of power are necessary to dislodge them from the seats of special privilege. Democratic revolutions, emancipation of slaves, improvement in the lot of workers, the development of constitutionalism and democratic machinery, expansion of the electorate, progress in civil and human rights, industrial protection of employees, the general extension of social and economic justice, enlarged educational opportunities, and advancement of women toward equality all have come about, in large part at least, because of coercive realities and norms. True, elements of compulsion were not sufficient, but the evidence of history indicates that they were necessary.

Coercion is an instrument. It is a causal agency. It may be a tool of justice or injustice, social change or social continuity, human solidarity or human estrangement, rationality or irrationality, dignity or misery, equality or inequality, freedom or tyranny, revolution or reaction. It can be a mighty servant of the Good Life. An adequate philosophy of the Good Life—involving means as well as ends—must include an ethic of coercion. The whole nexus and apparatus of power and the total resources at the disposal of men must be considered in the formulation of strategies and philosophies of social change and stability.

"A rational society," Niebuhr asserts, "will probably place a greater emphasis upon the ends and purposes for which coercion is used than upon the elimination of coercion and conflict. It will justify coercion if it is obviously in the service of a rationally acceptable social end, and condemn its use when it is in the service of momentary passions."[51] The real problem is always to make coercion the servant, not the master, of moral ideals and rational imperatives. Careful selection and discriminate use of the forms of force are crucial. Apart from the concerns of purpose, form, and consequence, the use of coercion should, of course, be regulated by con-

---

[51] Niebuhr, *op. cit.*, 234; also see 246.

stitutional processes—preferably those of democracy—and governed by reason, good will, civility, and the vision of an inclusive humanity. Coercion can be self-defeating, but so can noncoercive vitalities and forms of social control.

In the complicated context of social change, therefore, evaluation and justification of coercion cannot be made purely or primarily on *a priori* grounds. A multiplicity of considerations are important—moral, rational, pragmatic, and prudential. It is as important and necessary to tame and contain coercion as it is to use it in service of inclusive human ideals. The *ultima ratio* of the utilization of coercive power is the establishment and maintenance of a social and moral order in which coercion is minimized, if not virtually eliminated from the essential realms of human existence. But that goal and possibility presuppose a structure of social control and meaning which recognizes and respects the full dimensions of the richness and higher possibilities of human personality, selfhood, and community. The ultimate justification of coercion is, therefore, human freedom, justice, and enrichment of both individuality and the common good—a structure of existence and meaning that is not coercive. Democracy seeks, among other things, elimination of the worst forms and minimization of other forms of coercion in the interest of a richer, freer, and fuller life for men.

In a number of ways, various forms of coercion, sometimes exceedingly subtle and insidious, are pillars and allies of the *status quo*—institutionalized norms, symbols, sanctions, and incentives, customs, habits of obedience, sheer inertia, social and ecnomic pressures, intimidation, perceived perils and risks of adventure, and naked police power. A breakthrough is terribly difficult. Advocates of social change labor under the unfair burden of being the easy target of charges of undermining "law and order" and the peace and stability of the community. The *status quo* identifies the principles of law and order—and of justice—with its particular, partial, and narrow version and institutionalization of them.

In general, if not in virtually all instances, the very individuals and groups most vigorous in opposition to coercion in the direction of social change are enthusiastic supporters of, and apologists for, coercion—even naked, punitive, and repressive force—to maintain and strengthen the existing order of social arrangements and distribution of power, liberty, and privilege. There is no hesitation about coercion of the human will in order to preserve "law and order," curb "crime in the streets," curtail "permissiveness," intimidate, silence, crush or imprison radical activist dissenters, militant social critics, and irritating gadflies.

Privileged groups and their allies will quickly argue, in the face of demands for social change, that "you cannot legislate morals. Moral concerns are beyond compulsion. They are questions of inner life—heart, conscience, and attitude. I agree with the social goal, but there must first be a change in the hearts of men before there are changes in human relations." They are blind, or appear to be so, to the fact that the existing social order is based on certain moral conceptions, that law as a method of social control incorporates particular visions of what *ought to be* in man's relation to man, that coercion is a cornerstone of the prevailing structure of institutions, and that what exponents of social change have in mind are alternative or, at least, modified moral concerns and institutional patterns to govern the relations of men. The real question, therefore, is not the legislation and enforcement of morality but what and whose moral vision. Shall, for example, the morality of equality or that of inequality, the morality of the rich and privileged or that of the poor and mass of men and women, be institutionalized and coerced?

For a large number of people, naked force is *the* answer to problems of social dissatisfaction, protest, deep alienation of groups from the social order and political systems, and bitter and angry cries for justice. Unlike classic anarchists and pacifists, insensitive defenders of an oppressive order are not principled opponents of coercion; their approach is selective and self-serving.

Privileged groups, said Niebuhr, appoint themselves

> the apostles of law and order. Since every society has an instinctive desire for harmony and avoidance of strife, this is a very potent instrument of maintaining the unjust *status quo*. No society has ever achieved peace without incorporating injustice into its harmony. Those who would eliminate the injustice are therefore always placed at the moral disadvantage of imperilling its peace. The privileged groups will place them under the moral disadvantage even if the efforts toward justice are made in the most pacific terms. . . . They will furthermore be only partly conscious of the violence and

coercion by which their privileges are preserved and will therefore be particularly censorious of the use of force or the threat of violence by those who oppose them. The force they use is either the covert force of economic power or it is the police power of the state, seemingly sanctified by the supposedly impartial objectives of the government which wields it. . . .[52]

And Dewey observed that, to prevent economic changes, apostles of the *status quo*

resort to the use of the force that is placed in their hands by this very institution. They do not need to advocate the use of force; their only need is to employ it. Force, rather than intelligence, is built into the procedures of the existing social system, regularly as coercion, in times of crisis as overt violence. . . . But what we need to realize is that physical force is used, at least in the form of coercion, in the very set-up of our society. . . . It is not pleasant to face the extent to which. . . . coercive and violent force is relied upon in the present social system as a means of social control.[53]

Dewey goes on to point out that "at bottom social institutions have habituated us to the use of force in some veiled form."[54]

If coercion can be used and justified to maintain stability, continuity, and the *status quo,* it can be equally used and justified in the interest of social change and the establishment of a more just and humane social order. The *status quo,* with its vested interest, privilege, and symbolic moral prestige, does not hesitate to resort to coercive measures, even excessive ones. Preventive detention, puni-

[52] *Ibid.,* 129-30.
[53] Liberalism & Social Action, *op. cit.,* 63-64. Dewey goes to say that the failure to acknowledge the coercive elements of the present social system "signifies, among other things, failure to fealize that those who propagate the dogma of dependence upon force have the sanction of much that is already entrenched in the existing system. They would but turn the use of it to opposite ends. The assumption that the method of intelligence already rules and that those who urge the use of violence are introducing a new element into the social picture may not be hypocritical but it is unintelligently unaware of what is actually involved in intelligence as an alternative method of social action." *Ibid.,* 65.
[54] *Ibid.*

tive legislation and administration, and various forms of repression are resorted to with a sense of moral righteousness and indignation.

Order, for all its massive virtue, is not the highest social good.[55] "There is," said Hook, "a limit to the blessings of law and order if they become the law of the hangman and the order of the grave."[56] "Law and order" are not self-justifying phenomena. Whose law and order? To what ends? Divorced from justice and equality, law and order are not worthy objects of human loyalty and reason. There is no necessary connection between the existing order and the public good. "Order is good for what it implies and not for its own sake. To preserve order where the activities of the state are a perpetual outrage to its citizens is surely to sacrifice all that makes life worth living."[57] It has been well said that "justice and order are . . . dependent upon each other. They cannot be realized in a legal community except jointly."[58] A rational and ethical social order will not elevate order above liberty or subordinate justice and human rights to social peace and harmony.

Comprehensive and radical changes in the institutional scheme of things entail a variety of resources—intelligence, experimentation, moral vision, skill, leadership, organization. They also require a variety of tactics and strategies. Various forms of coercion must not be ruled out as a meaningful possibility and alternative. But they must be selected and used in context to supplement, complement, and reinforce voluntaristic resources and to be the servant of rational, moral, and humane ideals. Just as coercion contributed to social change and reform in the past, it can contribute to social transformation in the present and future. It is difficult to find in history a basic social change involving institutional power relations devoid of the push of coercion. Pragmatic considerations or prudential calculations, not formalistic moralism or rationalism, are crucial. Although not sufficient, coercion is a necessary factor in the structural modification of society.

[55] See Laski, *The State in Theory and Practice, op. cit.*, 68 and 77, and his *Liberty in the Modern State, op. cit.*, 92.

[56] Sidney Hook, *The Paradoxes of Freedom* (Berkeley and Los Angeles: University of California Press, 1964), 111.

[57] Harold J. Laski, *An Introduction to Politics,* new ed., prepared by Martin Wright (New York: Barnes and Noble, 1962), 31.

[58] Carl J. Friedrich, *The Philosophy of Law in Historical Perspective,* Phoenix ed. (Chicago: The University of Chicago Press, 1963), 214.

A crucial problem, of course, is the identification, evaluation, and selection of alternative forms of coercion. There are both governmental and nongovernmental types that can be utilized. The general principle is to use whatever institutions that exercise any form of coercive power and authority. In the nongovernmental sphere, economic, political, civic, education, professional, and social organizations and processes all have resources—both sanctions and incentives—at their command. They are particularly important in creating, bolstering, and sustaining the will for, and direction of, social change. Economic power and the political process are worthy of special emphasis.

The civil rights movement, the student movement, the peace movement, the new self-consciousness and thrust of the poor, and other organized forms of protest disclose a variety of coercive non-violent techniques of social and governmental change. Experience, thought, and imagination will create others. Martin Luther King, Jr. spoke of "constructive coercive power."[59] In creative ways and through persistent effort, he argued, America must be compelled to recognize and to institutionalize the black man's right to equality of citizenship and humanity.

> Nonviolent coercion always brings tension to the surface. This tension, however, must not be seen as destructive. There is a kind of tension that is both healthy and necessary for growth. Society needs nonviolent gadflies to bring its tensions into the open and force its citizens to confront the ugliness of their prejudices and tragedy of their racism.[60]

Hence Dr. King advocated various forms of nonviolent coercion: massive civil disobedience, boycotts, demonstrations, and other "confrontations" with established power.

The struggle for social change can seek to maximize the utilization of what Laski called "the supreme coercive power of the state."[61] In this it will inevitably be involved in a deep and sustained battle with the *status quo,* which desperately seeks to use the same power for the purpose of stability and continuity.

---

[59] Martin Luther King, Jr., *Where Do We Go From Here: Chaos or Community?* Bantam ed. (New York: Harper & Row, 1968), 152.

[60] *Ibid.,* 106.

[61] Laski, *The State in Theory and Practice, op. cit.,* 175.

Law is as important an instrument of social change as it is of social stability. It is more than a method of social control through coercive sanctions. It is a servant of community authority, cohesion, social and moral conscience, and aspirations. Law has the capacity of being more than a mere reflector of community attitudes and habits; it can also be their leader and influencer. It has an educational standard-setting, and persuasive function. Law not only formulates standards of behavior; it also establishes habits and attitudes of conformity to them. Conventional wisdom which insists that while law can control human behavior it cannot change attitudes is only partly valid. Because of the reciprocal relation of attitude and behavior, law, by controlling the latter, and alter at least part of the former. Indirectly, law is capable of changing *some* attitudes.

By the same token, the successful application and enforcement of law to the realm of human behavior is limited. Law is able to control only *some* behavior, not all; some conduct is beyond the reach of the law.[62] The effectiveness of law in regulating behavior and changing attitudes in the intricate web of human relations, moral imperatives, and social ideals is the function of a variety of factors, including the vigilance and skill of enforement.[63]

The improved status of black Americans, particularly in the South where racism was so deep and visible in institutional life, is a classic example of the use of coercion as an instrument of social change.[64] The South did not change voluntarily. In fact, voluntary compliance with the law of the land was not the general case. Various forms and degrees of resistance were asserted. But, as time passed the strong arm of the law carried the day, and had enforce-

[62] David Spitz, *Democracy and the Challenge of Power* (New York: Columbia University Press, 1958), 175.

[63] See, for example, John P. Roche and Milton M. Gordon, "Can Morality Be Legislated?" in Roche, *Shadow and Substance* (London: Collier Books, 1969), 351-58.

[64] See, in particular, Lois B. Moreland, *White Racism and the Law* (Columbus: Charles E. Merrill Publishing Company, 1970); Morroe Berger, *Equality by Statute: The Revolution in Civil Rights,* rev. ed. (New York: Doubleday and Company, Inc., 1967), esp. chap. 5; Frederick M. Wirt, *Politics of Southern Equality* (Chicago: Aldine Publishing Company, 1970), and Jack Greenberg, *Race Relations and American Law* (New York: Columbia University Press, 1959).

ment been more diligent, vigorous, and skillful that day would have been sooner. The main point, however, is that the South was compelled by the coercion of the law to eradicate racial barriers in voting, public institutions and facilities, public accommodations, and other sectors of its celebrated "way of life." Legislation, judicial decrees, executive orders, and administrative sanctions have, in convergence with other factors, produced radical changes in the life of black people.

Legal activism is gaining a foothold in the effectuation of social change in the related areas of the right of the poor, the rights of political dissenters, and the general public interest.[65] The implications and possibilities are of vast significance for structural changes in the legal system and consequent enlargement of human opportunity.

When a government defaults in its responsibilities to a large segment of the population in bringing about essential social change, say on the level of the basic rights of citizenship and humanity, what about the morality and utility of going "outside the system?" Is the use of coercion against government justifiable and, if so, under what conditions?

There is no compelling reason to assume that use of coercion on the part of government is necessarily morally better than resistance to government by coercion or other means. The use of coercive power by government can make no valid claim to intrinsic moral superiority. It all depends both on the form of government and on the actual behavior of that government. A crucial consideration is whether or not that government is democratic in principle and in fact. The intelligence, conscience, and prudence of the affected individuals and groups must judge and decide their course of action.

Rebellion is sometimes necessary to bring about the needed social changes. Oppressive and unjust social institutions can claim no moral right of survival. If a society does not respond with reason and good will to sustained and deep demands for a reconstruction of its institutions, then resort to various forms of coercion may be a rational and moral necessity. Coercion can be made a servant of rational and moral ideals. It may be necessary to energize the will and to sensitize the conscience of the community. "A government is hope-

---

[65] See David Riley, "The Antiestablishment Lawyers," *Washingtonian,* November, 1970, 53-57 and 76-79.

lessly bad when it has lost either the will or the capacity for sufficient self-correction."[66]

What of violent forms of coercion to bring about social change?
Clearly, a number of complex considerations are involved and must
be faced before a somewhat satisfactory answer can be given. Take
one crucial consideration—the form of government. In nondemocratic societies, where the doors of constitutional and peaceful
change are closed, violence or the threat of violence may be the
only method of effecting any sort of social change. In societies
which are in principle, if not always in fact, democratic, the issue of
violence is considerably more morally ambiguous.

But even in largely democratic societies, violent methods of social change cannot be ruled out on purely *a priori* grounds, apart
from the exhaustion of peaceful remedies, specific conditions, and
probable consequences. For American Indians or black Americans
—being overwhelmingly convinced by experience, reason, and conscience of the hopelessness of alternative approaches, and out of
sense of self-respect, frustration, and desperation—would it be
morally wrong to take the plunge into the treacherous and tragic
waters of violence in search of the pure gold of justice, liberation,
and full humanity? Doubtless, in terms of practical success, it would
be an act of futility. But, in the total dimension of what it means to
be truly human and in possession of personhood, cannot an act of
futility from one perspective also be, from another, an act of self-affirmation, of ultimate selfhood, of the assertion of the supreme radical freedom of the solitary and final human spirit over the oppressive structures of history and culture—structures which rob life of
much of its meaning, joy, and zest? Acts of desperation and despair
can be an ultimate way of saying "yes" and "no," of asserting a
form of final self-mastery, of "veto" and of clinging to an ultimate
enclave of alternatives and power of initiative, judgment, choice,
and action. "Instead of life," Cohen remarked, "we want the good
life."[67] There are minimal conditions that make life worth living.

Tragically, violence has been—and still is—one of man's most
common and enduring ways of settling disputes. Moore insists that
"it is not true that violence settles nothing. It would be closer to the
mark to assert that violence has settled all historical issues so far,

[66] Hocking, *op. cit.*, p. 447.
[67] Cohen, *Reason and Nature, op. cit.*, 457.

and most of them in the wrong way."[68] Since integral elements of violence are a vital and prominent feature of the landscape of the existing institutional structure and method of social control, the real issue is not the introduction of violence but (1) that of purposive direction, management, and utilization and (2) that of the establishment of a social order in which violence, if not eradicated, is minimized.

Long before the recent "discovery" of the deep and tangled roots of violence in our national heritage and character, John Dewey had observed that

> It is not surprising in view of our standing dependence upon the use of coercive force that at every time of crisis coercion breaks out into open violence. In this country, with its tradition of violence fostered by frontier conditions and by the conditions under which immigration went during the greater part of our history, resort to violence is especially recurrent on the part of those in power. In times of imminent change, our verbal and sentimental worship of the Constitution, with its guarantees of civil liberties of expression, publication and assemblage, readily goes overboard. Often the officials of the law are the worst offenders, acting as agents of some power that rules the economic life of a community. What is said about the value of free speech as a safety valve is then forgotten with the utmost of ease: a comment, perhaps, upon the weakness of the defense of freedom of expression that values it simply as a means of blowing-off steam.[69]

And Marcuse contends that

> Even in the advanced centers of civilization, violence actually prevails: it is practiced by the police, in the prisons and mental institutions, in the fight against racial minorities; it is carried, by the defenders of metropolitan freedom, into the backward countries. This violence indeed breeds violence.[70]

---

[68] Barrington Moore, Jr., "Thoughts on Violence and Democracy," in *Urban Riots: Violence and Social Change,* ed. Robert H. Connery (New York: The Academy of Political Science, Columbia University, 1968), 11.

[69] Dewey, *Liberalism & Social Action, op. cit.,* 64.

[70] Herbert Marcuse, "Repressive Tolerance," in Robert Paul Wolff, Barrington Moore, Jr., and Herbert Marcuse, *A Critique of Pure Tolerance,* Paperback ed. (Boston: Beacon Press, 1968), 102.

The violence-prone character of the *status quo* contributes to the creation of an atmosphere, syndrome, and mystique of violence—a chain of action and reaction, a self-feeding process. It tends to give violence the status of legitimacy.

Revolution and violent rebellion and insurrection, under a given set of historical circumstances, may be the only course of action for men who desire to be free, to be authentic human beings again. Violence cannot be ruled out on purely sentimental grounds.[71] The only *a priori* limitation is that the appeal of violence should be the method of last resort, the only alternative to the continuity of oppression and tyranny. When all other efforts have failed to provide a remedy for great social injustices or corporate wrongs, when the wielders of power are insensitive to the longings of the oppressed for social justice and freedom, when the will of the *status quo* is paralyzed and its conscience easy and complacent, violence, with all its dangers, may be rationally and morally justified.

But to assert that violence under particular conditions may be certified by reason, experience, and moral intelligence is not to affirm that it may also be wise. Sufficient cause is not the same thing as the utility or the practical wisdom of a specific course of action. Sober examination of all relevant objective conditions and the probable consequences of the resort to violence is indispensable. The point is, however, that coercive strategies and tactics must rest on empirical, pragmatic, and prudential as well as moral grounds. The issue at stake must be clear and fundamental, alternative remedies exhausted, the total cost counted, the conditions and prospect of success carefully analyzed and evaluated, and the highest human purposes espoused.[72] The slopes of violence are terribly treacherous. Even in extreme cases of injustice and oppression, there is no substitute for the creative encounter of human reason, imagination, and common sense with the existential circumstances. The probable consequences of recourse to violence are crucial. Romanticism, utopianism, outrage at injustice and oppression, and apocalyptic visions cannot be allowed to conceal the brutal facts of objective existence. Violent coercion can be more than counterproductive; it

---

[71] See, for example, *Ibid.*, 102-03, and Niebuhr, *op. cit.*, 238-52.

[72] David Spitz, "On Pure Tolerance: A Critique of Criticism," *Dissent* (September-October, 1966), 517-18, and Hook, *op. cit.*, esp. 109-110.

can be suicidal. The will of a group—even a strong and deep will —is not sufficient to create a revolutionary situation. Desire is not enough. A combination of conditions must be favorable.

In modern industrial states, with their vast and complicated network of social control created and sustained by technology, with their ability to dominate media of communication and transportation, and with their final virtual monopoly of the instruments of physical coercion, the odds are overwhelmingly against the success of a violent revolution. And surely violent attempts at social change in America are worse than futile. They simply play into the hands of the forces of reaction and repression and hence make the achievement of a freer, more just, and more humane society infinitely more difficult.

Coercion is as relevant and appropriate to social change as it is to social stability. In both, it is a means, not an end; it does not carry its own credentials. It must be justified in terms of a system of values beyond and above itself. We have tended to think of coercion in negative terms, as a hand of restraint and prohibition and a bulwark of order and stability—terms that make it an effective ally of the *status quo*. It can, however, serve positive and creative functions—as a foe of the established order and a friend of the excluded and disinherited. Coercion, properly informed, inspired, directed, and controlled can contribute mightily to the creation of a better life for all citizens and to the establishment of a more just and humane social order and political system. It can be a unique and infinitely precious servant of humanism, rationalism, and idealism.

8

IS COERCION "ETHICALLY NEUTRAL"?

Robert Paul Wolff

I agree with virtually all of Professor Cook's conclusions concerning the nature of coercion, its social and historical role, and criteria for its justification. However, I find his argument flawed by a serious internal inconsistency. At first, it may appear that the inconsistency is of purely academic interest, but I believe it bears upon issues of great importance in social philosophy. I should like, therefore, to devote my comment to sorting out this single confusion.

The thesis, or major argument of the paper, Cook tells us, "is the proposition that coercion, in itself, is ethically neutral." Coercion,

Editor's Note: Professor Wolff's comments were written on the basis of an earlier version of Professor Cook's paper. The statements quoted in the second paragraph, for instance, do not appear in Professor Cook's revised version. It seems to the editors desirable, however, to include Wolff's remarks both because tension still exists between his position and that of Cook, and because Wolff's point is worthy of presentation for its own sake.

as he puts it, is "a means, not an end, a servant, not a master." Professor Cook goes on to give examples in which coercion has been put to good social uses as well as bad. The clear implication of his argument is that in weighing the merits and demerits of a social policy or course of action, we should not place on either side of the scale the fact that it is *coercive* policy or course. As he asserts in his thesis, coercion is eithically neutral.

But when he comes, later on, to suggest some general principles for the adoption of social policies, Professor Cook speaks very differently about coercion. He says, for example, that "one of the justifications for the use of coercion (may be) the establishment of a social order in which coercion is minimized, if not eliminated." Two pages later, he warns that "if a society does not respond with reason and goodwill to sustained and deep demands for a reconstruction of its institutions, then resort to various forms of coercion may be a rational and moral necessity."

But why seek to eliminate, or at least to minimize coercion, if it is *not* intrinsically evil? And why view the use of coercion as a tactic to which one *resorts* if other tactics have failed? Presumably because coercion is *not* morally neutral (as persuasion perhaps is) but morally evil, and hence requires justification.

The tone and content of Cook's paper makes it clear, I think, that he really views coercion as evil, not as neutral. His target is not those who hold coercion to be evil, but rather those who hold it to be an *absolute* evil for which no justification can ever be found. He believes, as do I, that the evil of coercing men is frequently outweighed by the good which flows from the coercion. Indeed, as he quite correctly points out, very little that is good in human affairs has been brought about without coercion. Pacifists and others who refuse, under any circumstances, to employ techniques of physical coercion, are not saintly, or pure, or dedicated to a higher ethic. They are merely immoral. They permit ends to exist which they could eliminate by less evil means.

Why is coercion intrinsically evil? Surely not merely because it is painful, for many men find the pain of deliberation and self-determination much more severe than the pain of coercion. The low level of political participation even in small, face-to-face situations demonstrates the depressing truth that most men would rather be pushed about by others than make the effort to determine their own affairs in uncoerced fashion.

So if coercion is intrinsically evil, it is not merely because it is painful. The real reason is quite simply that coercion is degrading. To coerce a man rather than persuade him is to treat him as a thing governed by causes rather than as a person guided by reasons. Without pretending to offer an adequate analysis of the distinction between thinghood and personhood, I should like to suggest that Kant was quite correct when he asserted that one form of the highest moral principle is the injunction to treat men as persons and not simply as objects. Rational community, or the reciprocal discourse of persons equally situated, is the form of a truly moral human society.

Thus stated, the moral law abstracts from all the historical and social conditions for its realization. As Marx quite correctly pointed out, some classical philosophers of liberalism used the abstract principle as an ideological rationalization for social policies which served the economic and power interests of a single ascendant class. Nevertheless, as Marx also seems to have understood, the error of the classical liberals lay not in their abstract principle, but rather in their easy and false assumption that a capitalist society provided every man and woman with the material conditions required for being, and for being treated as, a person.

The truth, of course, is quite otherwise. So long as some men control access to the means by which other men gain a living, coercion of the worst sort will dominate the human relationships of a society. It is no accident that to plumbers and professors alike, job security is more sought after than even high pay or pleasant working conditions. Aristotle may have exhibited an unpleasant aristocratic bias in his discussion of the good life, but he was surely right in claiming that an assured income was an essential condition for the full and happy development of the human personality.

Professor Cook will no doubt wish to remind me that even the independently wealthy sometimes come into conflict with one another, and that when they do, coercion will occur. Since some men really do have fundamentally incompatible interests, which no amount of discussion can reconcile, there is no hope even in utopia of eliminating coercion.

Quite true. Nevertheless, there is no comparing the coercion suffered by the wage slave and the man of means. A poor man, tied to his job by a fear of poverty and starvation, submits to modes of coercion which the wealthy man never experiences. So, to put the matter in another way, coercive threats which the poor man perceives as matters of life and death, present themselves to the wealthy man as mere calculations of relative advantage.

Let me cite one simple, but urgent, example of this general truth by way of illustration. Parents of young children in Manhattan face a public school system which is so bad as to be a major threat to their children's well-being. Poor parents have no choice but to send their children to the public schools and pray that some improvement will occur soon enough to do them some good. Wealthy parents can send their children to private schools—at great expense, to be sure, but still at *manageable* expense. Both parents are, strictly speaking, coerced by the law which requires that their children go to school and by a system which offers inadequate schools. But the wealthy need make only peripheral sacrifices to avoid the evil, whereas the poor must resort to such heroic and hopeless measures as protests and defiance of the law.

Coercion, Professor Cook concludes, can "serve positive and creative functions—as a foe of the *status quo* and friend of the excluded and disinherited." I agree completely. But this does not alter the fact that coercion is evil. It merely points to the fundamental truth that the coercion of defiance, resistance, rebellion, and revolution, is frequently far less evil than the quiet, orderly, familiar, accepted coercion of established social institutions.

9

THE NEED FOR COERCION

J. Howard Sobel

Everyone knows that coercion is necessary for ordinary men, yet many philosophers have believed that perfectly good and wise men could do without it, that perfect men left alone would inhabit utopias. It is a pleasant thought, though I think not a true one. I believe that even perfect men could need coercion. In substantiation, however, I demonstrate here only a weaker thesis by considering hyperrational act-utilitarians and, without any attempt to defend or to assess their claim to perfection, by showing that they too could need coercion.

Two connected views will be opposed. The first holds that a community of supremely intelligent and well-informed men concerned only with the common good and possessed of strong wills could never need coercion. The second holds that a member of such a community could never need to be coerced to do his part; that knowing of the goodness of a given social arrangement and of the adequacy of its enforcement as regards others, such a man would do his part willingly; that from his point of view, sanctions—if and when needed by his community—would be needed only as guarantees that others would follow the rules and do their parts. Both views are mistaken. The need for coercion is more radical than they would suggest. Even hyperrational act-utilitarians could need it, and need it both collectively (a community of such men could need it in order that the common good be well-served) and individually (each such man could need it in order that he do his part). The two parts of this thesis are argued in turn after the men and communities in question are described in more detail.

THE COMMUNITY

We consider communities that satisfy the following conditions.

1.1. Act-teleology

Each member of the community holds that a person ought to do one of the best actions open to him. For more precision several technical terms are used.

An action x' is a *version* of an action x if and only if x' entails doing x—for example, returning serve backhand is a version of returning serve. An action is *open* to an agent if and only if he can do it by choice or "for sure." An action is a *most specific* action open to an agent if and only if it is open to him and no incompatible versions of it are open to him: returning serve is not a most specific action open to a player on an occasion if on this occasion he can choose to return backhand or forehand. A *minimal* action open to an agent is an action he can choose to do which, if chosen and initiated by him, could not be stopped short of completion. An agent cannot "change his mind" about an initiated minimal action.

An agent a's *expected value* for an event e that would take place at t is a probability-weighted average of the values of the possible futures from t were e to obtain, probabilities being relative to the past to t and the occurrence of e and such as a would assign after full consideration, and values being those that a would assign after full consideration. Suppose an event e has n possible futures,

$F_1 \ldots F_n$. Let an agent a's probability for future F_i given e and the past be p_i and let a's value for F_i be v_i. Then a's expected value for e is

$$\sum_{i=n}^{i=n} p_i \times v_i.$$

A *partition* of an agent's possibilities for action at t is a set of mutually exclusive actions he can do at t which actions are jointly exhaustive of his possibilities for action at t: An agent must do exactly one action from each partition of his possibilities for action. A partition, each member of which is a most specific action open to an agent, is a *finest analysis* of his possibilities for choice. A finest analysis of an agent's minimal options on an occasion is a finest analysis of his possibilities for choice, each member of which is a minimal action open to him on the occasion.

The practical principle now spelled out that is endorsed by each member of the community is that,

An action x is a *right* most specific minimal action open to choice by an agent on an occasion if and only if there is a finest analysis K of his minimal options on this occasion such that (i) x is in K, and (ii) for each action y in K, his expected value for doing x on this occasion is at least as great as his expected value for doing y on this occasion.

And each member holds that,

For any agent and occasion, if S is a set of actions containing all and only right actions from a finest analysis of his minimal options on this occasion, then he *ought* to do an action from S on this occasion.

(So each member holds that an agent ought to do an action x if and only if he ought to do an action from the unit-set that contains x.)

We cannot assume that there will always exist a unique finest analysis of an agent's minimal options. For example, if an agent can try to light a fire in a certain way and knows that it is raining, then both "trying to light a fire in this way" and "trying to light a fire in this way in the rain" may be for him most specific minimal options, one containing one of these actions, the other containing instead the other. But though there will not always be a unique finest and analysis of an agent's minimal options, the example just stated suggests —and we shall assume—that any two finest analyses of an agent's minimal open actions on an occasion will be *equivalent:* we assume that their members can be paired without remainder so that the agent performs one member of a pair on the occasion if and only if he performs the other. Furthermore, since actions paired will be open to the agent it follows that "in the end" he would know that he could not perform one without performing the other. So choices of paired actions will have for him the same expected values. But then for practical purposes it cannot matter how an agent's options are described. Applying his principle to different finest analyses of his minimal options cannot lead to incompatible or even substantially different directives. If applying it to one analysis established that he ought to do x and applying it to another analysis established that he ought to do y, then given our assumption that finest analyses of an agent's minimal options on an occasion are equivalent he would do x on this occasion if and only if he did y.

Each agent is a teleologist, a purely forward-looking teleologist. This has implications for his values. When assigning a value to a possible future, he does not regard what would be its past; the value assigned in no way depends upon what would be its past. For illustration, we consider what for us is an important consequence of this stipulation. Suppose that future F_1 would begin with the keeping of a promise that everyone knows was made, and that future F_2 would begin instead with the keeping of a promise that was not made but that everyone thinks was made. For a purely forward-looking agent, nothing has been said that makes F_1 "so far" or *ceteris paribus* more valuable than F_2. In all things our agents "look solely to the good to follow." So they do not value promise-keeping *per se*. Of course promise-keeping is only an important example. They do not value, or count as obligatory, acts of gratitude, reciprocity, or retribution either. A full list would be endless.

The forward-looking restriction is the *only* assumption we make about values. Thus we do not assume that our agents agree in their values. And we do not insist that they be benevolent. The men discussed always are universalists and impartially benevolent, but that they are is not essential to any arguments. Altruists or egotists would have served all arguments as well.

1.2. Practical rationality

Roughly, our agents do what they know they ought to do. More precisely, if one of them knows that he ought to do an action from a certain set, then he does an action from this set. And if he does a certain most specific minimal action open to him, then he knows that this action belongs to a set that contains all and only right actions from a finest analysis of his minimal options. *Our agents not only always do what they know they ought to do, they never act without such knowledge.*

Suppose that a finest analysis contains several right actions. Given the absence of reasons for doing one of these actions rather than another, we assume indifference (not impotence) and assume that any rational observer will judge each of the right actions equally probable. Other assumptions concerning expectations in cases of indifference suggest themselves: we might assume expectations fitted to the particular case and based, perhaps, on knowledge of causal determinants of the choice. But alternative assumptions need not be explored. When the assumption made plays a role, as in Section 2.2 below, the argument could be redirected so as to proceed without *any* assumption concerning expectations in cases of indifference. (See note 5 below.)

1.3. Theoretical rationality

We assume that our agents are reasonable in their assessments of probabilities, and, for simplicity, that they agree in these assessments. Further, each agent is to be an accurate and fast reasoner. If he knows certain premises, then he knows of whatever follows from them what he would like to know. Finally, our agents will be orderly in their deliberations, putting first issues first; difficult to characterize in general and with precision, what this comes to in at least one case will be apparent in Section 3.2 below.

1.4. Knowledge of situations

Each agent knows the past and the structure of the situation in which the community finds itself at a given moment: He knows a finest analysis of each agent's minimal options as well as what combinations of these actions are possible. In addition he knows how each agent views the several possible patterns of action—what expected values he assigns to them. Further he knows the extent (if any) to which these actions are dependent on, and apt to influence, one another.

1.5. Publicity of practical knowledge

In case it is not a consequence of other assumptions, we also assume that all matters relevant to what an agent ought to do are public and knowable by everyone if knowable by anyone. No one is to have special access to what anyone, even he himself, ought to do.

1.6. Community self-knowledge

That the community satisfies conditions 1.1 through 1.5 is to be "common knowledge" in the community: each member is to know that the community meets these conditions, know that this (i.e., that the community meets these conditions) is known by each member of the community, know that *this* is known by each member of the community, *and so on.*

This completes our specifications for the community. It is not an objection that *actual* men are never so well-informed and self-controlled. Our concern is not with the interaction and coordination problems of actual agents, or with solutions available to actual agents because of their imperfections.[1] Nor is it an objection that *perfect* agents would know more than we have explicitly assumed that ours know, for perfect agents would know at least the things assumed and, as I argue below, agents who know these things can be embroiled in difficulties from which additional information could not extricate them.

THE COMMUNITY'S NEED FOR COERCION

Reasonable and well-informed as they are our agents can need sanctions and coercive government. Two cases show this: in the first there is, in the second there is not, disagreement over values.

---

[1] I count conventions—see Lewis (1969)—as such solutions. Hyperrational agents unimpressed as they would be by "salience" and not prone to habits could not sustain what Lewis calls "convention."

2.1. The Farmer's Dilemma

2.1.1. Row and Column live on opposite sides of a chasm: they cannot cross it or move goods across it. Each can either plant wheat that he can eat or flowers that the other can view at a distance and enjoy—each enjoys flowers only when viewed from a distance, so neither can enjoy his own. To simplify, we assume that each must plant something, either only wheat or only flowers. And to complicate, we assume that each is capable not only of planting wheat, or flowers, "for sure," but also of making it probable to any degree p that he plant wheat and to the degree $(1 - p)$ that he plant flowers: we assume that a finest analysis of their minimal options contains as well as the two "pure" strategies every "mixed" strategy built upon them. (Strictly speaking, it is unlikely that, for example, planting would ever be a *minimal* action open to an agent. The case could be made more plausible by taking "planting wheat" as short for "starting to plant wheat;" similarly for "planting flowers.") Such finely-tuned agents, such virtuosi, are of course not encountered in real life. But it is good to see that even they can have problems, and it will be clear that the same problems could be more easily established for less well-endowed agents. Finally, regarding their actions, we assume that they are *fully independent*.

Row is a young man, unsubtle and quick to enjoy things of natural beauty. In contrast, Column is an older man, mature and possessed of refined sensibilities. Each would suffer from hunger without wheat, and would take pleasure in the other's flowers. As for their *values*, in many ways they are in agreement, but there is this difference: Row places a premium on the mature enjoyment that Column would get from looking at flowers, while he counts as relatively insignificant the sort of pleasure flowers afford him. Column values highly the innocent, spontaneous joy of which only Row happens to be capable, while taking a much dimmer view of the sophisticated pleasures that are apt to come his own way.

Row and Column rank the four possible planting patterns as follows: They agree that the pattern (W,W) in which each plants wheat is to be preferred to the pattern (F,F) in which each plants flowers. Neither feels that the other's aesthetic pleasures would be worth their *both* "starving." But they disagree as regards the two mixed patterns. Row assigns *highest* value to the pattern (F,W) in which he plants flowers and Column plants wheat: he ranks (F,W) even higher than (W,W)—he judges Column's aesthetic enjoyment worth one person's discomfort. Row assigns *lowest* value to the pattern (W,F) in which he plants wheat and Column plants flowers: he ranks (W,F) even lower than (F,F)—as has been said, he judges Column's aesthetic enjoyment worth one person's discomfort. Column, given the premium *he* places upon *Row's* sort of aesthetic pleasure, reverses these evaluations for the patterns (F,W) and (W,F). Their situation has the following structure:

The greater the number, the greater the expected value. (The magnitudes have been chosen arbitrarily but without prejudice. Any numbers similarly ordered would serve the argument as well.) Row's expected value for a pattern is entered in bold type in the lower left corner of the pattern's box; Column's in the upper right. Expected values for combinations of "mixed" strategies are computable. Consider a combination consisting of the "mixed" strategy $(1/3, 2/3)$ for Row—under it Row makes his W $1/3$ probable and his F $2/3$ probable— and the "mixed" strategy $(3/4, 1/4)$ for Column. Row's expected value for this pattern of strategies is, $(3 \cdot 1/3 \cdot 3/4)$ $+ (1 \cdot 1/3 \cdot 1/4) + (4 \cdot 2/3 \cdot 3/4) + (2 \cdot 2/3 \cdot 1/4)$, or, more simply, $3\frac{1}{6}$.

2.1.2. What will they do? It may seem that what they do should depend upon what they should expect each other to do, but this is not so. It will be clear to each that he should plant flowers *whatever* he should expect the other to do. This result follows from the independence of their actions and the "dominance" for each of the "pure" strategy in which he plants flowers "for sure." ("Dominance" alone would not support the argument. See Jeffrey (1965),

p. 8.) Row, for example, could reason: "What I should expect Column to do doesn't depend at all on what I do. So it does not matter what I should expect Column to do, my best bet in any case is to plant flowers "for sure." Suppose I should judge it probable to degree p that Column will plant wheat and to degree $(1 - p)$ that he will plant flowers. Then my expected value for my "pure" strategy $(0,1)$ in which I plant flowers "for sure" is $4p + 2(1 - p)$, or, $2 + 2p$, which is greater than my expected value for each of my other strategies $(q, 1 - q)$, $1 \geq q > 0$, in which I do not make my flower-planting certain: the expected value for such a strategy is, $3pq + q (1 - p) + 4(1 - q)p + 2(1 - q)(1 - p)$, or, $2 + 2p - q$."

The situation is one of frustration. It is as if nature had contrived a trap. Men caught in it might well feel that "there should be a law against such predicaments."[2] They could use a law "with teeth" against planting flowers, and if coercive law were their best remedy, we could say that they *needed* such a law. Of course, even if coercive law were their best remedy, they could prefer to live with their problem unsolved: Men can need things that they cannot afford and do not even *want* at the going price.

2.1.3. In the Farmer's Dilemma actions of reasonable agents operate to frustrate the ends they would have their actions serve. This has an air of paradox. Surely something has gone

[2] See Luce and Raiffa (1957), 97. The Farmer's Dilemma is a non-egoistic analogue of the well-known Prisoner's Dilemma. For an early consideration of a case of the same structure, see Hume (1888), 520-21: "Your corn is ripe today. . . ."

Though not "egocentric," Row and Column *are* "arrogant": neither in his values takes into consideration the values of the other. It is natural to wonder whether rational "nonarrogant" agents could find themselves in similar difficulties. Full consideration of such agents and their "value-composing" functions lies beyond the scope of this essay, but this much can be said: If there is just one reasonable way of taking into account the values of others when arriving at one's own values, then rational "nonarrogant" agents cannot be in *any* value-disagreement difficulties. If there are several reasonable ways, than value-disagreements are possible for such agents; whether a Farmer's Dilemma is possible depends on the exact characters of these several ways. And if there is no rational "value-composition" function for generating "nonarrogant" out of "arrogant" values, then there are no rational "nonarrogant" agents to consider. For strategic purposes, the important question regarding "nonarrogant" agents, as for agents of any value persuasion, is what kinds of value disagreements, if any, they can be in.

wrong. Some argument available to such men *must* have been over-looked. It cannot be that left to their own "natural" devices they are lost.

We consider two attempts to evade the conclusions reached in 2.12.

2.1.3.1. One wants to say, "There must be *something* wrong with the argument that purports to show that Row, for example, ought to plant flowers. For this argument can be met by one that contradicts its conclusion: 'If I were to plant wheat, then planting wheat would be what I ought to do: for I am a reasonable man—I do only what I know that I ought to do. But if planting wheat were what *I* ought to do, then it would be what *Column* ought to do: the situation is symmetrical. And if planting wheat were what Column ought to do, then that is what he would do, for he too is a reasonable and knowledgeable man. So, if I were to plant wheat, then Column would plant wheat and the pattern (W,W) would obtain: this follows by two applications of "hypothetical syllogism." By parity of reasoning, if I were to plant *flowers,* then *that* is what Column would do and the pattern (F,F) would obtain. So in actuality my choice is between these two patterns: the other two are not really possible. But then my choice is clear, and so is the conclusion that I ought to plant wheat, not flowers.' " (This argument might be compared to Rapoport (1966), pp. 141-42.)

Several objections suggest themselves. The main one concerns the argument's very first step. Row claims that if he were to plant wheat, then that would be what he ought to do. But in effect it has been argued that this conditional is false: according to the argument in Section 2.12, Row ought not to plant wheat, and *if* this is right, then one supposes that if he *were* to plant wheat (and he is *capable* of this, even if he should not and would not *do* this), then he would *not* be doing what he ought to do. We depict Row as seeking to determine what he ought to do, and yet, in the very first step of his argument we have him take for granted that, since he is a *reasonable* man, *whatever* he did would be right and what he ought to do! The difficulty, I think, is mainly with the notion of a reasonable man. This should be of a man who *does* only reasonable things, not of a man who *can* do only reasonable things. Everything that a reasonable man *does is* reasonable and Row is a reasonable man. But it does not follow that anything Row *did would be* reasonable.

This claim could be supported only in the totally bizarre circumstance in which, for any thing that is not what Row ought to do, doing it would not only be "out of character" but something of which he was *incapable*. To be brief, perhaps the following suffices against the present objection: Either planting wheat is not what Row ought to do or planting flowers is not what he ought to do, and Row knows this. So he cannot reason *both* that if he were to plant wheat he would be doing what he ought to do, *and* that if he were to plant flowers he would be doing what he ought to do. At the very least, his argument, since it requires both of these conditionals, fails for want of a premise. (Even granting its premises, the argument would be vulnerable. It involves applications of "hypothetical syllogism" to contrafactual conditionals, and there are in my view good reasons for thinking that this is not a valid form of inference for such conditionals.(See Sobel 1970, pp. 436-37.)

2.1.3.2. Even if (F,F) is the inevitable outcome of an isolated Farmer's Dilemma, it can seem that in practice one could in general anticipate repetition, and that given a series of Dilemmas reasonable agents would settle upon (W,W). But, at least under the only knowledge-assumption compatible with the spirit of this study, this is not so. The assumption made specific for agents confronted with a series of three Farmer's Dilemmas is:

> Each agent knows that (there are only three Farmer's Dilemmas to come and that when there are only two to come each agent will know that (there are only two to come and that when there is only one to come each agent will know that (there is only one to come))).

Consider agents confronted with a series of three Dilemmas. Each can see that the third one, when it comes, might as well be isolated: it will certainly resolve into (F,F). When it comes, each will know that there are no future Dilemmas to be considered and perhaps affected by performances in it; and past Dilemmas will be of no interest since they could matter only by generating expectations concerning the other's performance in the third Dilemma and, as was shown in Section 2.12, what an agent ought to do in a Farmer's Dilemma does not depend at all upon what he should expect the other to do.[3] So the last Dilemma will resolve into (F,F), and that it will, will be evident to our agents when in the second Dilemma. They will know that for all practical purposes it might as well be last and isolated; and so it too will resolve into (F,F). But then, turning to the first Dilemma, our agents will see that *it* might as well be last and isolated, and that each should and will plant flowers "for sure" in it and indeed in all three Dilemmas. (See Luce and Raiffa (1957) for a discussion of iterated Prisoner's Dilemmas: pp. 97-102.)

2.2. The Hunter's Dilemma

2.2.1. Row and Column are in value disagreement in the Farmer's Dilemma, and even if (as I think) this does not mean that either is in error, it is appropriate that we consider a value agreement case. It can seem especially implausible that men in value agreement and never at cross-purposes should have reason to wish themselves subject to coercion.

We consider a two-man hyperrational community and suppose that its members are wondering, somewhat anxiously, whether they will be able to cope with a situation they see headed their way. Here is the situation, described for simplicity as if it were already upon our agents.

Row and Column have left their fire. They are hunting separately and out of sight of one another, so their actions are independent. Under a "finest analysis" of minimal options each has available the "pure" strategies, continuing hunting and returning to the fire, as well as all "mixed" strategies "built upon" these "pure" strategies. The wind has freshened, making it important that someone return to the fire. But it does not matter who returns. Indeed, under the

[3] Past performances are not only irrelevant in Farmer's Dilemmas, but I think are irrelevant in general in hyperrational communities. It seems obvious, even if it is not easy to show with rigor, that precedent can play no role in such communities: An agent in a hyperrational community will expect a performance of another to be repeated only if, and to the extent that, it was dictated by reason in the first instance. So it seems that its reasonableness in the first instance *cannot* depend even in part upon another's being led by it to expect its repetition. For an attempt to articulate arguments against precedents, as well as threats and promises, in hyperrational communities, see Hodgson (1967), Chap. II and IV.

"finest analyses" stated, the situation is one of full *practical symmetry*: if a given man ought to employ a certain strategy or be indifferent as regards several, then the same is true of the other man. Still it is important that *someone* return, and it would be *best* if just one did, *next* best if both did, and *worst* if neither did. On these, as on all evaluations, the men are agreed. The situation has the following strucuture:

C

		F	H
R	F	2	3
	H	3	1

(Specific magnitudes are again unimportant.)

2.2.2. What will happen? It will be shown that either Row and Column will change and become less perfect before the Dilemma is upon them, or the Dilemma in its original form will somehow be "headed-off." Something will "give," this is certain, for hyperrational men cannot be in (and act through) a situation exactly like the one described. Hyperrational men always know what they ought to do, (see 1.2) and in a Hunter's Dilemma there is nothing *such* men *could* know that they ought to do. Every practical knowledge hypothesis can be eliminated as untenable. Row might, one supposes, know that he ought to employ a certain strategy $(p, 1 - p)$ in which he makes his returning to the fire probable to degree p and his continuing hunting probable to degree $(1 - p)$. Also, Row might, one supposes, know that he ought to choose indifferently from some nonunit subset of these strategies. We consider these two cases in turn:

First, suppose Row knows that he ought to employ strategy $(p, 1 - p)$ where $1 \geq p \geq 0$. There are three possibilities: $1 > p > \frac{2}{3}$; $p = \frac{2}{3}$; $\frac{2}{3} > p \geq 0$. (Given the magnitudes chosen for the structure of the case, $\frac{2}{3}$ is a pivotal value for p.)

Let $1 \geq p > \frac{2}{3}$. That is, assume Row knows that he ought to employ strategy $(p, 1 - p)$ where $1 \geq p > \frac{2}{3}$. Then given the practical symmetry of the situation this is also the strategy that Column ought to employ, so Column ought to make his own hunting probable to a degree *less* than 1. But given Column's knowledge of Row's practical knowledge and practical rationality (see 1.5, 1.2, and 1.6), Column knows that Row will employ strategy $(p, 1 - p)$ thus making Column's expected value for his own "pure" strategies F and H, respectively,

$$EV_c(F) = 2p + 3(1 - p)$$

and,

$$EV_c(H) = 3p + 1(1 - p),$$

and Column's expected value for $M(q)$, a "mixed" strategy $(q, 1 - q)$ on his part in which $1 > q > 0$,

$$EV_c[M(q)] = 2\,pq + 3p\,(1 - q) + 3\,(1 - p)q + (1 - p)(1 - q)$$

or, regrouping, factoring, and putting equals for equals,

$$EV_c[M(q)] = q[EV_c(F)] + (1 - q)[EV_c(H)]$$

It is obvious that unless $EV_c(F) = EV_c(H)$, either $EV_c(F) > EV_c(H)$ and $EV_c(F) > EV_c[M(q)]$ for any q such that $1 > q > 0$, or $EV_c(H) > EV_c(F)$ and $EV_c(H) > EV_c[M(q)]$ for any such q. And so, given that $1 \geq p > \frac{2}{3}$, $EV_c(H) > EV_c(F)$ and $EV_c(H) > EV_c[M(q)]$ for any q such that $1 > q > 0$. But then Column ought to do H "for sure," which contradicts the conclusion reached above that he ought to make it probable to a degree *less* than 1 that he hunts. That $1 \geq p > \frac{2}{3}$ is thus eliminated. That $\frac{2}{3} > p \geq 0$ is eliminated by a similar argument.

It remains only to suppose that Row knows he ought to employ the strategy $(\frac{2}{3}, \frac{1}{3})$. Under this supposition, since Column would know that Row was employing this strategy, Column's expected value for *each* of his possible strategies, F, H, and $M(q)$ for every q such that $1 > q > 0$, would be the same, namely, $2\frac{1}{3}$. But then it would not be true that Column ought to employ the strategy $(\frac{2}{3}, \frac{1}{3})$: it would not be true that this would be Column's *only* right action. And so, given the "practical symmetry" of the situation, it would not be true that Row ought to employ this strategy, which means that, contrary to the supposition being examined, Row could not know that he ought to employ the strategy $(\frac{2}{3}, \frac{1}{3})$.

The conclusion to this point is that there is *not* a certain strategy $(p, 1 - p)$ that Row knows he ought to employ.

Second, suppose Row knows that he ought to choose "indifferently" from some nonunit set of his available strategies. Then Column will judge the strategies in this set equally probable and arrive at probability expectations p and $(1 - p)$ for Row's F and Row's H. (Simple averaging determines p if the set is finite; more sophisticated calculations will be required in case the set is infinite.) There are, again, three possibilities: $p > ⅔$; $p = ⅔$; $⅔ > p$. Let $p > ⅔$. Then Column ought to do H, Row knows that Column is going to do H, and F is Row's *sole* right action, which contradicts the assumption that Row knows he ought to choose indifferently from some nonunit set of strategies. That $⅔ > p$ is eliminated by a similar argument. It remains only to let $p = ⅔$. But then, as was seen above, each of Column's strategies would have an expected value of $2⅓$ and Column would choose "indifferently" from them. Knowing this, Row would judge it probable to degree ½ that Column would return to the fire: Column's choosing indifferently from *all* his strategies is equivalent, as far as Row's expectations are concerned, to Column's employing the "mixed" strategy (½, ½).[4] But then F would be Row's *sole* right action, which would again contradict the supposition that Row knows he ought to choose "indifferently" from some nonunit set of his possible actions.

So there is *nothing* that Row knows he ought to do. There is nothing he *could* know that he ought to do: each possibility has been eliminated. Of course the same holds of Column. But then as long as we suppose that Row and Column compose a hyperrational community that satisfies conditions 1.1—1.6, we cannot consist-

[4] A proof: Consider finite choice-sets in which probabilities for F are "evenly spaced" from 0 through 1. Given size n of such a set, its members can be computed. For $n = 3$ they are, (0,1), (½,½), and (1,0); for $n = 5$ they are, (0,1), (1/4,3/4), (2/4,2/4), (3/4,1/4), and (1,0). Suppose that Row will choose indifferently from such a set. Knowing this Column will make the probability of Row's eventually, after choosing a strategy and exercising it, doing F equal the simple average of the probabilities for F contained in the strategies in the choice-set. If the set contains n strategies, then Column will set the probability p of Row's F so that,

$$p = \frac{\sum_{i=o}^{i=n} \frac{(n - 1) - i}{n - 1}}{n}$$

The "average" for the infinite case in which Row chooses indifferently from the set of all strategies should be the limit as n "goes to infinity" of the averages for finite n. Since each average in the series has the value ½, the series limit is of course also ½.

ently also suppose that they are in (and acting through) a Hunter's Dilemma: hyperrational agents always know what they ought to do and only do what they know they ought to do (see 1.2). Our conclusion, put most briefly, is that such men cannot be in (and act through) such situations—such situations are for such men not possible.

2.2.3 "But," one wants to protest, "if Hunter's Dilemmas are not *possible* for hyperrational men, surely they cannot be *problems* for them. Could not *such* men dismiss such situations with the simple, true observation, 'that can't happen to us?' " The reply is, No. For men who are at a certain time hyperrational, though necessarily not then in a Hunter's Dilemma, cannot by anything that we have assumed be sure that their condition will continue or that they never will be in a Hunter's Dilemma. Indeed, they could realize that they were threatened, that a Hunter's Dilemma lay in their "natural" future, that one would befall them unless it was somehow "headed off." And they could see that were it to descend upon them they would not remain the men that they are but would change, and change for the worse, at least in their own, present eyes: moral deterioration would be one possibility—they could experience a weakening of resolve or a falling away from pure act-teleology; intellectual deterioration would be another—they could come to know less. It is in this way that a Hunter's Dilemma, just *because* impossible for hyperrational agents, can be a problem for them.[5] It is for *this* reason that they would like Hunter's dilemmas

---

[5] The argument in the text involves an assumption of equal probabilities in cases of indifferent choices. If this assumption were dropped, then perhaps Hunter's Dilemmas could not be shown to be impossible, but they would remain problematic. Let the assumption be dropped. Then perhaps each agent could know that all his actions were right and that it did not matter what he did, and perhaps each agent would judge the other's F probable to degree $2/3$. No *other* practical knowledge and no *other* expectations concerning F would be possible, but this knowledge and these expectations just might be—at least they could be supposed without immediate and obvious contradiction (even if how they could be "reached" remains a puzzle). However, even allowing this knowledge and these expectations and so allowing Hunter's Dilemmas to be *possible* for hyperrational agents, Hunter's Dilemmas would remain *problematic* for such agents. Allowing the stated expectations, each agent would judge it to be $2/3$-probable that the other would F, and $2/3$-probable that he himself would F. So each agent would view the emergence of one of the best, mixed patterns of action as only $4/9$-probable. With coercive organization a best pattern could be *guaranteed*.

to be in some way by someone advoided. This could be accomplished by judiciously applied coercion. A law against fires would provide one radical solution. A better, perhaps the best, solution would be an enforced system of social roles and special duties.

"But, again, surely laws and threats of sanctions are not needed. Desiring coordination and being reasonable, these men could *talk* things out. Since they are out of sight they might need to shout or to settle things in advance, but in any case, with words they could make necessary arrangements. It is false that Hunter's Dilemmas would pose problems for hyperrational men or be impossible for them. Such situations would be child's play for them." Not so. They could talk, but there is nothing helpful that they could say to each other—they know each other and their situation too well. Neither could have any news for the other; neither could, even if he wanted to, deceive the other; and they would know that neither values an action just because he has said that he would do it. Thus, if one said, "I'll take care of the fire," a response would be, "How do you *know* you will?" And if one said, "I'll take care of the fire if I can be sure that you will not," a response would be, "True, but not very helpful." While if one said, "I'll tend the fire no matter what," a proper response would be, "No you wouldn't, not if you were sure that I would!" And finally, if one said, "I'll take care of the fire and that's a promise," a proper response would be, "Empty words as you well know." Even allowing that they could talk, draft documents, post notices, and in general do with words the things we do with words, hyperrational men would have problems with impending Hunter's Dilemmas—problems coercive laws could solve. In this essential respect, the Hunter's Dilemma is like the Farmer's Dilemma. (Of course there are differences: most notable here is that Farmer's Dilemmas are not impossible for hyperrational agents; such agents can cope with Farmer's Dilemmas, they simply cannot cope well with them.)[6]

---

[6] Hyperrational agents could need coercive government. But it is not clear that when they needed it and wanted it they would have it. For one thing, it is possible that hyperrational agents would be incapable of coercive self-government. It has been said that every coercive government needs a inner governing cadre that is not itself coerced (see Lucas (1966), 76-77), and given the nature of such a cadre's work it seems likely that it would need to negotiate situations that hyperrational agents either could not handle or could not handle well. (Forward-looking teleologists would have other prob-

THE INDIVIDUAL'S NEED FOR COERCION

Communities composed of good and wise men can have use
for sanctions and coercive government, as we have seen. But one
can still think that if a good and wise man knows that everyone else
is subject to adequate sanctions he will never himself need to be
under threat. It can seem that, if a pattern of threatened sanctions
solves a certain social problem, then the sanctions directed against
any given good and wise man will invariably be *superfluous,* that
any such man would do his part unasked and uncoerced as long as
he knew (as he would) of the sanctions to which all *others* were
subject. So it can seem, but it is not so. It does not hold for the
Farmer's Dilemma, and seems not to hold even for the Hunter's Dilemma. We consider each in turn.

3.1 To simplify, we assume that each pattern of "pure"
strategies has a future that is known to each agent, a future to
which each agent assigns a probability of 1. Under this simplifica-
tion we represent a Farmer's Dilemma by future-structure I:

I   C   II   C

	W	F
R W	A	B
F	D	E

	W	F
R W	3 3	4 1
F	1 4	2 2

A is the future of the pattern of actions *(W, W):* each agent judges
it probable to degree 1 that if the pattern *(W, W)* were to obtain,

---

A would be its future. *"B," "D"* and *"E"* are used in similar ways. The value matrix for the case, we recall, is as in II, above.

The *problem* in the Farmer's Dilemma is that as things stand "in nature" the pattern *(F, F)* will obtain even though all concerned would prefer pattern *(W, W)*. We shall say that a sanctioned law that secures the jointly preferred pattern *(W, W) solves* the problem of the case. A law against planting flowers, if adequately sanctioned, could accomplish such a solution. Establishing this law and making certain its enforcement would change the futures of three of the four patterns in a manner depicted in III:

III   C   IV   C

		W	F
R	W	*A*	*B + S*
	F	*D + S*	*E + 2S*

		W		F	
R	W		4		3
		4		2	
	F		2		1
		3		1	

Let B + S be the future of the pattern *(W, F)* given the sanction against Column's planting flowers. *B + S* can be thought of as the result of changing the "natural" future *B* of pattern *(W, F)* by the introduction of a sanction *S* at a certain point. Similarly, *D + S* can be thought of as the result of introducing a similar sanction into *D* at a certain point, and *E + 2S* can be thought of as resulting from *E* by the introduction of two similar sanctions at certain points.

Suppose the sanction *S* would induce the reordering of values that is depicted in IV above. Under this assumption the problem of the case is solved: planting wheat is now "dominant" for each man. The *issue* is whether or not it is essential to this solution that each man is subject to sanction in case he plants flowers. The answer is that perhaps it is essential. Alternatively, the question is: would Row, for example, have sufficient reasons, the sanctions against him aside, for participating in the solution pattern *(W, W)?* The answer here is, Not necessarily.

Suppose that the sanction against Row's planting flowers was literally set aside, while the sanction against Column's planting flowers was maintained. The futures of the four patterns would be as in V:

V   C

		W	F
R	W	A	B + S
	F	D	E + S

VI   C

		W	F
R	W	3 3	1 2
	F	4 2	2 1

What values might Row and Column assign to these futures? Recalling that Row and Column are benevolent universalists, and supposing that each takes as dim a view of S imposed on the other man as he does of S imposed upon himself, several necessary or at least plausible restrictions flow from structures II and IV: It is necessary that the values assigned by each man to A and $B + S$ be ordered as they are in IV, and that the values assigned by each man to A and D be ordered as they are in II. One may expect, though it is not necessary, that the values assigned by each man to D and $E + S$ should be ordered as are the values assigned by him in IV to $D + S$ and $E + 2S$; and one may expect the values assigned by each man to $B + S$ and $E + S$ to be ordered as are the values assigned by him in II to B and E. Further, perhaps S would be a strange sanction if the values assigned by either man to A and $E + S$ were ordered differently from those assigned by him in II to A and E, or if the values assigned by Row to D and $B + S$ were ordered differently from those assigned by him in II to D and B. But subject even to these restrictions, and certainly no others are *necessary*, it is possible that the value matrix for future-structure V should be VI, above.

But given the values in VI, Row would not participate in the solution pattern *(W, W)* even though he knew of the sanctions against Column's F and indeed knew that Column was going to participate in this pattern in the sense that he was going to perform W. Column would plant wheat in this civil state in which only he was coerced. Thanks to the sanction against his planting flowers, planting wheat would be "dominant" for him, so he would do "his part." And Row could know this. But it would not matter, for even knowing it he would plant flowers: planting flowers would still be "dominant" for him.

So when communities that meet our specifications have use for sanctions it is not necessarily sufficient to a man's reasons for participating in a well-sanctioned solution pattern that he be sure everyone else is subject to sanction. It can be essential to a given sanction solution in which each man is subject to sanction that each man be subject to sanction.

3.2 Let the future-structure and value matrix for a Hunter's Dilemma be,

	VII	C			VIII	C
	F	H			F	H
R F	A	B	R F		2	3
H	D	E	H		3	1

The problem with the Hunter's Dilemma is not that our agents would not do well in it—without corruption of one sort or another our agents could do nothing at all in it. We consider a solution in which "would-be" Hunter's Dilemmas are converted by an arrangement of sanctions into situations that are not only possible for hyperrational agents but that in their resolutions would leave nothing to be desired. A certain penalty sufficient to secure the optimum pattern *(F, H)* is imposed against Row's continuing hunting and Column's returning to the fire. The future-structure and value matrix for the converted Hunter's Dilemma are, we assume,

	IX	C		X	C	
	F	H			F	H
R F	$A+S$	B	R F		3	4
H	$D+2S$	$E+S$	H		1	2

In a Hunter's Dilemma so converted, each agent has a "dominant" action that brings him into the solution pattern: tending the fire is "dominant" for Row; hunting is "dominant" for Column.

Could the sanctions against Row be set aside without destroying the solution? The answer again is, Maybe not. Setting aside the sanction against Row's hunting yields future-structure XI:

XI

	C	
	F	H
R F	A + S	B
R H	D + S	E

XII

	C	
	F	H
R F	1	3
R H	2	1

It is necessary that the (agreed) values assigned to $A + S$ and B should be ordered as in X, and that those assigned to B and E should be ordered as in VIII. And it would be strange if $D + S$ were not assigned a lower value than B. Further, one is apt to expect the values assigned to $A + S$ and $D + S$ to be ordered as are those assigned in VIII to A and B. But even subject to these restrictions (and no others are *necessary)* the value matrix for structure XI could be XII, above. And Row would not, I think, have sufficient reasons in this partially converted Hunter's Dilemma for doing his part in the solution pattern *(F, H);* nor for that matter would Column. This partially converted Dilemma would be, though for different and perhaps less clear and compelling reasons, as problematic (indeed, "as impossible") for hyperrational agents as the original one.

The partially converted Dilemma is not marked by practical symmetry. Here is one difference from the original Dilemma. And in the partially converted Dilemma there is a unique best pattern of actions. Here is another difference. Given these differences, especially the second one, it can seem that the partially converted Dilemma ought not to be impossible, ought not to be in *any* way problematic, for our men. They are concerned to do what is best, and they will know which pattern is best. "Surely they will manage to realize this pattern." But recall that our agents are not "pattern-utilitarians," each concerned to do his part in a best pattern, but act-utilitarians, each concerned to do *a* best act. So it is *not* clear and obvious that they would manage to realize the best pattern. On the contrary, it is tolerably clear that they would not so manage.

Whether Row, for example, ought to return to the fire *depends:* it depends on what he should expect Column to do. Row should tend the fire and not hunt if and only if he should judge it probable to a degree greater than ⅓ that Column will continue to hunt. But it is at least not necessary that Row should have this expectation. It would be necessary if this expectation could be "reached," and if *only* it could be *supposed* without immediate contradiction: but in the partially converted Dilemma *several* expectations could be supposed without immediate contradiction. It could be supposed without immediate contradiction that Row should assign to Column's hunting either a probability of 1 or a probability of 0, and if the assumption of equal probabilities in cases of indifference were dropped, a probability of ⅓ could also be supposed without immediate contradiction. So it is not necessary that Row assign a particular probability to Column's hunting, and what is more important, it seems that no such assignment is *possible*. Given his knowledge of his community and the structure of the situation, Row would realize that in order to decide what to expect of Column he needed *first* to discover what Column in the end would expect of him: Row knows that Column never acts without knowledge of his duties, and that what Column ought to do in this situation depends upon what Column should expect him to do. So it seems that in order to decide what to expect of Column, Row must *first* determine what Column should expect of him: at least this seems right if the decision concerning what to expect is reasonably and responsibly taken, as for our men it must be. Of course, this could only be the beginning, and there could be no end! Row would know that Column was locked into the same process. Row would be driven to attempt to replicate Column's deliberations, and in particular Column's attempt to replicate Row's deliberations, and in particular Row's attempt to replicate Column's deliberations, *and so on!* Row's impossible task cannot even be put into words. Such labyrinths of mutually dependent expectations are ordinarily terminated by flagging interest, fatigue, lack of time, acts of faith, the assumption of one of these things, the assumption of the assumption of one of these things, and so on. But none of the ordinary terminations are possible for hyperrational agents. Row could, it seems, given the nature of the situation and the character of his community, especially its extensive self-knowledge and the determination of its members to deliberate reasonably and responsibly, putting first questions first neither avoid nor escape from the "labyrinth," (See 1.3 and 1.6.)

It is not necessary that our men should have any particular expectations in a partially converted Hunter's Dilemma, and given the feedback traced above it seems not *possible* that they should have expectations regarding each other. When men are so related in principle and circumstance that their actions depend mutually upon their expectations regarding each other's actions, a regress is generated which, in the limiting case of a hyperrational community, precludes the formation of such expectations. The argument given for this conclusion lacks the rigor one might desire. In particular it would be nice to have explicit general premises concerning exactly how, under various circumstances, hyperrational agents deliberate and order issues. Still, a case has been made that makes tolerably clear that hyperrational agents in a partially converted Dilemma would not know what to expect of each other and so would not know what they ought to do. And since this is not possible for our agents (see 1.2), we conclude that the converted Dilemma is "as impossible" and as problematic for them as the original unconverted Dilemma.[7]

Our thesis is thus reinforced: A good and wise man *cannot* always ignore the sanctions he is under and still find sufficient reasons for participating in a desirable and adequately sanctioned arrangement. We *cannot* say, with Hart, that when coercion is needed, "what reason demands is *voluntary* cooperation in a *coercive* system." (Hart (1961), p. 193.) We cannot say this, at any rate, of our men. For them at least, the need for coercion is more complete. They can need it not only *collectively* as a community, as was argued in Section 2, but also *individually* as participating members, as has been argued in the present section.

APPENDIX: THE FARMER'S DILEMMA AND MUTUAL TRUST

In the Farmer's Dilemma what each agent ought to do does not depend at all upon what he should expect the other to do. Even

---

[7] The same conclusion could be reached with no more, and no less, difficulty if the sanctions against Column were set aside. The resultant partially converted Dilemma would have future-structure XIII, and could have value matrix XIV:

XIII   C

		F	H
R	F	A	B
	H	D + S	E + S

XIV   C

		F	H
R	F	2	4
	H	3	1

if Row, for example, could trust Column and could be sure that Column would plant wheat, Row would still plant flowers. One is tempted to think that lack of trust is in this case not at all the problem. *(Tullock* (1967), p. 229.) But there is a sense in which the problem in the case is one of "want of mutual confidence and security." *(Hume* (1888), p. 521.) Let a *trustworthy* man be a deontologist who recognizes two *ceteris paribus* duties, a duty to maximize expected value, and a duty—a more stringent duty—to keep promises. Trustworthy men would have a way out of Farmer's Dilemmas. They could, by exchanging promises, convert would-be Farmer's Dilemmas into situations in which planting wheat was reasonable for each. The relatively natural promise-based reasons available at will to trustworthy men could serve in place of the more artificial sanction-reasons we have been considering. (See *Gauthier* (1967), p. 471.)

But there is a small and soluble puzzle. Suppose that Row and Column were trustworthy and that they could solve their problem by exchanging promises to plant wheat. How could they make the exchange? Though each would prefer that both rather than neither promise to plant wheat, each would most prefer that just the other make this promise. Apparently, just as not planting wheat is "dominant" in the Farmer's Dilemma, so not promising to plant wheat would be "dominant" in a preliminary situation in which each could either make this promise or not make it. But then how could they arrange to exchange promises to plant wheat?

The puzzle has a number of solutions. We consider first a simple but inelegant solution. Suppose there were a document containing the words, "The undersigned agree, agreement effective when two have signed, to plant wheat." Now let it be settled that the document is to be presented first to Row and then to Column. Their problems are solved. Row by signing can guarantee that Column will sign, that they will both be bound by promises to plant wheat, and that they will both plant wheat. So Row will sign. And then Column will sign. The desired exchange of promises will be accomplished.

Must a document be produced? No. Is it essential that moves be ordered in the contract situation, with Row (Column) "going first" and Column (Row) "going second?" The answer is again, No. Dispensing with the document and with order, each could say in any order or simultaneously, "I promise to plant wheat, my promise effective as soon as both of us have said this." Let S be saying this and $\overline{S}$ not saying this and suppose each is in a position to S or $\overline{S}$. Their situation has the structure displayed below. That it has this structure is explained, and then it is shown that in such a structure each would S:

XV   C

		S	$\overline{S}$
R	S	1 1	1 0
	$\overline{S}$	0 0	0 0

The numbers represent the presence or absence of duties overall or *sans phrase*. (The numbers do not represent expected values, though it can happen that a duty *sans phrase* to do an action can derive from an unopposed expected value-based duty *ceteris paribus* to do it.) For example, if Column does S, then (as we shall see) Row has a duty overall to do S—the **1** in the box for *(S, S)* expresses this fact. We now turn to the justification of the numbers. Note that if both do S, then each has a promissory duty to plant wheat and each will plant wheat. But if only one does S or if neither does $\overline{S}$, then no promises result and each will plant flowers. Thus, if Column does $\overline{S}$, Row has a duty overall to S and no duty overall to $\overline{S}$, for by doing S Row can maximize expected value: the **1** in the *(S, $\overline{S}$)* box and the **0** in the *($\overline{S}$, S)* express these facts. If Column does S, then it does not matter what Row does—he has no duty overall to do S or to do $\overline{S}$: the **0**'s in the *(S, $\overline{S}$)* and *($\overline{S}$, $\overline{S}$)* boxes express these facts.

Assuming that Row and Column are hyperrational trustworthy agents, what would they do in a situation of this structure? Each would do S, for each would know that he ought to do S. This is the only practical knowledge that can be supposed without contradiction. Suppose that Row knows that he ought to do S. Then Column knows that Row will do S and knowing this knows that he, Column, ought to do S. Knowing this Row knows that he, Row, ought to do S. The hypothesis that Row knows that he ought to do S "leads back to itself." In contrast, suppose that Row knew that he ought to do S. Then, as Row would know, Column would know this and be indifferent between his own alternatives. Knowing *this* Row would judge Column's S and S equally probable and so know that he, Row, ought to do S. The hypothesis that Row knows that he ought to do S leads to a contradiction and can thus be eliminated. It could be shown in a similar fashion that each "mixed" strategy $(p, 1 - p)$ regarding S and S, where $1 > p > 0$, can be eliminated: if Row knew that he ought to employ such a strategy, then Column would know that he ought to do S "for sure," and so, contrary to the present hypothesis, Row would know that *he* ought to do S "for sure." Similarly, Row cannot know that he ought to choose "indifferently" from some nonunit set of his strategies: from Column's point of view any such choice is equivalent to Row's employing a "mixed" strategy; so if Row knew that he was to choose "indifferently" from some nonunit set of strategies, he would on the contrary (!) know that he ought to do S "for sure." So Row would know that he ought to do S. He knows what he ought to do. (He knows what he ought to do in every situation in which he finds himself.) And every other practical-knowledge hypothesis leads to contradiction and can be eliminated. Row would know that he ought to do S and would therefore do S. (But how would he *come* to know that he ought to do S? He could reason in the way I have and come *by elimination* to know that he ought to do S. He would know that he knew what he ought to do—we suppose that he is in the situation and he knows that he knows what to do in every situation in which he finds himself. See 1.2 and 1.6. And he would know that every other practical-knowledge hypothesis was eliminable.)

The exchange puzzle can be solved by exchanging mutually dependent unconditional promises to plant wheat. Only formally different solutions would consist in the exchange of independent conditional promises: for example, in signing a certain document, each could promise to plant wheat if the other signs the document. But many superficially similar exchanges would not constitute solutions. We consider two inadequate exchanges. *First,* it would not help for each to promise to plant wheat if the other plants wheat. The structure of a would-be Farmer's Dilemma given such promises would be,

XVI   C

		W	F
R	W	1 **1**	0 **0**
	F	0 **0**	1 **1**

If either plants wheat the other has an overriding promissory duty to plant wheat; whereas if either plants flowers the other has no promissory duty to plant wheat, can maximize expected value by planting flowers, and so has a duty overall to plant flowers. For reasons rehearsed in Section 3.2 above, I think that situations of structure XVI are problematic for hyperrational agents. Though trustworthy agents would have a way out of, they could have no reason for getting into, such a situation. *Second,* it would be no advance for each to promise to plant wheat if the other promises to plant wheat. Given such conditional promises, promise based duties to plant wheat would exist were either, or both, to make a further unconditional promise to plant wheat. But the situation *vis-a-vis* these further unconditional promises would have the following structure:

XVII   C

		P	$\overline{P}$
R	P	0 **0**	0 **1**
	$\overline{P}$	1 **0**	0 **0**

Both will plant wheat if and only if at least one makes a further unconditional promise to plant wheat. Both will plant flowers if and only if neither makes this further unconditional promise. The crucial point is that nothing is gained by *both* making a further unconditional promise. This is why a further promise is called for from Row, for example, only in case it is *not* forthcoming from Column. Given the practical symmetry of this situation, *every* practical-knowledge hypothesis can be eliminated. In particular, neither could know that he ought to make a further unconditional promise to plant wheat. For if he knew this, then he would know that the same was required and to be expected of the other. But knowing that the other would make a further promise, he would know—contrary to the hypothesis being tested—that it did not matter whether or not *he* made a further promise. Every *other* practical-knowledge hypothesis is similarly eliminable. A situation of structure XVII would be problematic for hyperrational agents, and trustworthy agents could have no reason for getting into such a situation, though again they would have a way out.

Hyperrational trustworthy agents would find their way out of Farmer's Dilemmas. They could count on each other's promises and they would know what promises to make and how to make them. Probably such agents would find their way out of all interaction problems. It seems they could never need coercion. But they pay a price for their self-sufficiency: Insofar as they are trustworthy and thus committed to keeping promises regardless of costs and benefits, they are unreasonable. At least this is the judgment of a forward-looking teleologist.

REFERENCES

Gauthier, David P. "Morality and Advantage," *Philosophical Review* LXXVI (October, 1967), 460-75.

Hart, H. L. A. *The Concept of Law* (Oxford: Clarendon Press, 1961).

Hodgson, D. H. *Consequences of Utilitarianism: A Study in Normative Ethics and Legal Theory* (Oxford: Clarendon Press, 1967).

Hume, David. *A Treatise of Human Nature* edited by L. A. Selby-Bigge (Oxford: Clarendon Press, 1888).

Jeffrey, R. C. *The Logic of Decision* (New York: McGraw-Hill Book Company, 1965).

Lewis, David K. *Convention: A Philosophical Study* (Cambridge, Mass.: Harvard University Press, 1969).

Lucas, J. R. *The Principles of Politics* (Oxford: Clarendon Press, 1966).

Luce, R. Duncan and Raiffa, Howard. *Games and Decisions: Introduction and Critical Survey* (New York: John Wiley & Sons, Inc., 1957).

Rapoport, Anatol. *Two-Person Game Theory: The Essential Ideas* (Ann Arbor: University of Michigan Press, 1966).

Sobel, J. Howard. "Utilitarianisms: Simple and General," *Inquiry* 13 (Winter, 1970), 394-450.

Tullock, Gordon. "The Prisoner's Dilemma and Mutual Trust," *Ethics* (April, 1967), 229-30.

10

NONCOERCIVE SOCIETY: SOME DOUBTS, LENINIST AND CONTEMPORARY

William Leon McBride

V. I. Lenin, in *The State and Revolution,* suggests some revealing dilemmas for every student of the phenomenon of coercion. Lenin was unquestionably an authority on the subject in his own right; it is therefore unimportant for our present purposes to decide whether Lenin was simply explicating, removing ambiguities from, or drastically distorting the classical Marxist conceptions of the state and of post-political society. By way of anticipation, I maintain that if we accept Lenin's analysis, we shall be very hard put to avoid the pessimistic conclusion of theologians and others (reported elsewhere in this volume by Professor Cook) that coercion is an all-pervasive, non-eliminable feature of life, with its roots, perhaps, in being itself. My ultimate purpose in this essay, written at a time in American history at which daily events seem to furnish the most utterly incontrovertible evidence in favor of this same conclusion, is to try to leave open the possibility of the conclusion's being false.

Toward this end, I propose to deal with some of the principal issues (as I conceive them) under three main headings: (1) Leninist dilemmas; (2) the ideal of a noncoercive society in light of present attitudes; and (3) suggestions for rendering the ideal more easily imaginable.

I

Following Engels, Lenin begins by insisting on the fundamental separability of the concept of "state" from that of "society." Anthropological evidence supplements philosophical argument to the effect that the state "is a product of society at a certain stage of development,"[1] not some peculiar type of eternal Form or Idea that has taken up permanent residence in the historical world of men. If there once were primitive societies in which there existed nothing resembling what could be called state structures, then future, post-political societies are also meaningful conceptual possibilities. It follows from this that the strongly rooted and still almost universal prejudice—which was raised to an unrivaled height of sophisticated, systematic justification in the political philosophy of Hegel —in favor of some form of state as a *sine qua non* of *civilized* human existence may in fact be nothing but a prejudice, rather than a kind of necessary truth. So far, I take it, so good. Whether a post-political society would be *desirable* is, of course, a further question; but regardless of the answer to this latter question, I regard as essentially sound the Marxian-Engelsian-Leninist critique of those who would Platonize the Idea of the State.

In the treatise in question, Lenin's principal philosophical problem then becomes one of defining what is meant by "state." Here the concept of coercion, or oppressive force, is crucial. "According to Marx," Lenin says approvingly, "the state is an organ of class

---

[1] This is a citation by Lenin from Engels, *Der Ursprung der Familie, des Privateigentums und des Staats* (Marx-Engels *Werke*, Band 21, Berlin: Dietz Verlag, 1962) 165; cf. *The State and Revolution*, in Lenin, *Selected Works*, Vol. 2 (Moscow: Foreign Languages Publishing House, 1960), 306.

rule, an organ for the *oppression* of one class by another; it is the creation of 'order,' which legalises and perpetuates this oppression by moderating the conflict between the classes."[2] Later, in discussing the political notion concerning which his writings seem to me always to reveal the greatest personal ambivalence, even if not formal inconsistency—namely, "democracy"[3]—Lenin makes a useful additional contribution to clarifying his understanding of the term "state." He writes: "Democracy is a form of state, one of its varieties. Consequently, it, like every state, represents on the one hand the organised, systematic use of violence against persons. . . ."[4] To summarize, then, the state as Lenin understands it is a collection of institutions (or a "machine," as he often calls it) characterized by the organized, systematic application of coercion for the purpose of maintaining economic inequalities among groups within a single society. (I do not intend to enter here into the complex of issues surrounding the identification of these groups as "classes," except to comment that the word "economic" should not be interpreted in a narrow, technical sense.) At the same time, a successful state will perform the ideological function of masking its fundamentally coercive nature by "creating order" and using a legal system in order to "moderate the conflict" among groups that would presumably ensue if the society's members were to be educated to an awareness of the coercive reality in a thoroughgoing, completely overt fashion.

What, then, does Lenin see as the future alternative (since primitive, pre-political societies are now only of antiquarian interest) to societies characterized by inherently coercive state structures? His answer is complicated and constitutes, I think, the very honest grappling[5] of a man of great practical wisdom with basic problems

---

[2] *Ibid.,* 307.

[3] See the interesting and by now rather classical discussion of this by A. G. Meyer, *Leninism* (Cambridge: Harvard University Press, 1957), Chap. 3, 57-77.

[4] *The State and Revolution,* 382. The sentence continues: "but on the other hand it signifies the formal recognition of equality of citizens, the equal right of all to determine the structure of, and to administer, the state." Lenin further implies that the transition to the "democratic dictatorship of the proletariat" is facilitated by the growing consciousness of the gap that must necessarily exist between this formal recognition of equality and the built-in social inequalities in any *capitalist* democracy.

[5] I cannot agree with Karl Wittfogel's contention that, "By discussing Marx' views of the state without reproducing Marx' ideas of the Asiatic state and the Oriental despotism of Tsarist Russia, Lenin wrote what prob-

of reconciling his theory with what seemed feasible. If the political system of the contemporary Soviet Union can legitimately be regarded as in large measure Lenin's responsibility, then we must conclude that there were serious deficiencies in his practice; here, I shall be concerned with dilemmas of his theory, without intending to denigrate either his character or his acumen. Communist society, which by definition would be noncoercive, remains Lenin's long-range alternative to the present state of affairs, but it is clear that he considers this so remote as to be almost impossible to discuss.[6] Prior to this, he foresees the need both for a transitional stage of historical development, the period of the famous "dictatorship of the proletariat," and for an intermediate stage which he identifies as "the first phase of communist society." The technical distinction between these two periods, based on the assumption that class divisions could be abolished while the unequal distribution of goods in accordance with bourgeois notions of right still prevailed, need not concern us greatly here. Of greater interest is the role given to coercion in Lenin's conception of the dictatorship of the proletariat. For, from a formal point of view, it is practically indistinguishable from the role that has already been assigned to the same concept in Lenin's definition of the state.

As we have seen, Lenin has maintained that there can be no such thing as a noncoercive state, and this thesis would undoubtedly find wide acceptance. But now it becomes apparent that the dictatorship of the proletariat, as he conceives it, is to be equally coercive, the primary difference (at least at the beginning) being one of "who" is coercing "whom." (Lenin stresses, for instance, the replacement of the standing army by the "armed people.") The word "dictatorship" seems particularly well chosen when viewed as a way of contrasting a post-revolutionary government with a more traditional type still characterized by the ideological superstructure of a legal system, since the root notion of a *"Diktat"* (decree) differs so fun-

---

ably is the most dishonest book of his political career: *State and Revolution." Oriental Despotism* (New Haven: Yale University Press, 1957), 7.

[6] "In fact, when [certain writers, philistines, etc.] talk of unreasonable utopias, of the demagogic promises of the Bolsheviks, of the impossibility of 'introducing' socialism, it is the higher stage or phase of communism they have in mind, which no one has ever promised or even thought to 'introduce,' because generally speaking it cannot be 'introduced'." *The State and Revolution,* 380.

damentally from that of "law."[7] The dictatorial rule of the newly-victorious proletariat over members of other classes would have the advantage of eliminating the mystifying mask of "law and order" worn by the coercers in capitalist society. But the *reality* of coercion would in no way be diminished at this point in time. (Quantitatively speaking, of course, Lenin supposes that coercion would be diminished, since the proletariat would rule in the name of the vast majority of people, but this rather idealistic and optimistic view of the situation must be modified considerably when such further complexities as Lenin's theory of the proletariat's elite party vanguard and the comparative paucity of members of the proletariat in Tsarist Russia are taken into account.) Although the ultimate goal of reducing the level and use of force within society is certainly never formally abandoned by Lenin, his essay tends to give prominence to the role of violence and of the less overtly physical forms of coercion during both the envisioned proletarian revolution and its foreseeable aftermath. Thus it is that he makes repeated references to the need for hierarchy and subordination, command and obedience—in short, what he himself revealingly calls "factory discipline," generalized over the entire post-revolutionary society.[8]

The most famous of Lenin's references to such discipline is immediately followed by the assurance that this is not the ultimate goal. But the three paragraphs in which Lenin elaborates on this as-

[7] In his famous anti-Bolshevik tract, against which Lenin in turn directed one of his fiercest polemics, Karl Kautsky says: "Taken literally, the word ['dictatorship'] signifies the suspension of democracy. But taken literally it also means the sovereignty of a single person, who is bound by no laws. . . ." *The Dictatorship of the Proletariat,* tr. by H. J. Stenning (Manchester: The National Labour Press, Ltd., no date), 43.

Lenin takes issue with two elements of this definition (the suspension of democracy and the sovereignty of a single person), but concedes that "Kautsky accidentally stumbled upon *one* true idea (namely, that dictatorship is rule unrestricted by any laws). . . ." This is then repeated and amplified in Lenin's own proposed definition:

"Dictatorship is rule based directly upon force and unrestricted by any laws.

"The revolutionary dictatorship of the proletariat is rule won and maintained by the use of violence by the proletariat against the bourgeoisie, rule that is unrestricted by any laws." *The Proletarian Revolution and the Renegade Kautsky,* in *Collected Works,* Vol. 28 (Moscow: Progress Publishers, 1965), 235-236.

[8] "The whole of society will have become a single office and a single factory."—*The State and Revolution,* 384.

surance, with which the substantive part of *The State and Revolution* closes (since the final, incomplete Chapter VI is concerned with certain particular controversies and polemics), leave serious doubts as to whether there is really any room within the theory of Leninism for a conception of a genuinely noncoercive society. For here Lenin makes it clear that he envisages the Marxian notion of "the withering away of the state" through the category of *habituation* (which, it must in all honesty be pointed out, has very little importance in the major works of Marx himself). When *"the necessity* of observing the simple, fundamental rules of human intercourse will . . . become a *habit,"* Lenin concludes, "Then the door will be wide open for the transition from the first phase of communist society to its higher phase, and with it to the complete withering away of the state."[9] The image that he has just drawn seems to be one of a society in which coercion—though its manifestations would not usually need to be overtly, dramatically violent—has attained a very high degree of completeness. Once the approved "rules of human intercourse" have become fully *habitual,* of course, then there will surely be no need for police or armed forces. But such a society can hardly be regarded as one in which coercion has been eliminated, and there is no hint that Lenin envisages a dramatic reversal with respect to the employment of this subtle but total, internalized coercion in the highest phase of communist society.[10]

[9] *Ibid.*

[10] In what is perhaps his clearest and most revealing statement in favor, supposedly, of a noncoercive society, Lenin says the following:

"We set ourselves the ultimate aim of abolishing the state, i.e., all organised and systematic violence, all use of violence against man in general. We do not expect the advent of a system of society in which the principle of the subordination of the minority to the majority will not be observed. In striving for socialism, however, we are convinced that it will develop into communism and, therefore, that the need for violence against people in general, for the *subordination* of one man to another, and of one section of the population to another, will vanish altogether since people will *become accustomed* to observing the elementary conditions of social life *without violence* and *without subordination."*

The succeeding paragraph then begins with this explanatory clause: "In order to emphasise this element of habit. . . ."—*The State and Revolution,* 368.

My point is that, when carefully considered, Lenin's ultimate vision will in fact be seen to be one of a very subtly and thoroughly coerced society.

In terms of Lenin's overall theoretical aims, the most basic defect of this final result is that it trivializes, in an important respect, the social goal to which he is supposedly committed. If, following Lenin, one is compelled to answer my question concerning the future alternative to coercive state structures by speaking of thoroughly habituated societies in which coercion has at best been internalized rather than eliminated, then there are no grounds for regarding the alternative as "qualitatively different" (to use an expression of which Lenin is rather fond) from the original with respect to coercion. If this is so, then in a crucial sense Leninism remains socially conservative. If it is conceded that current Soviet practice is closely tied to Leninist theory, then the confirmatory evidence for this conclusion is abundant. And "it is no accident" (as the consecrated phrase of the historical determinists goes) that the highly undialectical behavioral psychology of Pavlov, with its overriding emphasis on habituation, became an accepted and honored part of official Soviet ideology.

Much of twentieth-century Western philosophy has emphasized the fundamental incompatibility between the advocacy of social habituation and the espousal of a nonrepressive society as an ideal. This emphasis is shared by existentialists such as Sartre, in his contrast between the alienated, "serial" form of social existence and the revolutionary *praxis* of the "group,"[11] by philosophers in the Wittgensteinian tradition, who frequently oppose habitual to rule-governed behavior,[12] and by such neo-Marxists as Marcuse, in whose writings the preference for a free society over an habituated one is so clearly delineated.[13]

On the other hand, within the context of traditional philosophy and especially educational theory, Lenin's position is not at all new. Aristotle, for instance, conceives of the virtuous man as one who

[11] In *Critique de la raison dialectique,* Tome I (Paris: Librairie Gallimard, 1961).

[12] For instance, H. L. A. Hart, in *The Concept of Law* (Oxford: Clarendon Press, 1961), 9-11 and *passim.*

[13] I have briefly developed a contrast on this point between Marcuse and B. F. Skinner, who forthrightly espouses the path of habituation, in an article entitled, "The Nature of Political Philosophy and the Attempt to Go beyond Politics", in *Akten des XIV. Internationalen Kongresses für Philosophie* (1968), Band V (Vienna: Verlag Herder, 1970).

has learned, and has become endowed with, good habits.[14] Habituation in its earliest stages (notably in children) is commonly taken to entail a considerable amount of overt coercion; later, followers of this time-honored way of thinking maintain, a successful process of habituation will permit the coercion to be internalized. Therefore, precious little is novel about this aspect of Leninism; what is distressing is that it should have retained such a prominent position in the thinking of one who was, in so many other respects, such a distinguished revolutionary theorist. The various dilemmas that we have been considering in *The State and Revolution* are reducible to the fact that Lenin seems not to have regarded a noncoercive society, in which individuals would act out of free choice rather than out of external compulsion or internalized habit, as a real human possibility.

II

The realization of a noncoercive society, whether or not it is a real possibility, would in any event have to await the universalization of the belief that such a society is supremely desirable. This belief is by no means universal at present. As long as individuals holding opposed values continue to exist, then the achievement of a noncoercive society will depend on efforts to coerce such individuals into agreement—to "force them to be free," if one wishes to express the paradox in this way, but at any rate to coerce them. Let us consider these contentions for a moment.

There is abundant empirical evidence for the existence of individuals in the contemporary world who are opposed to the noncoer-

---

[14] "Some people believe that it is nature that makes men good, others that is habit, and others again that it is teaching. Now, whatever goodness comes from nature is obviously not in our power, but is present in truly fortunate men as the result of some divine cause. Argument and teaching, I am afraid, are not effective in all cases: the soul of the listener must first have been conditioned by habits to the right kind of likes and dislikes, just as land to foster the seed."—*Nicomachean Ethics* (1179b 20-27), tr. by M. Ostwald (Indianapolis: Bobbs-Merrill, 1962), 296.

Interestingly, the context of these remarks is Aristotle's justification, at the end of the book, for making the transition from the study of ethics to that of politics. Since men need to be coerced in order to be virtuous, he argues, and since neither fathers nor other single individuals generally have sufficient coercive powers, we must look to the enactment of proper laws to do the job.

cive social ideal. If, for example, one admits that "sadism" is a real phenomenon, then the case for the present non-universality of a value commitment to a noncoercive society has already been made. Sadists are particularly good examples to point to in order to counter the contention that everyone favors the minimization of coercion in principle, and regards coercion as at best a *pis aller*. It may of course be objected that sadists and other such individuals are mentally ill and must therefore, with respect to coercion, be regarded as being in an entirely different category from the rest of mankind. However, the notorious oversimplification involved in the assumption that it is possible to draw clear guidelines to distinguish the well from the ill, with borderline cases constituting a troublesome but statistically insignificant minority, is now widely recognized.[15] Once it is seen that the differences between practitioners of the most easily isolable and bizarre forms of sadism, and "ordinary" individuals who take some small but genuine delight in, for example, journalistic accounts of the torture of enemy war prisoners, are differences of degree and not of conceptual kind, then the way has been opened to a realization of just how widespread the popular sentiment *against* a noncoercive society may in fact be.

When critics say, in the phrase that one hears with increasing frequency at present, that contemporary American society is "sick," one useful way of rendering this vague, rhetorical charge more precise is to translate it into an observation concerning the high incidence of preferences (to the extent to which these can in fact be measured) for forcing others into "life styles" not of their own choosing. Such preferences, of course, become more visible and issue in more overt, violent actions in periods in which significant minorities begin to adopt radically different styles from the dominant one; in epochs more completely dominated by tradition, the coercive "pressures to conform" were so great as often to prevent even the mere emergence of alternatives that could evoke calls for their suppression. Whether the ideal of a noncoercive society faces

[15] See, for example, Thomas Szasz' influential book, *The Myth of Mental Illness* (New York: Harper & Row, 1961).
    Lenin's political successors, by their well-documented practice of placing social dissidents under psychiatric care, have provided much food for thought on this very question. The lesson they teach is lost if this abhorrent practice is regarded as being merely an act of complete cynicism, with no logical or theoretical basis whatever.

more numerous, or simply more vocal, opposition now than at any given past time is really not of great importance for present purposes. What is essential is to recognize this opposition as such and to see its manifestations in many of the recent historical developments that have evoked the most virulent and widespread protests in this country.

It appears to be a widely-held conviction, especially on the part of some of our more idealistic youth, that an educational process of "awakening people to the dangers" of implementing such coercive attitudes towards segments of the population is more or less guaranteed success in advance, if it is properly conducted. But the passage from acquiring a deeper understanding of the pro-coercion tendencies of some current social and political developments to upholding the supreme desirability of a noncoercive society, while frequent, is by no means automatic. Even after they have acquired such an understanding, some individuals may still prefer to see others coerced, even while having some sense of the "bad faith" inherent in this position; others, like the common people in Dostoevsky's fable of the Grand Inquisitor, may prefer to remain dominated. If a noncoercive society is ever to be achieved, then, as I have already indicated, such individuals will somehow have to be coerced into accepting it. But of course, to the extent to which this occurs the new society will not truly be noncoercive. This paradox is inescapable, and lies at the base of many of our contemporary dilemmas concerning the use of violence to achieve allegedly nonviolent ends.

It is saddening, but hardly surprising, to find that important segments of those protesting against the growth of repression appear to share the same general pro-coercion attitudes as their antagonists, even while differing sharply from them with respect to the kinds of life styles, actions, and beliefs into which they would like to see other individuals coerced. Regardless of this development, however, it remains true that there exists a meaningful and clear-cut conceptual distinction between those, on the one hand, who regard a noncoercive society as supremely desirable and yet are willing to live with the uncomfortable paradox to which I have just alluded, and those who, on the other hand, whether they call themselves radicals, moderates, or conservatives, do not cherish a noncoercive society as an ideal. This is so even though the distinction may sometimes tend to become blurred (even within the mind of a single individual) in the heat of political activity.[16] By way of illustrating this distinction, it is useful to consider the special but familiar case of relations with young children: it is not always feasible to refrain entirely from coercing them, in however restrained and nonviolent a fashion, and yet parents may well have as their ideal—indeed, as I would argue, *should* have as their ideal, since the family is a sub-group within the total society—the minimization of coercive relations with their children. On the other hand, abundant evidence exists to the effect that families are often fertile grounds for the cultivation of sadistic behavior.

And so, as this illustration again reminds us, we remain confronted with the brute empirical fact that there exist widespread preferences running counter to the ideal of a noncoercive society. Predictions as to the likelihood of future society's advancing towards this goal by such-and-such a degree are certainly beyond the scope of this paper, and any such predictions based on projections from past experience would be of dubious significance at best. It *can* legitimately be pointed out here, however, that the sort of fact in question is indeed a contingent one, not itself universal, and not ultimately rooted in any demostrable necessity about "human nature." If there are some individuals who are committed to the goal of a noncoercive society and who act, as far as possible, in accordance with this goal, then there is no logical argument against the possibility of *all* individuals' sharing this commitment and acting accordingly at some future time.

Lenin, unfortunately, did not pause to consider systematically the general philosophical issue of what might be necessary and what contingent about the attitudes of individuals. The greatness of his theory of political practice (as developed especially in his masterful *What Is To Be Done?*) surely lies in his recognition that attitudes and, ultimately, social structures themselves can be changed by education and agitation, and in his concomitant refusal to take as seriously as his "Economist" opponents the tenets of strong historical determinism. However, to a surprisingly large extent he did share

---

[16] I exclude from consideration here a third group, the consistent pacifists, who advocate a nonviolent society and at the same time attempt to escape from the basic paradox to which I have called attention. Their situation is too complicated to consider in this essay; I shall only remark that it is a profound delusion to think that massive *satyagraha,* simply because its practitioners eschew all overtly violent acts, is therefore immune from being characterized as "coercive."

the conservative conception of human nature as a set of fixed characteristics that are more or less unalterable, at least for the foreseeable future.[17] This endows Leninism with a determinism of a different sort, one that is thoroughly at odds with the radical spirit of the Bolshevik Revolution and with the enthusiastic eulogists of its early days. Herein lies an important clue to Lenin's failure to take seriously, in the final analysis, the possibility of moving toward a genuinely noncoercive society. There is no need, however, to acquiesce in Lenin's premises in this respect.

III

Just because of the rather banal character of some of his views about "human nature" or "people as they are now," Lenin would have found enormous difficulty in accepting, or perhaps even in understanding, the Marcusean and French student revolutionary slogan, "Power to the imagination!"[18] He did, it is true, muse in one long passage in *What Is To Be Done?* on the strikingly similar phrase, "We should dream!"[19]—but this passage is not typical. Perhaps he would have regarded the noncoercive society of which I have been speaking—noncoercive even in the sense of being nonhabituated—as strictly unimaginable. But let us reconsider, briefly, whether some of the strongest objections to imagining it are really so insurmountable.

Marcuse, who was concerned with these sorts of issues at a time when very few other writers seemed to be, has analyzed at length the possibilities of a nonrepressive but still "civilized" form of society in which creativity (which is often said, by critics of radical change, to depend for its existence on conditions of scarcity or even of repression) would flourish instead of drying up. His perspective in *Eros and Civilization*[20] is, of course, primarily psychological.

[17] "There is no trace of utopianism in Marx in the sense that he made up or invented a 'new' society. . . . We are not utopians . . .; these anarchist dreams . . . serve only to postpone the socialist revolution until people are different. We want the socialist revolution with people as they are now, with people who cannot dispense with subordination, control, and 'foremen and accountants.' "—*The State and Revolution,* 340.

[18] "*L' imagination au pouvoir!*"—See Herbert Marcuse, *An Essay on Liberation* (Boston: Beacon Press, 1969), 22.

[19] *What Is To Be Done?,* in *Selected Works,* Vol. I (Moscow: Foreign Languages Publishing House, 1960), 267.

[20] Boston: Beacon Press, 1955.

There is no reason to go back over the same ground here. I shall content myself with observing that certain small groups larger than families—for example, some types of "communes," with which so much experimentation is currently being conducted in sections of the United States—seem to provide partial evidence in support of his contention. While these groups frequently have additional, more specific objectives, an adherence to the ideal of noncoerciveness, though of course never perfectly maintained and often (I have no doubt) rather flagrantly violated in practice, is fairly widespread among them. If small noncoercive societies actually do exist and "work" for substantial periods of time, then there is no reason *in principle* why the same way of life could not be extended indefinitely over the larger societies of which these are parts. However, the practical obstacles to such a development are often thought to be so great as to cause the entire conception to be dismissed out of hand. What can a proponent of the ideal of a noncoercive society say by way of reply?

The practical obstacles in question are essentially the same as those with which Lenin, who was usually a very practical man, was most concerned at the time of his taking power. How can the vast and complicated technical systems—industrial, distributional, communications, etc.—required to maintain a modern country be run without the employment of substantial amounts of coercion, contrary to the ideal which we have been considering? To respond with Engels' famous pat phrase about making the transition from administration over persons to administration over things is to leave some of the most difficult questions still unanswered. Lenin himself shows an almost disastrously oversimplistic conception of the magnitude of the problems: in *The State and Revolution,* for example, he returns several times to his contention that, at least as concerns former governmental operations not connected with scientific technology, "the great majority of the functions . . . have become so simplified and can be reduced to such exceedingly simple operations of registration, filing, and checking that they can easily be performed by every literate person."[21] As for the more technologically

---

[21] *The State and Revolution,* 336.

advanced sorts of functions, "the question of the scientifically educated staff of engineers, agronomists, and so on," Lenin rather air-
ily dispenses with raising the important questions and, in so doing,
once again betrays the ideal of a noncoercive society. "These gen-
tlemen," he says, "are working today in obedience with the wishes
of the capitalists; they will work even better tomorrow in obedience
with the wishes of the armed workers."[22] He does not seem even to
recognize the discrepancy between his supposed long-range goals
and his casual reallocation of this class of individuals from one
coercive relationship to another. But we, who are trying to render
plausible the very conception of a noncoercive society, cannot afford to be so casual.

The key to imagining the possibility of a noncoercive society that
would function at a high level of technological development lies in
taking a more careful look at the related concepts of rule-following
and law. Law is one of the most important forms of socially relevant rules and, more often than not, it has traditionally been associated with enforcement and coercion. This certainly holds true for
Lenin, as we have seen, and it is for this reason that he feels compelled, as a good Marxist, to advocate the abolition of "mystifying"
legal systems. But has Lenin really succeeded in eliminating all
traces of law-like phenomena even in his vision of a more distant
future society? I think not. In a passage that I cited earlier, Lenin
speaks of what he calls the "rules of human intercourse." To me
these sound suspiciously like present-day legal rules, except that
Lenin regards them as becoming, in the envisioned future, matters
of habit and even of *"necessity"*, which law as we know it at present
is not. The inherent conservatism of this conception of the "rules"
that would replace present-day "laws" undoubtedly served as a partial basis for justifying, under Stalin, the suppression of the brilliant,
diverse, and creative endeavors in the field of legal philosophy that
flourished in the Soviet Union while Lenin himself was still alive.
Lenin, while making abundant use of Marx's insight into the ideological function of law in pre-revolutionary societies, apparently
failed to ask himself some crucial questions about the relationship

---

[22] *Ibid.*, 383.

between rule-following and coercion.[23] To do so would have been to challenge not that correct insight, but the seemingly inevitable Marxist conclusion—which so greatly concerned those early Soviet legal philosophers—that there could be no place for institutions resembling law in a fully developed postrevolutionary and postpolitical society.[24]

By contrast, a conception of systems of legal rules as potential objects of *acceptance* rather than as instruments for facilitating coercion into passive obedience, invites us to take a more radical perspective on the phenomenon of law, regarded as rule-governed social activity. From this perspective, we may be able to imagine a noncoercive society that would at the same time avoid the total anarchism and consequent breakdown of modern technology so feared by Lenin and other opponents of the noncoercive ideal. It is possible for laws to be accepted—not passively, out of a mixture of fear and force of habit, but actively, in the sense of their being recognized as the best for achieving certain desirable goals and followed for that reason alone.[25] In some "law-abiding" societies and smaller groups, the degree of such active acceptance has at times been quite high, so that the members have regarded their rules, in accordance with the formula common to Rousseau and Kant, as having been "prescribed to themselves." Since circumstances are continually changing, the continuance of such a situation over time assumes the constant possibility of members' deciding to alter the rules by which they abide. Within a group or even a whole society,

[23] One Russian legal theorist who *did* do so, with the result that I am suggesting, was M. A. Reisner, in an early (1908) attempt to bring together his version of Marxism with the legal philosophy of Petrazhitskii. See the excerpt from his *The Theory of Petrazhitskii: Marxism and Social Ideology,* in *Soviet Legal Philosophy,* tr. by H. W. Babb (Cambridge: Harvard University Press, 1951), esp. 71-75. During the 1920s, however, Reisner was criticized for his alleged "idealism," and backed away from a number of the positions taken in his previous work.

[24] See Ivo Lapenna, *State and Law: Soviet and Yugoslav Theory* (New Haven: Yale University Press, 1964). Lapenna mentions one theorist, Ye. Korovin, who upheld the maxim, "Where there is society there is law," in the 1920s, and implies that he may not have been unique in this respect (84-85). Korovin maintained this without at the same time abandoning the doctrine of the projected future "withering away of the state." He was correct, I think, to keep the two questions distinct.

[25] See my article, "The Acceptance of a Legal System," *The Monist* 49, 3 (July 1965), 377-396.

to the extent to which participation in decision-making is general and complete in this sense, then—even though different members may have different aptitudes and fulfill different roles in accordance with these differences, and even though opinions about the desirability of certain given rules may not be unanimous—that group or society can be called a "voluntary association." I have discussed this concept in some detail in a previous volume of NOMOS.[26]

But these conditions, if met, are still not sufficient to make a society a noncoercive one. For, beyond the coercions that may be imposed by others—which would be obviated in a society organized on the principles of voluntary association—lie the more subtle, less easily discernible coercions of the existing social structures themselves. Here the clear, critical intellects of a Marx or of a Lenin can provide us with especially useful enlightenment. The overt manifestations of coercion in favor of perpetuating social inequalities that are not based on natural aptitudes and propensities, or of replacing one set of such inequalities with another, are few in number (even in times of great turmoil) by comparison with the instances that are acquiesced in—or, better still, not even recognized as such—by those coerced. No single individual or class can be said to be *responsible* for such a state of affairs: the category of responsibility, so important in discussing the principle of voluntary association,[27] simply does not apply at this level, except perhaps in the rather contentless sense in which *all* the members of society may be said to be responsible. Successful coercive social structures do, indeed, have the function of *mystification* that Marx and Lenin ascribed to the law, but this does not mean, except in quite extraordinary cases, that they are the creation of some mystifier or mystifiers (for example, "the capitalists") who, with full consciousness of what they were doing, made them this way.[28] Their coerciveness actually

---

[26] "Voluntary Association: The Basis of an Ideal Model, and the 'Democratic' Failure," in J. R. Pennock and J. W. Chapman, eds., *Voluntary Associations* (NOMOS XI) (New York: Atherton Press, 1969), 202-232.

[27] *Ibid.,* 214 ff.

[28] "To prevent possible misunderstanding, a word. I paint the capitalist and the landlord in no sense *couleur de rose*. But here individuals are dealt with only in so far as they are the personifications of economic categories, embodiments of particular class-relations and class-interests. My standpoint, from which the evolution of the economic formation of society is viewed as a process of natural history, can less than any other make the individual

(continued)

functions at a much deeper level than this, and it is proportionately more difficult to discover and to remove.

Thus in order for a society to be truly noncoercive it must have the characteristics of a fully voluntary association, plus an important additional one. It must abide, in short, not just by *any* agreed-upon rules, but rather by rules that ensure the minimization of all relationships of dominance and subordination, *even* on occasions when such relationships might meet with the acquiescence of every single member of the society. In a noncoercive society no great man or party or other group, however highly regarded by all other members of the society, would be able to exercise control over others except when the others are recognizably incompetent (as in the cases of young children or of persons with brain damage), and in limited areas of special, acknowledged technical competence. The rules of such a society would be formulated and constantly revised by all the members, with a view not just to ensuring universal participation in this self-governing process, but also to maintaining the basic objective of minimizing coercive structures and relationships in every domain of life. Such a procedure would presuppose the recognition by all that the ultimate bastions of social coercion are likely to be not a dominant individual or a group external to the rest, but practices internal to the society itself.

Of course, all this remains an ideal. "Minimization," not total "elimination," of coercive structures is the operative concept.[29] It will of course come into conflict at times with other worthwhile ideals, and then some adjudication will be needed. A number of seemingly unrelated contemporary developments have shown that the ideal is not, however, as unimaginable as Lenin would have thought

---

responsible for relations whose creature he socially remains, however much he may subjectively raise himself above them."—Karl Marx, *Capital,* Vol. I (Preface to the First German Edition) (Moscow: Foreign Languages Publishing House, 1961), 10.

[29] I find myself in substantial agreement with, though perhaps slightly less optimistic than, Christian Bay when he says:

"The total abolition of coercion is an ideal that can possibly never be fully vindicated in practice, but it can be approached in practice and is not unattainable in principle. . . . A society within which all children go to school motivated by a spontaneous quest for knowledge, in which there are no criminals to lock up, and in which reasonable taxes are paid willingly— such a conception strains the imagination but does not surpass it."—*The Structure of Freedom* (New York: Atheneum, 1968), 94.

it. For example, experiments with workers' self-management of industrial enterprises in Yugoslavia have provided some useful models, however ambiguous and subject to diverse interpretations. In France, during the events of May and June 1968, short-lived workers' and technicians' takeovers of huge business, industrial, and communications enterprises (for instance, the Assurance Générale de France, the Atomic Energy Center in Saclay, and even the Organisation de la Radiodiffusion Télévision Française) pointed at least to the *existence* of possibilities for the successful operation even of highly centralized industries in a less fundamentally coercive fashion than is currently characteristic of the most advanced countries of East and West.[30] In the United States, usually in poor areas, a few efforts at something approaching "community control" over professions as highly technical as those connected with mental and physical health have proved remarkably successful, even while others have failed.[31] With respect to nontechnical areas of everyday existence, I have already mentioned the resurgence of interest in communal living; likewise, some of the contemporary "women's liberation" movements seem to be based on the assumption that the noncoercive ideal can be extended even to social structures in which subtle coercions are so deeply ingrained as to have passed almost unnoticed, until recently, by those coerced.

Among the lessons suggested by these developments is that Lenin's stresses on *centralization* and *professionalism* (at least on the part of the Party leadership), while understandable in the context of a backward, early twentieth-century Russia, are incompatible (unless they are subjected to the most radical reinterpretation) with

[30] For a number of interesting observations, with which I generally agree, concerning both the French events of 1968 and (esp. in Chap. 10) the subject of "self-management" *("autogestion"),* see Henri Lefebvre, *The Explosion: Marxism and the French Upheaval,* tr. by A. Ehrenfeld (New York: Monthly Review Press, 1969). For brief references to the takeovers to which I have alluded, see Gabriel and Daniel Cohn-Bendit, *Obsolete Communism: The Left-Wing Alternative,* tr. by A. Pomerans (London: Penguin Books, 1968), esp. 91-112 ("The Workers") and 76 (mention of the ORTF strike).

[31] See, for example, Nancy Milio, *7229 Kercheval: The Storefront That Didn't Burn* (Ann Arbor: University of Michigan Press, 1970). Apropos of this same topic, a fascinating institute, the proceedings of which are eventually to be published, took place from April 17-21, 1970, at the Yale University School of Nursing on the subject of "Community Control: Realities and Possibilities."

the noncoercive ideal, and show the same conservative lack of imagination as do some of the other aspects of his theories of social organization with which I have been concerned here. At the same time, I think it becomes clear that the alternatives to a whole society's becoming "a single office and a single factory" during some indefinitely long transitional stage, and a habit-governed agglomeration later on, are not either a continuation of old ways, on the one hand, or anarchy, on the other. In short, we can imagine a society that would be both rule-governed and noncoercive.

IV

As I have already suggested, there is no way of *proving* the supreme desirability of a noncoercive society. Some of Professor Wolff's agonized reflections on the question of why coercion is to be considered intrinsically evil point to the same conclusion. Nevertheless, it seems to me to be extremely illuminating—not only for purposes of purely academic discussion but also, and more importantly, for understanding some of our contemporary crises—to try to sort out fundamental issues about social and political action in light of the ideal of a noncoercive society. In today's global political context, V. I. Lenin looms as an enormously influential thinker and practitioner with regard to these issues; his many brilliant insights, so frequently accurate when he is critically analyzing his own social world, seem to me time and again just barely to miss the mark and then to lead to drastically distorted conclusions concerning the desirable future organization of our advanced industrial society. That is why I have felt it important to consider these matters in the context of some of his theoretical principles.

If one shares my conviction concerning the supreme desirability of the noncoercive ideal, what is called for and what is in fact taking place in many areas of daily life at present—is a massive educational effort to develop a deeper understanding of the coercive features of many of our present social structures, in particular those that are more covert. This effort cannot successfully be conducted in accordance with Lenin's Platonic-Guardian conception of the elite professional revolutionary agitator; rather, it must aim at a radical growth in awareness concerning the nature of those social structures on the part of all elements of society.

The underlying assumption of this process of education is, I re-peat, that the achievement of such a more comprehensive knowl-edge will *probably* lead to a more widespread recognition of the desirability of a society in which such features are absent. Presuma-bly, this recognition could be achieved not only by those who have come to see themselves as most obviously oppressed by present structures, but also by those with more apparently dominant posi-tions within the structures. The latter would come to see the truth (though not necessarily in the same technical terms) of the inescap-able dialectical logic of the master-slave relationship, so brilliantly analyzed by Hegel, in the development of which reflection brings about a kind of reversal, at least within consciousness, of the re-spective positions. Ultimately, if the underlying assumption should prove accurate, the further development of this unequal dialetic could then proceed toward its own elimination by moving beyond the domain of consciousness into that of social practice, as Marx advocated. This would take place, however, without involving *coer-cion* to nearly the same degree as that presupposed in Leninism's Jacobin reinterpretation of Marxism.

11

TRUST AS AN ALTERNATIVE TO COERCION

William H. Riker

"Covenants, without the Sword, are but words, and of no strength to secure a man at all." All careful observers of society have always known that this sentence is false.[1] Even the most Machiavellian politician or the most Austinian jurist has known that some bargains are kept without the sword. At almost every level and kind of bargaining there are well-known examples of bargains that are kept out of mutual self-interest and even perhaps out of affection. One can instance, for example, marriage and other family agreements and market bargains which in every society are

The research for and writing of this paper was supported by a grant from the National Science Foundation
[1] For a recent and excellent discussion of this point, see Michael Barkun, *Law Without Sanctions: Order in Primitive Societies and the World Community* (New Haven, Yale University Press, 1968).

typically concluded with a conventional sign, like a ring or a handshake, and enforced by custom and not by the sword. The Hobbesian could assert, however, that these many billions of bargains kept without coercion are not good examples because the authority of the sheriff and the judge is always lurking in the background. More compelling examples can be drawn, therefore, from the realm of international politics, where the absence of coercive authority guarantees that, if a covenant is kept at all, it is kept without coercion. One such example is the peacetime alliance (for example, the 1939 alliance between England and France and Poland) which develops into an alliance for waging war even though only one of the peacetime allies is attacked by a prospective enemy. There is hardly any way to say that the unattacked ally comes to the aid of the attacked ally because of some sort of coercive authority. Surely England and France did not fear Poland in 1939. And generally, since a government at war can hardly take time off from fighting an enemy to coerce an ally, the unattacked ally has no present fear of reprisals for failure to keep the bargain. Typically also the unattacked ally has no fear of future reprisals. It is hard to imagine that England or France could have feared future coercion from Poland. Common sense assures us that the object of English and French fears was the common enemy, not the common friend and not any conceivable international authority. They kept their agreement with Poland because they believed it was advantageous to do so—and they kept it with no possible enforcement in sight.

Alliances kept when only one ally is attacked are probably relatively rare events and as such are not a very good example of the falsity of Hobbes' assertion. A much more common example, however, is the agreement between the government of an undeveloped country and a corporate citizen of a developed country for the exploitation of resources within the boundaries the government controls. Since governments commonly recognize no international authority in these business matters and since all the force is in the hands of the government—which is only one party to the bargain —it follows that there can be no possible coercion to enforce against a breach of contract by the government. (It may be that in the heyday of imperialism the home government of the developer corporation served as the enforcer against breaches by the undeveloped government. But that era is long since past, as massive and substantially unprotested nationalizations in Eastern Europe, Cuba, Mexico, Peru, Chile, Indonesia, Iran, etc. have demonstrated. So it may be truly said that today there is no possible coercive authority to support these business covenants.) Nevertheless, American, German, Japanese, British, French, Scandanavian, Dutch, Canadian, and Belgian corporations continue to make such covenants with a fair amount of eagerness—not perhaps with the eagerness of, say, the old East India Company, whose armies were better than the armies of the undeveloped countries they bargained with, but still with the more tempered and calculating eagerness of, say, Jersey Standard. (It is, of course, a sad thing for the undeveloped world that it has frightened corporate developers, for these are the only good source of the venture capital that undeveloped countries need more than anything else. Such is the price that all the undeveloped world must pay for the senseless braggadocio of a Sukarno, the impulsive pride of a Mossadegh, and the insane rantings of a Castro.) The fact that corporations do continue to make such covenants in the face of known nationalizations is the best possible evidence that Hobbes' sentence is false. In the long run, the only possible motive that corporate managers can have for making contracts with governments of undeveloped lands is to make money for the corporation and themselves. And they can make money from such contracts only if a substantial portion of the contracts are kept. That developers continue to make such contracts—even though frightened by nationalization—is therefore sufficient evidence that governments—however tempted by the short-run gains of nationalization—resist the temptation to break covenants because of the long-run gain such bargains bring. There is no common power to enforce these covenants; yet they are kept simply because they are advantageous to both parties.

I

Even this superficial glance at the world of international politics and international business indicates that some covenants are kept without coercion. Clearly, Hobbes' sentence is a poor description of behavior, and hence Austinian jurisprudence, which also makes this behavioral premise, is clearly false. To rebuild political theory and jurisprudence one needs to know something about what really occurs in nature. If coercion is not the root of the matter, why do people really keep bargains?

I have some evidence that indicates some of the answers to this extraordinarily complex question. The remainder of this paper is devoted to explaining and explicating this evidence.

For several years now I have been studying politics through the medium of a game which, for reasons that will soon be obvious, I call *Couples*. In this game the central action is making bargains to form coalitions. In my opinion Couples is a simplified version of politics in the real world. Because it is simplified, it is not, of course, quite the same as politics; but it contains enough of the central kind of political action to give us some valuable hints about why people keep contracts in the larger political world.

From the point of view of our present concerns, the main feature of Couples is that, although it requires that a pair of players keep an agreement for either to win, still there is, as in international politics, no possible coercive authority. A brief statement of the rules will make this point clear:

1. There are three players (1, 2, and 3) who vote privately for a partner and a division of the payoff to the partnership. If the pair (1, 2) forms—that is, if 1 votes for 2 and 2 votes for 1, and if they agree on the division—then (1, 2) receives $4.00 from the referee. If the pair (1, 3) forms and the members agree on the division, it receives $5.00. If the pair (2, 3) forms and the members agree on the division, it receives $6.00. In each case the referee pays the individual members of the pair according to the agreement. In any one of these cases, the omitted player receives nothing. Of course, it may also happen that no pair forms, that is, for example, 1 may vote for 2, 2 may vote for 3, and 3 may vote for 1. In this case, the players receive nothing.

2. Before they vote, players negotiate privately by pairs in (mostly) five minute conversations. A typical sequence of conversations is: (1, 2), (1, 3), (2, 3), (1, 2), (1, 3), (2, 3), (1, 2), (1, 3), (2, 3), which amounts to a maximum of 45 minutes of negotiation. The main thing discussed in these conversations is, of course, whether or not the players in the pair should vote for each other and, if so, how they should divide the money.

Since the subjects I have used as players in this game are college undergraduates for whom the sums of $1 to $4 are reasonably substantial, the subjects clearly have a strong motive to come to an agreement so that they can get something rather than nothing. But there is nothing coercive in the situation. If 1 agrees to vote for 2 and 2 agrees to vote for 1 and then they both actually do so, it is because they have chosen to do so, not because anyone forced them. I must admit that subjects often find this situation quite frustrating, but their frustration only serves to underline the absence of coercion.

If the world were constructed along Hobbesian lines, there would be a sword to enforce every contract and, once two players agreed, they would not need to worry whether or not the agreement would be carried out. Accustomed to living under governments with judges and sheriffs, subjects at first anticipated the same kind of situation in the game. On first hearing the rules explained, a number of subjects noted the absence of enforcement procedures and asked what the substitute would be. Some initially found it hard to believe that trust alone was to determine the result. During the play the subjects often tried to turn the experimenters into an enforcement mechanism comparable to the state. They asked, for example, that the experimenter hold money as a bond of the performance of an agreement. That is, if 1 and 2 agreed to vote for each other, they then agreed each to give a relatively large amount—say, $5.00—to the experimenter for him to hold with the following instructions which he supposedly agreed to obey: If both voted as promised or both reneged, to return the deposit to both and, if only one reneged, to give the entire $10.00 to the player who kept his word. To allow the posting of a performance bond would require that a bondholder act as a kind of judge, an action thus comparable to the mechanism of the state. Although my assistants and I always emphatically refused to be bondholders (stating, "If you give us the money, we keep it"), some desperate subjects persisted with the proposal that we watch them hide the money. Again we refused to be custodians in any way, remarking that one of the graduate student assistants might take the money if it were left lying around. We thus deprived the subjects of an objective enforcement procedure, which did frustrate them. That it did so suggests the degree to which the Hobbesian emphasis on coercion is correct.

So far I have observed 223 matches of this game, and of these 210, or 94%, have resulted in payments to the subjects. Hence, in a very large portion of the experiments the subjects have made and kept agreements without any coercion at all. Their behavior is not frivolous, however. They keep the agreements for what appear to be good reasons. I turn now to a catalogue of those reasons in order to demonstrate how many things besides coercion are involved in keeping agreements.

II

The main thing that subjects are concerned with in this game is finding another player whom they can trust. The early conversations of any particular match, especially after subjects become somewhat experienced, are chiefly devoted to probing for trustworthiness, and most of the innovations of play involve ways of generating trust, which appears to be the main alternative to coercion.

Most of the time players make judgments about trustworthiness on the basis of cues from manners, voice tones, etc. As they always find this unpleasant, they search for better indicators and guarantees of trust. It does not take much experience to discover that, regardless of how nice and decent a player seems, he cannot keep an agreement with *two* players. Hence, many of the social cues for trustworthiness are unreliable in this game. In their place my subjects find at least the following ways to establish bases of trust.

1. Generation of Mutual Advantage

The most obvious basis for trust between two players in this game is the occurrence of bargains such that each person in a pair makes more with the other in the pair than with the player outside. Consider the following circumstance: In the first round of conversations, that is, one conversation for each pair, the result was:

1 and 2 agreed to split $4.00 so that 1 got $1.50 and 2 got $2.50;

1 and 3 agreed to split $5.00 so that 1 got $1.60 and 3 got $3.40;

2 and 3 agreed to split $6.00 so that 2 got $2.50 and 3 got $3.50.

At the end of this round each player privately expressed himself as likely to vote as follows:

Player 1: for 2, 25%; for 3, 75%;

Player 2: for 1, 50%; for 3, 50%;

Player 3: for 1, 10%; for 2, 90%.

That is, at this initial point no bargain was established. But by the end of the third round, that is, the third conversation for each pair, the agreements were:

1 and 2: $1.65 for 1 and $2.35 for 2

1 and 3: $1.60 for 1   and $3.40 for 3

2 and 3: $2.45 for 2 and $3.55 for 3.

At this more definite stage, each player was furthermore able to compare his position in each of two potential contracts. Owing to the exchange of information among players, which in this case was accurate, players 2 and 3 knew what each other would receive from 1, although of course they could not be certain that this information was truthful. Players 2 and 3 expressed their chance of voting for each other as 100% and 95% respectively, so that one can regard a bargain as made. Player 1 did not know what he was going to do, and expressed himself as equally likely to vote for 2 and 3.

In the actual vote, 2 and 3 did vote for each other, presumably because 2 received 10¢ more from 3 than from 1 and because 3 received 15¢ more from 2 than from 1. The bargain between 2 and 3 was easy to cement presumably because each felt certain that the other would rather vote for him than for player 1.

In part this resulted from the foolishness of player 1, who often seemed unable to comprehend the way other people might look at the world. Player 1, in his naive greed, made agreements that were excessively advantageous to himself in the sense that his share, while smaller than the shares for other people, were larger than his strategic position warranted. Had he not been so greedy and so poor a bargainer, 2 and 3 would not have so easily trusted one another.

2. Arriving at Principal Points of the Solution

Typically, among experienced and good players, it is not possible to find a basis of trust so easily, because no player is willing to make himself a patsy by asking for more than the solution of the game indicates he is worth. Nevertheless, the solution itself is something to stick by. The principal points of the von Neumann-Morgenstern nondiscriminatory solution are:

if (1,2) forms, 1 gets $1.50 and 2 gets $2.50

if (1,3) forms, 1 gets $1.50 and 3 gets $3.50

if (2,3) forms, 2 gets $2.50 and 3 gets $3.50.

In addition, that solution contains infinites of other points for three-person winning coalitions. If (1,2,3) forms, either

a) 1 gets from $1.50 to $3.50, 2 gets from $2.50 to $4.50, 3 gets from 0 to $2.00, and the payments sum to $6.00; or

b) 1 gets from $1.50 to $2.50, 2 gets from 0 to 1.00, 3 gets from $3.50 to $4.50, and the payments sum to $6.00.

Incidentally, it is appropriate to use the nondiscriminatory solution because the social situation of the three players is symmetric. Indeed, in most groups they were people who had never previously known each other.

Since forming a three-person winning coalition is quite difficult (but not impossible) when negotiations occur in paris, most of the time only two-person winning coalitions occur. Hence, among experienced players—even if they know nothing about the mathematical theory—the values $1.50, $2.50, and $3.50 soon took on special significance. Players gradually realize that these values are in a sense quotas for the three positions, and that to deviate from these quotas is asking for trouble unless some special circumstance justifies the deviation.

And the trouble is there. Suppose that in the first round of conversations each pair arrives at a division in the solution. (As my subjects became experienced, they tended to do exactly this because it seemed "fair.") Then suppose that in the second round 1 accepts an arrangement with 2 in which 1 gets $1.60 and 2 gets $2.40. This is not totally unreasonable for 1. As long as all three pairs are at points in the solution, voting may well be random. Hence, to avoid randomness, some pair may break the pattern. But they do so at their peril. By this deviation 1 invites 2 to prefer 3 to 1. Indeed, half of the situation previously described in which 1 is a patsy has thus been created. Thus 2 distrusts 1 and, if 3 learns of this situation from either or both of 1 and 2, then 3 has good reason to distrust 1. Thus the coalition of 2 and 3 is cemented, in good part because it is at the quota, while one of the coalitions involving 1 is not. Therefore, one method of generating trust is to arrive and *stay* at a principal point of the solution. In a sense, the person who *stays* most determinedly is the most likely to win.

3. Generating spurious rationales for trustworthiness

It is possible for a skillful player, typically in the 1 position, to generate the special circumstances for deviation from the quota by convincing another player, say 2, of his (1's) belief in the disadvantage of the 1 position, thereby presumably justifying a division such that 1 receives less than his quota. Thus, 1 might offer to divide the $4.00 payment to (1,2) so that 1 gets $1.25 and 2 gets $2.75. Typically, player 2 is led to believe that he can trust 1 to stick with the deal, even though 1 receives less than his quota, because 1 is desperate to assure himself membership in a winning coalition. Elsewhere I have called this a strategy of "shaving the quota."[2] Of course, this may be a trap for 2, in the sense that 1 may be making a quota deal (that is, $1.50 for 1 and $3.50 for 3) with 3 and may leave 2 out altogether. Nevertheless, "shaving the quota" in this fashion seems to work well, at least with partly experienced players, and especially for players in the 1 position.

Eventually, however, players come to understand that greed for amounts in excess of the quotas for the positions is likely to lead to disaster, so no one will accept more than his quota; this makes shaving the quota impossible. Hence, also, it is not possible for players to base their trust in each other on any manipulation of the payoff. Indeed, among experienced players, even if they are not sophisticated, it is common for all three pairs to arrive at agreements on principal points in the solution and to stay with those agreements determinedly. When this occurs no player has any financial reason to prefer one of his possible coalitions to another. Indeed, voting is no more than random choice. What basis for trust exists then?

[2] William H. Riker, "Bargaining in a Three Person Game," *American Political Science Review*, 61 (1967), 642-56. See also, William H. Riker and William James Zavoina "Rational Behavior in Politics: Evidence from a Three Person Game," *American Political Science Review*, 64 (1970), 48-60, and William H. Riker, "Experimental Verification of Two Theories about in-Person Games" in Joseph Bernd, ed., *Mathematical Applications in Political Science*, III (University Press of Virginia, 1968), 52-66.

4. Generating Conspiracies

Looking constantly for some basis for trust, experienced players have found that some overt form of conspiracy is very helpful in generating trust among the conspirators. Our subjects have invented the following kinds of conspiracies, all of which work to some degree in generating trust.

a) Conspiracy to vote together and to lie to the third party. This procedure words in the following way: Two players, say 1 and 2, agree in the first conversation to vote for each other, typically at the quota of $1.50 for 1 and $2.50 for 2. At the same time they agree to lie to 3 about this agreement, saying, for example, that the (1,2) deal is $1.25 for 1 and $2.75 for 2. This lie has several important consequences. For one thing, it confuses the bargaining so that (2,3) is likely to come to a deal which is unbelievably advantageous to 2—for example, (0,$3.00, $3.00)—so that (1,3) is likely to come to a disadvantageous deal for 1—for example, ($1.40, 0, $3.60). Neither of these is likely to be kept—simply because they are so far from points in the solution—so the (1,2) deal is thereby strengthened. For another thing, the lie permits a test of trust. In subsequent conversations 2 can ask 3 what 1 said the (1,2) deal was, and, if 3 reports hearsay of a split $1.25-$2.75, 2 can conclude that 1 is trustworthy in all things because he has been trustworthy in keeping the conspiracy to lie to 3. Similarly, 1 can check on 2's lie to 3. (Of course, by his own more or less random lies 3 can undermine this test, but he cannot plan to do so unless, as happened once, 2 makes a conspiracy with 3 to lie to 1 after having previously made a conspiracy with 1 to lie to 3.) Since the test is hard to throw off, it has the effect of generating trust simply by setting up a pre-vote "proof" of trustworthiness.

b) Conspiracy to exchange articles of value as evidence of good faith. This procedure works in the following way: Two players, say 1 and 2, agree to exchange objects that will be returned when both have kept the agreement to vote for each other. If one of the pair breaks the agreement on voting, then it is understood that the other may keep or destroy the object of value. Of course, if both break the agreement, then presumably the objects would be re-exchanged.

Two sets out of seven of my subjects have discovered this possibility of exchange and have traded such objects as keys to rooms and cars, college ID cards (which cost $2.00 to replace), meal tickets, books, glasses, rings, driver's license, etc. Of course, a mere trade such as I have described is objectively meaningless, though not apparently to the subjects when they make the agreements. For one thing, most of my subjects had sufficiently deep respect for rights of property that they could not keep or destroy valuable objects forfeited in the game. Thus, one player put up his glasses as security, forfeited them, and demanded them back. The loser, whom he had thus cheated, did reluctantly return them.

While there is no real security in a simple exchange, my subjects did work out one exchange that was relatively secure. In this case, 1 and 2 agreed on a division of $1.50 for 1 and $2.50 for 2. Then 2 gave 1 the $1.50 immediately out of 2's own private funds, and 1 gave 2 his (1's) driver's license—worth about $2.00 to player 1 and substantially non-negotiable for 2. (Ideally, the collateral should be worth no more than $1.50 to 1 and nothing to 2; but my subjects never found quite the perfect object.) Finally, of course, it was agreed that, when it came to voting, they would vote for the coalition (1,2) with a split of zero for 1 and $4.00 for 2. Given the previous payment from 2 to 1, this would result in a division in the solution; $1.50 for 1 and $2.50 for 2.

This agreement was realtively secure because both 1 and 2 had good reason to trust each other. Player 1 could trust 2 either to vote for (1,2) at the agreed division or to form a new coalition with 3 for a three-person coalition of the sort described in the next subsection. In either event, 1 had his money and needed to worry only about the return of his collateral. If he voted as agreed, he would earn the return of his license. In any event, 1 could trust 2, simply because 1 already had his payoff. Thus, 1 knew that he could not be hurt by the actions 2 could take to earn back the capital he (2) had advanced. On the other hand, 2 could trust 1 to vote as agreed simply to earn back the collateral. Specifically, 2 could trust 1 not to deal with 3 because the formation of (1,3) would mean that 2 would tear up 1's driver's license.

There is a disadvantage for 1 in this agreement—namely, that player 2 might sell the driver's license back to 1 after the division of the rewards for an amount up to $2.00, the charge for a replacement. My subjects discussed this possibility but never attempted it.

Apparently players in the 2 position were constrained by public opinion. That being the case, here we have a deal that captures the spirit of our original basis of confidence—mutual advantage—without depending on the cooperation of a stupid third player.

c) Conspiracy to form a three-person coalition. I think it is remarkable that the von Neumann and Morgenstern solution predicts an occurrence that none of my subjects, many of whom were thoughtful and experienced game players, found until the sixth experimental group. The three-person coalitions among my subjects always occurred in the following way as a development out of the exchange-of-objects strategy which has just been described. Players 1 and 2 agreed that 2 give 1 the quota for the 1 position and that 1 give 2 a guarantee (for example, a driver's license) of his (1's) intention to vote for 2. Typically also player 1 agreed to tell player 3 the nature of the agreement and to refuse to bargain with him. Player 2 then negotiated an agreement with player 3 for a division of $5.00 for 2 and $1.00 for 3. Thus, player 2—who had already given $1.50 to player 1—has $3.50, which is $1.00 more than his quota. In the voting, 1 votes for 2 at a split of zero for 1 and $4.00 for 2; 2 votes for 3 and 3 votes for 2 at a split of $5.00 for 2 and $1.00 for 3. The situation of trust is quite complicated here. Player 1 must trust 2 to give him (1) back his driver's license. Since the license is worthless to 2—except perhaps to sell it back to 1—1 can fairly surely trust 2 for it. Players 2 and 3, who must trust each other in the vote, both have good reasons to do so. Player 3 trusts 2 because 3 knows that 2's vote for 3 is the only way that 2 can profit heavily from the elaborate scheme which, typically, 2 has instigated. Because 1 refuses to bargain with 3, 2 trusts player 3 for 2 knows that 3 has no place to turn even though he is not getting anywhere near his quota. In few matches of this game have players been as justifiably confident of the behavior of others as in these matches with a three-way coalition.

III

To return now to the subject of coercion, Couples does not admit coercion; yet, to play it most effectively, people must make and keep agreements. In this respect it is very much like society, which also depends on honored promises and in which there is not enough coercion to go around. In Couples, the subjects have found ways to make their trust more certain, mostly by redefining the situation so that all parties to the bargain receive an advantage from the bargain. I suspect that this is also what happens in society generally, in that custom and public opinion are, alone and often, the guarantee of mutually advantageous bargains.

In Chapter 9 Professor Sobel apparently agrees that real people behave in this way, but he suggests that if they were *perfectly* reasonable they would have to use coercion to enforce agreements. And doubtless it is true that coercion is useful—indeed its usefulness shines through every example I have offered. Contrary to Professor Sobel's first claim, however, coercion is not always necessary for effective agreements. Even Professor Sobel's *perfectly* reasonable (and imaginary) people would probably behave the same way as my *very* reasonable (and real) subjects. Professor Sobel has been misled by his failure to consider situations in which there are absolute gains from organization and absolute gains from trade.

Professor Sobel remarks that he is not sure how his perfectly reasonable people would behave in the circumstances of Couples. If they could cope with it all all, he says, they might randomize among available alternatives. Let us examine this possibility by making the situation as initially advantageous for them as possible. Hence, each player is restricted to two alternatives—namely, to make a division in the solution with either of the other two. Thus, player 1's alternatives are

    (a) to vote for 2 at a division of $1.50 for 1 and $2.50 for 2;
    (b) to vote for 3 at a division of $1.50 for 1 and $3.50 for 3.
Then, to randomize, 1 chooses (a) with some probability p (for convenience, say $p = \frac{1}{2}$), and (b) with probability $1 - p$. If all three players randomize with $p = \frac{1}{2}$, as they must if we are to avoid assuming that agreements are made and kept, then there are eight possible outcomes:

(1 for 2, 2 for 1, 3 for 1)		($1.50, $2.50, 0)
(1 for 2, 2 for 1, 3 for 2)		($1.50, $2.50, 0)
(1 for 2, 2 for 3, 3 for 1)		(0, 0, 0)
(1 for 2, 2 for 3, 3 for 2)	with the payoff	(0, $2.50, $3.50)
(1 for 3, 2 for 1, 3 for 1)		($1.50, 0, $3.50)
(1 for 3, 2 for 1, 3 for 2)		(0, 0, 0)
(1 for 3, 2 for 3, 3 for 1)		($1.50, 0, $3.50)
(1 for 3, 2 for 3, 3 for 2)		(0, $2.50, $3.50)

If these outcomes are equiprobable—as in the case when $p = \frac{1}{2}$ for all three players—then player 1's expectation is $\frac{4}{8}(1.50) + \frac{4}{8}(0) = .75$. Similarly, 2's expectation is $1.25 and 3's is $1.75. (One could, of course, complicate matters by adding alternatives —such as not voting, or voting for divisions other than the quotas —but such additions would simply lower the expected value by making more opportunities for the zero payoff. This would be contrary to the intention of giving these perfectly reasonable men the best chance possible in their world.)

Assuming that the other two randomize, player 1 has the same expected value *whether he randomizes or not*. If he chooses (a) for certain, his expected value is .75; and if he chooses $\frac{1}{2}$(a) + $\frac{1}{2}$(b) it is also .75. To choose (a) for certain or (b) for certain (the essence of making and keeping an agreement) is then *just as good as randomizing,* provided that the other two players are randomizing. In other words, it is costless to make agreements. When you make them you cannot do worse than when you refuse to make them or break them.

At the other extreme, suppose that players are making firm agreements, so that the chance of either the event (1 for 2, 2 for 3, 3 for 1) or the event (1 for 3, 3 for 2, 2 for 1) is zero. Then player 1's expectation is: $\frac{4}{6}$ ($1.50) + $\frac{2}{6}$ (0) = $1.00; 2's is $1.67; and 3's is $2.33. In this case, then, to choose one alternative for certain is more profitable by one-third than to randomize. And, of course, if there are more than two alternatives the increase in profitability from making agreements is correspondingly larger.

Thus, in Couples, it cannot hurt to try to make and keep agreements and, if at least one other person does so, it is profitable. Since agreements—without coercion—are both costless and potentially advantageous, one can expect them to be made by perfectly rational people.

Of course, it remains possible that Professor Sobel's perfectly rational people could not cope with Couples because they are by definition incapable of agreement. If so, it is difficult to describe them as being purely forward-looking teleologists, for they are too pathologically suspicious to take advantage of a costless opportunity.

Couples is then a counterexample to Professor Sobel's claim that perfectly reasonable men cannot make effective unenforced agreements. His claim is doubtless true when such men live in a world of prisoners' dilemmas, for in that world agreement is less profitable than breaking agreements. In the world of Couples, however, even though it does not have a core,[3] the act of agreement is potentially more profitable than disagreement, even for perfectly reasonable men.

Whether the real world outside the laboratory (our ultimate interest) is composed more of situations on the model of prisoners' dilemmas or of situations on the model of Couples is an empirical question that deserves much study. It appears likely that situations involving public goods, such as the purchase of national defense or law enforcement, are very like prisoners' dilemmas.[4] On the other hand, market situations are typically like games with cores; in a sense, everybody wins because there are gains from trade. The situations modeled by Couples—in which it is not the case that everybody wins but in which there are nevertheless gains from organization—are essentially political situations. The political situations are somewhat in between law enforcement and the market in quality; but nevertheless, as I have shown, effective agreements can be made in them without coercion, even among perfectly reasonable people. Thus there are many kinds of situations in the world, in some of which coercion is necessary for effective agreement and in some of which it is not. Consequently it is incorrect to assert that coercion is either necessary (as Hobbes said) or unnecessary (as anarchists say) for effective agreements. The correct view is more balanced: Coercion is necessary in some kinds of situations and not in others.

---

[3] A division of rewards is the core—a strong kind of solution—if, in the division, the sum of payments to individuals in each possible coalition is at least as good as that coalition could do under the most adverse circumstances. Clearly the form of Couples I have used does not have a core. The most that can be made out of it is $6.00 while the sum of the individual quotas is $7.50. No matter how the money is divided, some person is not going to get all he expects. One could change Couples into a game with a core by making the payment to the three-person coalition not $6.00, as it now is, but $8.00. In such a game the potential profit in agreement over disagreement must surely wipe out suspiciousness.

[4] See my discussion of this matter in a paper entitled "Public Order as a Public Good" in Eugene Rostow (ed.), *Is Law Dead?* New York: Simon and Shuster, 1971.

12

POLITICAL COERCION AND POLITICAL OBLIGATION

Alan P. Wertheimer

The purpose of this paper is to consider the claim that there is a contradiction, tension, or inverse relationship between political coercion and political obligation. More specifically, I will examine the adequacy of two claims: first, that if one consents to a political system, that system is not coercive, and therefore men may have obligations to it; second, that because membership in the polity is involuntary and coercive—without consent—one could not have political obligations. Both claims assume an incompatibility between political obligation and political coercion, and neither claim stands up for the following reasons: the conception of the sources of obligation upon which these claims rest is too limited; the consent theory is virtually irrelevant in the modern polity; the terms in which political coercion are usually defined are misleading and biased; and neither claim sufficiently accounts for the relationship between the political and the economic systems.

213

In Part I the concept "obligation" will be analyzed; this will serve as a framework for the rest of the paper. Further, the merits of the "consent" theory of political obligation will be considered. Part II will discuss "political coercion" with a view to exploring the nature and limitations of the concept. In Part III I will suggest that the political system has no monopoly on coercion and that depending upon one's socioeconomic status, the economic system may be understood as primarily coercive. Relying heavily on the "theory of public goods," I will develop in Part IV a framework for the justification of political coercion. In Part V I will draw some conclusions from the argument and suggest why our theories of political obligation must be formulated along new lines.

I

While it is often claimed that the problem of political obligation is the central problem of political philosophy, recently both the "possibility" and "appropriateness" of theories of political obligation have been strongly attacked. Several authors have argued (for different reasons) that political philosophers can and should dispense with either the concept or the consideration of the problem. I accept the assertion that it is possible to develop a political philosophy "that neither makes explicit use of this concept nor requires it."[1] From a collectivist or organic perspective of society, the problem of obligation need not even arise. The significance of the problem is closely tied to an individualistic or liberal perspective—a perspective which understands society as a source of restraints and coercion, not as an arena for the development of one's potentialities. Because much of this paper is quite critical of liberal assumptions, I wish to anticipate the objection that I am therefore inconsistent. An organic perspective can facilitate understanding and analysis of important social and political problems which an individualistic or liberal perspective ignores. So too with a liberal perspective. While political theories can be developed that neither use

[1] Thomas McPherson, *Political Obligation* (London: Routledge and Kegan Paul, 1967), 84-5. Also see the article by John Ladd, "Legal and Moral Obligation" in J. Roland Pennock and John W. Chapman, eds., *Nomos XII: Political and Legal Obligation* (New York: Atherton Press, 1970).

nor require a discussion of "obligation," this does not preclude the appropriateness or possibility of raising the problem. Political philosophers must adopt the perspective most appropriate for the problem under consideration. This implies a willingness to use a variety of perspectives, not just one.

Political philosophers have rarely found it necessary or important to base their theories about the sources and limits of political obligation on a prior analysis of the concept "obligation." "Power," "rights," "authority," "public interest,"—we can certainly profit from careful analysis of the ambiguities and intricacies of these concepts. But surely we all know what "obligation" means—the only interesting problems concern when, if, and why it is correct to say that persons have obligations. This assumption is partially correct. It is correct because we certainly do ordinarily understand what a person means when he says that he has an obligation to do something. It is only partially correct because while the concept is sufficiently clear for most non-philosophical discourse, a philosophical treatment requires more careful analysis. The context in which "obligation" is most obviously used is that of a promise or contract.[2] When A promises B to do X, we do not say that A "ought" to do X, but that he is "obligated" or "bound" to do X. It is clear that obligations are often created by prior acts or transactions; the act which one is "obligated" to perform may itself be morally neutral. If A promises B to mow B's lawn, he is obligated to mow the lawn not because mowing the lawn has moral significance, but because promises have moral significance. The "consent" theory of political obligation assumes or argues that obligations can only occur in such contexts and that it is always improper to infer obligations when no prior act has taken place. Thus, Michael Walzer suggests that "obligations can only derive from willful undertakings . . . ."[3] There can

[2] I have relied heavily on the article by R. B. Brandt, "The Concepts of Obligation and Duty," *Mind,* LXXII (1964). Brandt distinguishes between the "paradigm" and "extended" senses of these concepts, and argues that both senses are legitimate. I have developed this argument in greater detail in my paper, "Political Legitimacy, Political Obligation and Political Size," delivered at the Sixty-Sixth Annual Meeting of the American Political Science Association, Los Angeles, 1970.

[3] Michael Walzer, "The Obligation to Disobey," *Ethics,* LXXVII (1967), 166-67. This article is reprinted in A. de Crespigny and A. Wertheimer, eds., *Contemporary Political Theory* (New York: Atherton Press, 1970).

(continued)

be, of course, much dispute as to what constitutes a prior act, commitment, or "willful undertaking," but my present concern is with the presupposition that obligations always require such acts.

It might be said that A has an obligation to help a drowning man, that a doctor has an obligation to aid an injured party (that he might not have a legal obligation is beside the point), or that a son has an obligation to provide for his elderly and dependent parents. It could be argued that such uses are only "parasitic" and that they are not genuine cases of obligation. I do not think that is the case, and to adopt such a view would be to beg the question. Persons acquire obligations by virtue of a special status, position, or relationship with other persons. Relationships may be entered into voluntarily (as in a promise or contract), or they may be acquired quite accidentally or involuntarily. It is the nature of the "special relationship" not the manner in which the relationship is acquired that created the obligation.

However, since we do not use "obligation" to describe all moral relationships, what then distinguishes the context in which "obligation" is appropriate from the context in which other moral terms—for instance, "ought"—are more appropriate? We might say that a millionaire "ought" to distribute his fortune among the needy, although we might not say that he has an "obligation" to do so. To do so might be "ideally" what he ought to do, but it would be strange to say that he was "bound" to do it. Therein lies the nature of the distinction. We say that an act is obligatory only when failure to perform it constitutes sufficient grounds for moral condemnation, and not when performance would result only in praise. Our moral vocabulary reflects the important social practice of distinguishing acts whose nonperformance subjects the individual to blame from acts which entitle the individual only to praise.[4]

Persons have obligations when others have good moral reasons to expect them to perform (or not perform) some act and to sanction

---

Walzer has developed a most interesting set of esays, all from the perspective of "consent theory," in his recent book, *Obligations* (Cambridge, Mass.: Harvard University Press, 1970).

[4] Lon Fuller makes a similar distinction between a "morality of aspiration" and a "morality of duty" in *The Morality of Law* (New Haven, Conn.: Yale University Press, 1964).

them if they do not (or do).[5] In order to avoid sanction, persons under obligations must supply the relevant person(s) with good reasons why they did not or could not perform the act. While we must give the millionaire good reasons why he should distribute his fortune, he must give us good reasons for failure to keep a promise or to aid a drowning man. "Obligation," then, has a reasonably clear and precise meaning that can be elucidated without recourse to prior acts or transactions. Clearly, while A's promise to do X constitutes one good reason to expect A to do X, there may be other good reasons for expecting A to perform some act. What is to count as a good reason necessarily depends upon the social context in which the relationship occurs. When we say that persons who promise to do something acquire obligations, we merely reflect our social practice of establishing relationships by the act of promising. The strength of the obligation a son has to his elderly parents depends in part upon the kinds of provisions the society makes for the elderly. Bonds between people develop in many ways, and most important for this analysis, we should not assume that moral relationships in the political context are or must be acquired in the same fashion as moral relationships in "face-to-face" contexts.[6]

The consent theory of political obligation claims that when giving consent to the government, by giving agreement to be governed, the citizen thereby makes the government legitimate and incurs an obligation to abide by its laws and policies. It is our own will that creates the obligation; we are not, in fact, bound to an "alien" will. Thus the apparent contradiction between individual autonomy and political coercion is reconciled. The theory presupposes that this mode of acquiring obligations is the only one consistent with our autonomy and natural rights. Men cannot have obligations that they did not agree to accept. Political obligations are created in much the same way that we acquire obligations to keep our promises. The theory can be presented in syllogistic form:

[5] Stephen Toulmin has developed the concept of "good moral reasons" at length in *The Place of Reason in Ethics* (Cambridge: Cambridge University Press, 1953). He makes a strong case for claiming that moral noncognitivists are wrong in assuming that moral reasoning is impossible.

[6] See Peter Laslett, "The Face to Face Society" in Peter Laslett, ed. *Philosophy, Politics, and Society,* First Series (Oxford: Basil Blackwell, 1956).

Major Premise:	One is under an obligation to one's political system *if* and only if one consents to the system.	
Minor Premises:	(A) One consents.	(B) One does not consent.

Conclusions:	(A) One has obligations.	(B) One has no obligations.

If the major premise is accepted, in order to reach conclusion A one must show that minor premise A in true; otherwise one must reach conclusion B. More important (this was Locke's problem), if one wants to avoid conclusion B, one must show minor premise A to be true. However, if it is the case that minor premise B is true (as I intend to argue), we are forced to accept conclusion B only if we assume the major premise is valid. As the previous analysis demonstrates, there are good reasons for *not* accepting the major premise.

The consent theory makes sense only if the meaning of consent is identical in both the major and minor premises. It would be a mistake to assert the validity of the major premise employing one definition of consent and the minor premise while employing another. It is certainly possible, appropriate, and consistent with ordinary language to employ different senses of "consent" in different contexts. There may well be a sense in which all governments, or all democratic governments, rule by "consent of the governed." There may well be a sense in which people consent by participating in a system, voting in elections, accepting the benefits of a system, or even quietly acquiescing in the face of political power. *But,* such uses of consent are not consistent with the purpose of the theory. I do not wish to argue that such uses are wrong, but that they would not serve to fulfill the purpose of the theory, that is, to provide for political obligations. If the objection is made, then, that my account of consent in unduly rigorous, it is because I find it the only account consistent with the theory's major premise.

To say "I consent to X" is to make what J. L. Austin calls a "performative utterance," for one is "*doing* something rather than merely saying something."[7] Just as to say "I do thee wed" under

---

[7] J. L. Austin, "Performative Utterances," in Austin, *Philosophical Papers* (Oxford: Clarendon Press, 1961), 222.

the appropriate circumstances *is* to marry, to say "I promise" or "I consent" under the appropriate circumstances *is* to promise or consent. Austin reminds us that the words do have to be uttered in the "appropriate circumstances." Since performative utterances owe their meaning to the existence of social conventions, it will be necessary to examine the nature of these conventions. Austin also reminds us that "there are many nonverbal procedures by which we can perform exactly the same acts. . . ."[8] It will, then, be necessary to establish under what conditions "nonverbal" or "tacit" consent is possible, and whether those conditions obtain in the polity.

I will briefly state what I take to be the most important and relevant conditions that are normally present in an act of consent. First, consent must be given voluntarily.[9] Just as a coerced confession is not legally binding, consent which is given under the threat of severe deprivation or harm is not voluntary and is not morally binding. Secondly, "a necessary precondition for anyone's consenting to anything is that he be asked first for his consent. . . ."[10] One cannot consent to something of which one is unaware, and one must be given the opportunity not to consent. Thirdly, since there have been several attempts to redefine consent in terms of "dispositions" or "attitudes" it is best to keep in mind that consent is an action. For an obligation to be created, a person must actually give consent, and it is not sufficient to argue that he is predisposed to give consent. There is a world of difference between saying that a person thinks that his is a good or just government and saying that he consents to it.

As consent is an act of communication, there must be an available means for such communication. The medium may not be the message, but without an available medium there is no message. Locke was surely right that consent can be given tacitly. In some contexts tacit consent is possible, but only when it is generally understood that in such contexts silence does constitute consent, and only if the previously mentioned criteria are met. If a book club which I have joined sends a card with the instructions, "We will

---

[8] *Ibid.*, 223-24.

[9] See H. L. A. Hart "The Ascription of Responsibility and Rights," *Proceedings of the Aristotelian Society,* XLIX (1948-49), 171-194. Hart distinguishes between "voluntary" and "involuntary" actions in terms of the concept of "defeasibility."

[10] Burton M. Leiser, *Custom Law and Morality* (Garden City, N.Y. Doubleday, 1969), 153.

send the next book unless you return this card marked 'no book wanted,' " and if I do not return the card, I have tacitly consented and am obligated to pay. Locke, however, was surely wrong in arguing that "travelling freely on the highway. . . ." and accepting the benefits of a social system are cases of tacit consent. To make that argument stick, Locke would have had to show that such acts are generally understood to constitute voluntary consent, and that he did not do. Tacit consent is not a "weaker" form of consent; the strength of consent (and the obligation) is a function of the substance of the communications and the degree to which the mentioned criteria are met, not the form of communication.

Unless it can be established that these conditions obtain in the political context, there could be no political consent and no obligations which would follow from consent. There are two facts about modern political systems which preclude their being based on consent in this sense: the populations of such systems are quite large; and membership in political systems is involuntary, unselective, and coercive. In this part I wish to elaborate upon the first observation, that is, the matter of size. Rousseau and Plato are obvious examples of philosophers who recognized the importance of political size; their conceptions of a moral political society required polities of extremely small dimensions. Groups of different size are distinguished (of course, not exclusively) by their "interaction possibilities," for interactions which occur in small groups "inevitably disappear when the groups grow larger."[11] Consent is one such "interaction possibility" which disappears when groups grow larger. In examining the manner in which consent creates obligations, I relied on examples involving only a few persons. In the face-to-face context it was possible to show how persons can be asked for their consent, how consent is (or is not) given voluntarily, and how it can be communicated verbally or nonverbally. When the conditions are met, the act of consent changes people's mutual expectations and creates a moral relationship. The size of the modern nation, however, precludes the interactions that consent requires. No one can give consent because no one is in a position to note whether or not it has been given. It also seems to make little difference in determining the nature of the moral expectations we have of our fellow

---

[11] Quotation from George Simmel in A. Paul Hare, *et al.*, eds., *Small Groups* (New York: Alfred A. Knopf, 1965), 9-10. For a more detailed discussion of political size see my paper, "Political Legitimacy," *op. cit.*

citizens. While I am not expected to help my neighbor paint his house unless I agree to do so, I am expected to obey the laws no matter what I do. Political actions do not generally affect the moral expectations that others have about my behavior. To say "I consent to my political system" in the modern polity is like saying "I do thee wed" when one is alone. It is an absurd act, and has about the same consequences: None.

As the size of collectivities to which we belong increase, and as the members of those collectivities become more remote, we nevertheless continue to employ the concepts that we use in understanding and relating to those in the more immediate environment. In attempting to describe political relationships in terms of consent, we have transferred a concept from the "face-to-face" context to the political context and have assumed that this could be done without any significant loss in meaning. It does not work. The conditions which give consent its meaning in the face-to-face context are totally absent in the polity. Political consent becomes totally symbolic, mythical, irrelevant, and without moral force. It could be objected that in the modern polity it is the electoral process that serves to articulate consent. I do not think this claim can be seriously argued. Even if one could establish that elections and the representational process articulate a kind of consent, it would be far removed from the account of consent that occurs in the major premise of the consent theory. To vote in an election has very little relationship with the act of promising. I do not dispute that the availability of an electoral process may create obligations, nor do I disagree with Walzer that a *prima facie* obligation to the polity may exist "so long as the state provides equally to all its members certain essential services."[12] I argue only that obligations which arise from participation or the receipt of services have nothing to do with consent. I have not argued that there can be no political obligations, but that the attempt of the consent theory to establish them must fail.

II

Coercion belongs to a family of "power" or "influence" concepts and thus must be distinguished from other forms of power.

---

[12] Walzer, "The Obligation to Disobey," 170.

"When A exercises coercive power, B complies with A's intentions because A has made doing so less unattractive to him, at the time of his compliance, than anything else."[13] A coerces B when A uses or threatens to use deprivations, sanctions, or physical harm to change B's behavior in accordance with A's intentions. Coercion is distinguished from persuasive power which involves appealing to B's reason, and inducive power which involves offering B rewards for compliance. A coerces B when B complies to avoid being made worse off; A induces B when B complies in order to become better off. The use of coercive power by political systems is the source of the present philosophical problem. If one is persuaded by reason or receives remuneration for acting in a certain way, there is generally little need for elaborate moral justification. However, when one is compelled to act in accordance with another's intentions due to the use or threat of physical harm, an important moral problem may arise.

There are several additional defining characteristics of "coercive power." When A coerces B, we usually assume "deliberate activity" on A's part, although coercion may occur without A knowing so— for example, "the authorities of a state do not generally know when particular subjects are deterred by the penalties. . . . "[14] Noncoercive power, on the other hand, can be nondeliberate: the power may be diffuse, as when the informal norms of a group change the behavior of new members; power may be anticipatory, reactional, or nonintentional, as when B acts against his wishes for fear of A's adverse reaction. Secondly, coercion implies social conflict, "since one actor is compelled to subordinate his wishes to those of another."[15] However, when A exercises inducive power over B, B complies because there is a commonality of purpose, that is, there is no social conflict. Thirdly, because coercive power limits our choices and opportunities, there is a sense in which it is "incompatible with our liberty"; inducive power, because it increases our opportunities, is compatible with our liberty. When it is most effective, coercive power does not involve the actual use of force or bod-

---

[13] Anthony de Crespigny, "Power and Its Forms," *Political Studies,* XVI (1968), reprinted in de Crespigny and Wertheimer, eds., *Contemporary Political Theory,* 43.

[14] *Ibid.,* 44.

[15] *Ibid.,* 44.

ily harm. The rarity with which Americans are jailed for failure to pay their income tax does not negate the effectiveness of incarceration as a coercive threat. Rather, it confirms its effectiveness.

Our political vocabulary defines and shapes our perceptions of political phenomena, and can both enlighten and conceal. Robert Dahl suggests that references to power as coercive generally imply a fourth characteristic—that is, that its use is illegitimate. To refer to power that involves the use of threat of severe deprivations as both legitimate and coercive is "so counter to the usual meaning of our language as to be confusing."[16] To accept Dahl's analysis would be to avoid the vital problem of justifying coercion, for to call power coercive, says Dahl, is to say that it is thereby not justified. Dahl would have us say that a political system is not employing coercion when it jails a murderer. I do not find the locution, "legitimate coercion," to be contradictory, confusing, or even unusual. Therefore, when I refer to power as coercive I do not imply anything about its legitimacy. Note that it follows from Dahl's analysis that coercion is evil and "ought to be minimized."[17] I wish to disagree with that conclusion, but most important, I maintain that the justification of coercion is a philosophical problem, one that needs to be discussed, and one that should not be solved by fiat of definition.

Our language, no doubt, reflects the distinction between power based on sanctions, physical harm, or deprivation (that is, coercive) and power based on rewards or benefits (that is, inducive). One could argue, however, that this distinction is not important— that it matters little whether B is threatened with the loss of X dollars or offered X dollars from compliance with A's wishes. The net difference in each case is X dollars.[18] But we do often want to distinguish between making a person "better off" and "worse off," and this is a distinction that should be preserved. It is clear, however, that if we employ the distinction, it is intelligible only in terms of a shifting or floating "baseline." Removing television privileges for A is a deprivation, but not for B who has no television. The

---

[16] Robert Dahl, *Modern Political Analysis* (Englewood Cliffs, N.J.: Prentice-Hall, 1970), 33.

[17] *Ibid.,* 33.

[18] Peter Blau, *Exchange and Power in Social Life* (New York: John Wiley, 1964) reprinted in Roderick Bell, *et al.,* eds., *Political Power* (New York: Free Press, 1969), 293.

offer of a $10,000 salary is a deprivation for C who earns $15,000, but an inducement for A who earns $5,000. It is true, as Blau reminds us, that "regular rewards . . . create expectations that redefine the baseline in terms of which positive sanctions are distinquished from negative sanctions."[19]

Of the various deprivations that we may endure, we generally "view attacks on our persons as different in kind from other sorts of harm. . . ."[20] When we refer to power as coercive, we often mean to point to this fact. It may also generally be true, as Wagner suggests, "that gaining inducements lies lower on everyone's schedule of preferences than avoiding sanctions."[21] The question, then, is not whether or not the distinction between coercive and inducive power can be made, for it certainly can. Nor is the question whether or not the distinction is even useful, for it often is. The vital question is whether or not the distinction is appropriate for the present problem. I wish to argue that the terms in which the distinction is generally made, conceal more than they reveal, reflect and reinforce certain basic (but mistaken) assumptions of liberal ideology, and have the consequence of diverting our attention from the extraordinary social power that nonpolitical systems can exert.

Let us imagine a continuum in which we place sanctions (ranging from severe to mild) at one extreme and inducements (ranging from small to large) at the other. The continuum would encompass: one, sanctions such as loss of life, incarceration, physical harm, removal from a particular location, or loss of material goods; two, rewards such as small amounts of money, provision for basic necessities, or larger rewards, both material and psychic. If we exercise power over B's behavior through the use of any sanction, we are employing coercion, whereas if we exercise power through the promise of any reward, we are not coercing him. The major difficulty with this line of thought is that it assumes that everyone starts equally, that is, the various sanctions and rewards will be experienced or perceived similarly by all persons. This is plainly untrue. If B were poor, the promise of food, shelter, and clothing exerts far

[19] *Ibid.*, 294.

[20] Robert Paul Wolff, "On Violence," *The Journal of Philosophy*, LXVI (1969), 606.

[21] R. Harrison Wagner, "The Concept of Power and the Study of Politics," in Bell, *et al.*, eds., *Political Power*, 7.

more power over his behavior than it would over C, who has moderate means. In addition, B might well experience the threat of physical harm as less of a deprivation than C.

This is not a new discovery. It is obvious that the strength of any sanction or reward may be experienced differently by persons of different socioeconomic status. What is not so obvious is that our political vocabulary obscures this vital fact. The distinction between coercive and inducive power seems to serve a rather clear ideological purpose: to label the political system as primarily coercive.[22] That would be all right if it did not serve an additional purpose: to label the economic system of a capitalist society as primarily noncoercive. Whereas the coercive power of the political system is "incompatible with our freedom," the inducive power of the economic system is not.[23] However, not to be made better off, not to be induced, leaves some people in a condition of severe deprivation—a condition of perpetual coercion as it were. The coercive-inducive distinction seems to ignore the existence of social class. In the analysis to follow, I will explore the implications of this obvious, but often unrecognized, fact.

III

For the purposes of this paper I want to propose three ways of characterizing the groups, organizations, and systems in which men live: selectivity of membership; voluntariness of membership; and mode of compliance. By selectivity of membership, I mean to point to the fact that there are some groups that we do not select to join, for example, a family, religion, race, and nationality, while there are other groups in which membership is selective. By voluntariness I mean to point to the ease with which membership in a group can be avoided or dissolved and to the kinds of consequences which follow nonmembership or resignation. While membership in a religion may be unselective, it is voluntary. At adulthood one may leave a religion with relative ease, without enduring any harmful (terrestrial) consequences. In a similar vein, one may even sever

---

[22] I am certainly not contending that the distinction was "created" to serve that purpose.

[23] See pp. 12-13. For a fuller discussion of the relationship between power and liberty, see the article by de Crespigny, "Power and Its Forms."

ties with one's family. Some groups are considerably "more voluntary" than others. For a political scientist, joining the American Political Science Association is a voluntary act because the consequences of nonmembership or resignation are not too severe. On the other hand, for a lawyer, joining the bar association may be an involuntary act because the consequences of nonmembership or resignation may be quite severe. In some states, lawyers who do not join the American Bar Association may be unable to practice law. But I do not know that any political scientists are compelled to join the American Political Science Association in order to practice their profession. If one is a bricklayer or barber in a locale where all bricklayers and barbers are unionized, joining or leaving the respective union is not entirely voluntary, although we might not want to say that it was entirely involuntary. If one must abandon one's trade or profession in order not to maintain membership in a particular group, the group's claim to be voluntary is weakened. There are, of course, other groups in which membership is entirely involuntary—for example, a prison, or concentration camp.

The mode of compliance refers to the manner in which an organization creates conformity with its norms. Etzioni has suggested that compliance can be "coercive," "utilitarian," and "normative."[24] Normative organizations, such as church, employ moral commitments to obtain compliance, whereas utilitarian organizations, such as professional associations, use various rewards (both material and psychic) to gain compliance. Coercive organizations, such as prisons and concentration camps, use physical force or the threat of such force to gain compliance. Of course, it is often the case that organizations rely on more than one mode of compliance, as when a prison uses rewards such as better conditions, jobs, and status to gain compliance from the inmates. In characterizing an organization's mode of compliance, therefore, we refer only to the predominant mode.

With regard to these distinctions, there are two claims I wish to advance: one, that there is no necessary relationship between the voluntariness of membership and the mode of compliance, although there may well be an empirical relationship; two, the tendency to

[24] Amitai Etzioni, *A Comparative Analysis of Complex Organizations* (New York: Free Press, 1969), 27ff.

demand moral justification for the use of power increases as one moves toward the involuntary and coercive ends of the continuum. To support my first claim I have demonstrated that all six possibilities are also emprical facts by the examples in the diagram below. Just as voluntary organizations can use coercion, involuntary organizations can use normative compliance.[25]

FORMS OF COMPLIANCE		MEMBERSHIP	
	Voluntary		Involuntary
Coercive	Voluntary Army Street gang	Mafia	Prison
Ultilitarian	Prof. Assoc.	Labor Union	Elementary Schools
Normative	N.A.A.C.P.	Church	Ethnic Association

It is apparent that our tendency to demand moral justification is higher when an organization is either involuntary or coercive. We are more likely to demand justification for a prison's use of coercive techniques than for its utilitarian techniques. On the other hand, when membership is voluntary we are not apt to be disturbed at the use of coercion. If a member of a voluntary army does not like coercive discipline, he can leave. On the other hand, we may demand that even a utilitarian organization justify its use of power if it is involuntary, as in the case of the debate over "union shops" and "right to work" laws. We are not likely to demand similar justification when a utilitarian organization is voluntary, as when a professional association exacts fees from its members.

I do not think it difficult to show that political systems are both involuntary and coercive. While Joseph Tussman argues that there are "sufficient alternatives" to citizenship so that continued residence in a polity can be construed as a voluntary commitment, his claim has little force.[26] I suppose that residence in a political system is more voluntary than residence in a prison—escape is easier,

---

[25] As Etzioni points out, coercive organizations are usually characterized by high alienation among the participants, making normative commitments very difficult.

[26] Joseph Tussman, *Obligation and the Body Politic* (New York: Oxford University Press, 1960), 39. Tussman's is one of the few serious attempts to argue that the state can be perceived as "voluntary."

although only for some. Even if one is legally able to leave a political system, many persons lack the economic mobility to make emigration a remote possibility. And unlike a prison, the alternative to residence in one political system is residence in another. If we went so far as to accept Tussman's claim that residence in a polity is not entirely involuntary, I would agree with Michael Walzer that "the willfulness of that membership does not seem to have even the most minimal moral significance."[27] If it were the case that residence in a political system were voluntary, the problem of its moral justification would not even arise. The problem of political obligation would not be a problem.

The claim that political systems employ coercion requires even less discussion. While it is certainly true that political systems do seek and obtain compliance through utilitarian and normative techniques, as Max Weber has stated, it is the distinctive characteristic of political systems that "the enforcement of its order is carried out continually within a given territorial area by the application and threat of physical force. . . ."[28] The necessity, desirability, and justification of political coercion is, of course, another matter. While it seems fair to assume that all societies must employ sanctions to establish conformity with the society's norms, we do not know that societies must employ negative sanctions, that is, coercion.[29] These questions aside, however, it seems fair to assume that when we speak of political systems, we speak of systems that do employ coercive power in creating conformity with its norms.

Whereas the political system may enforce its rules with coercive power, a capitalist economy does not. Those with the preponderance of economic resources—those who hire, fire, sell, lend, rent, and produce—offer rewards or inducements to obtain compliance with their decisions. If an economic agreement is violated, the reward may cease (as when one is fired or has one's electricity cut

[27] Walzer, "The Obligation to Disobey," 172.

[28] Max Weber, *The Theory of Social and Economic Organizations,* translated A. M. Henderson and Talcott Parsons (New York: Oxford University Press, 1947), 154. It is interesting that Dahl, in *Modern Political Analysis,* has no problem defining the political system as coercive in his introduction, despite the objections he raises in his discussion of power.

[29] On the inevitability of sanctions in a society, see Rolf Dahrendorf, "On the Origin of Social Inequality" in *Philosophy, Politics, and Society,* Second Series (eds. Peter Laslett and W.G. Runciman) (Oxford: Basil Blackwell, 1962).

off) or an agent of the political system may enforce the agreement (as when the police evict a tenant for failure to pay the rent). In either case, agents of the economic system exert no visible coercion, and since inducive power (the economy's dominant mode of power) is compatible with liberty, it seems that the economic system (unlike the political system) is a realm of freedom, choice, opportunities, rewards, and cooperative exchanges. But this is not quite the way it really is, and there are again two questions that must be answered: to what extent is participation in economic roles voluntary? to what extent does the economic system employ coercion?

We are born into an economic system just as we are born citizens, and as we must obey the polity's laws or suffer the consequences, so must we work in order to live. There is, however, an important sense in which our economic life is voluntary. One is free to choose one's means of employment, the products to be consumed, the places where one lives, etc. However, this characterization of our economic roles as voluntary can easily be overdrawn.[30] In entering the employment market men must devote significant amounts of time and energy to the acquisition of a trade, skill, or profession. Once accomplished, one may well be tied to that means of employment for life. If a barber should be out of work for want of his services, it is not only anlytically wrong but quite mean to insist that he could voluntarily find another means of employment. A member of the Board of Trustees at the University of Vermont insisted that if the faculty did not like the Board's decisions, they could "go elsewhere," insisting that the faculty's decision to stay was altogether voluntary. More as a worker than a philosopher I find this attitude appalling, for in a market with few opportunities for mobility one cannot easily "go elsewhere." One must often stay where one is. In addition, in order to maintain one's job, as I pointed out above, one is often compelled to join certain organizations. The question is not whether compulsory membership in such organizations is ever justifiable, but whether these facts are sufficient to render the economic system involuntary. I think that they are.

If there is a sense in which economic life is involuntary, is it also

[30] In this paper I point to only a limited number of ways in which it can be said that the economic system is "involuntary."

coercive? On the surface it would seem not, for the economic system relies primarily on inducive power. I argued previously that the distinction between coercive and inducive power is often misleading and conceals more than it reveals, as in the following example: X has a family of five and has been laid off his job, but unemployment compensation is inadequate to provide for his family's needs. He finds an employer willing to hire him for a subsistence wage, and X accepts the job. This is a job that X does not enjoy, nor does it adequately provide for his family's needs, yet X prefers this job to no job at all. To not accept the job would render X and his family subject to severe deprivation (material and psychic)—deprivations slightly alleviated by the new employment. Although no threat or use of physical force compelled X to take the job, we could say that X was nevertheless "coerced by the market," for as I have argued, to suffer extreme deprivation is the essence of coercion. The economy may well render the normal (or abnormal) situation of many persons one of severe deprivation. Their relationship with the system through its employers, sellers, money-lenders, credit managers, and landlords is primarily coercive because they either cooperate or suffer extreme deprivation. To say that coercion always means making someone worse off is to forget that there are many whose present situation is already intolerable. The distinction between coercive and inducive power, when used for political analysis, seems to assume that everyone's "baseline" is either similar or tolerable. It is a distinction without a conception of class structure and conceals what is all too clear—that the "baseline" for some is one of great deprivation, that one man's inducement is another's coercion.

If we often fail to see the reality of economic coercion because our conceptual distinctions tend to conceal it, there are still other reasons for this misconception. The rule makers and enforcers of the political system are far more visible or public than the agents of economic coercion. We know who is responsible for enforcing selective service laws, but who compels a family to starve? The diffuseness of economic roles, the lack of concentration of power in clearly defined offices and places, makes identification and understanding of economic coercion all the more difficult. The media, too, play their role. Public officials gain far more attention than economic leaders, although they may exercise far less power. The quasi-dramatic contests by which our political offices are filled lend themselves to the media and public consumption in a way that competition for economic power does not. Those who feel the squeeze of political coercion more severely than economic coercion are also more apt to be knowledgeable, articulate, able to determine the agents responsible for the coercion, and ready to make a response of some kind.[31]

Most interesting is the tendency among those who are most critical of this society's institutions to concentrate on political coercion and repression rather than economic coercion and exploitation. Even those who have read their Marx seem to be enamored with the political. Among the "New Left" there seems to be far more emphasis on anarchism than socialism, and more emphasis on civil disobedience and resistance than workers' strikes and economic change. Perhaps working class attitudes on certain domestic and international issues have either distracted or destroyed the "New Left's" concerns for the subjects of economic coercion. Again, it is not that we are unaware of all this, nor is it that we think the concepts and presuppositions of liberal-individualism are entirely correct or adequate. The problem seems to be that we have no alternative political theory through which to understand this problem and that in a theorectical vacuum, any theory will do, even an inadequate one.

IV

If it is to be argued that one could have obligations within an involuntary and coervice system, then first I must attempt to justify such coercion. Christian Bay has argued that political coercion can be justified "only if it in fact serves to reduce coercion or prevent increased coercion."[32] So long as we are willing to employ a sufficiently broad conception of coercion (one that would accept the reality of economic coercion), Bay's statement provides a suita-

[31] It is also possible that since most philosophers are "middle-class," they write from their own "baseline," and that since they are not apt to feel the squeeze of economic coercion, they tend to view political coercion as more significant.

[32] Christian Bay, *The Structure of Freedom* (Stanford, Calif.: Stanford University Press, 1958), 133.

ble framework. One way of approaching the justification of political coercion is to show that the political system provides for basic needs and wants of its citizens in a way that no other social system can attempt to do, and that it serves to reduce the coercion imposed by other social systems. Most of the things that we need and want are either "free" (for example, air, affection, self-esteem) or are obtained through the economic system as "private goods." Goods are labeled "private" when their use is restricted to the persons) paying for them. Automobiles, televisions, airline travel, apartments, etc. are "private" goods, because unless payment is made, the good or service cannot be enjoyed.

When it is impossible to exclude someone from the use of a good, regardless of whether or not payment is made, the good is labelled "collective" or "public." Schools, parks, museums, police, fire protection, highways, and national defense are public goods because they are available to all without regard to the amount of contribution. It is true that many public goods, such as those just mentioned, are not equally provided for nor consumed by all segments of the society, but they are public goods because their consumption by one citizen does not generally preclude consumption by another. Many goods can be (and often are) provided both publicly and privately—for example, education, medical care, museums, highways and bridges, even police protection. Some communities have even provided fire protection privately on a "pay as you burn" or "burn unless you pay" basis. There are several reasons for providing goods publicly: economies of scale; convenience; and most important, there are many goods which if not provided publicly would not be provided at all, or would not be provided in sufficient quantities.

The private actions of individuals affect others in ways which are both negative and positive, intended and unintended, significant and insignificant. One additional reason for having public goods is that they either provide protection or compensation for the "costs" which social interaction imposes. Our behavior as motorists, producers of waste products, and builders are examples of contexts in which our private actions may harm others, thereby necessitating either protection or compensation. There is another class of goods, such as education, national defense, interstate highways, which would not be available to us at all were they not available as public goods. If there were needs which we could not satisfy through the private market, it would be rational for us to create groups or organizations to provide them as public goods. However it is not the case that rational, self-interested individuals can always provide public goods voluntarily, as the "prisoner's dilemma" model vividly demonstrates.

A and B commit a crime together, are apprehended and held separately for interrogation. The District Attorney tells each prisoner that he has sufficient evidence to convict them both on a charge carrying a two-year sentence, but that he prefers to obtain a conviction on a major charge carrying a fifty-year sentence. The District Attorney offers each prisoner a deal: if he will turn state's evidence against his partner, the prisoner will be granted immunity and set free. Since the same deal is offered to each prisoner, the Distrinct Attorney indicates that if both prisoners turn state's evidence, the sentence will be reduced to forty years. If neither should turn state's evidence, they will both be procuted and if convicted, will receive the two-year sentence.

		Prisoner B	
		Talks	Does Not Talk
A	Talks	-40, -40	0, -50
	Does Not Talk	-50, 0	-2, -2

The penalty for A is indicated first in each cell. Assuming that each prisoner pursues a strategy of maximizing his own interest, it will be rational for him to talk. Regardless of the strategy his partner adopts, each prisoner's penalty is less if he talks. Consider the problem from A's point of view. If B *does not talk,* A gets no sentence if he talks, and a two-year sentence if he does not talk. The preferred strategy is to talk. Assuming that B *does talk,* A gets a forty-year sentence if he talks and a fifty-year sentence if he does not talk. Again, the preferred strategy is to talk. Of course the same holds true from B's point of view. If both prisoners pursue the rational strategy they will both talk and will receive forty-year sentences— the worst solution for both when considered as a group. More important, there seems to be no way for A and B to voluntarily adopt the solution which provides the least total harm, even if they should be allowed to communicate.

> The 'general will' of the prisoners . . . is to avoid confession, but each person's 'particular will' is to confess. Since, in the absence of successful collusion their self-seeking wills

take them to a situation worse for both, what is needed is an enforceable contract between them. In the absence of sanction . . . each prisoner may be driven by rational self-seeking to break the contract which is to the common advantage of both.[33]

The "prisoner's dilemma" model illustrates a simple but vital social fact: the collective actions of rational individuals do not always yield the most rational result. Adam Smith was simply wrong. The notion of collective rationality cannot be understood in terms of nor derived from a notion of individual rationality. Perhaps, Runciman and Sen suggest, this is what Rousseau had in mind in distinguishing the "will of all" from the "general will."

The "prisoner's dilemma" is certaintly not a model for all social relations, as agreement can often be reached in the absence of coercion. This model does demonstrate that there are contexts in which agreement may be impossible, that it may be impossible for rational, self-interested individuals to voluntarily provide collective goods, even when doing so is in their own interest. As Mancur Olson states: "Unless . . . a group is quite small, or unless there is coercion . . . to make individuals act in their common interest, rational self-interested individuals will not act to achieve their common or group interests."[34] Let us assume that if one hundred families live on an unpaved road, and if each contributed $200.00, the road could be paved. While none could afford (or would be willing to pay) the entire $20,000.00, all would be willing to contribute an equal share, having calculated that the benefits of a paved road are worth the cost. However, since no family could be denied use of the road were it to be paved, the rational strategy would be not to contribute one's own share and to have the road paved at the expense of the other families. Because each family would be unsure that the other families would pay their share (in the absence of a binding agreement, supported by the coercive powers of the state), it is possible that none would contribute, and if Olson is correct, there is a

[33] W. G. Runciman and Amartya K. Sen, "Games, Justice, and the General Will," *Mind,* LXXIV (1965), 556-57. For a more detailed and empirical treatment of the game, see Anatol Rapoport and Albert Chammah, *Prisoners Dilemma* (Ann Arbor, Mich.: University of Michigan Press, 1965).
[34] Mancur Olson, Jr., *The Logic of Collective Action* (New York: Schocken Books, 1965), 2.

high probability that the road will not be paved. It could be objected that in this case the desire to preserve friendships in the community, or the fear of adverse social pressure, might be sufficient to provide the collective good. The objection is sound, because in small groups the probability of providing collective goods without coercion is relatively high, other kinds of sanctions and rewards being quite powerful. In larger groups where there are no strong personal ties and where the power of social pressure or personal rewards is low, there is an extremely low probability that collective goods could be provided without coercion. Thus, the fact that the collective good might be provided in the above example serves to illustrate Olson's contention.[35]

If adequate provision for many of our needs and wants requires significant amounts of public goods, and if there is a direct relationship between the size of a group and the necessity for coercion in producing such goods, it is apparent that the more public goods we desire the more we may be coerced. The provide larger amounts of public goods, we must endure larger costs (money, time, lives) and we will pay those costs only when we are coerced into doing so. In large social systems, coercive power may be used to force us to do what we want to do (that is, what we recognize as in our interest), but would not do unless we were forced to do it. The need for political coercion is not a function of evil or irrationality inherent in our souls, but is simply a function of the difference between individual and collective rationality in large social systems.[36]

Unfortunately, the problem is not quite so simple. While I might conclude that my needs and wants can be fulfilled only through public goods provided by a coercive organization, and while I might (if given the opportunity) voluntarily place myself in such a coercive system, I am not so willing to be coerced for public goods which I do not need or want. I do not desire to travel at supersonic speeds, nor to the moon, nor do I believe that my security from attack by other nations requires the current level of military expenditures. It is an obvious fact that we do not all agree as to which pub-

---

[35] Olson has developed the relationship between size and public goods in considerably more detail in *The Logic of Collective Action.*

[36] This assumes, of course, that human beings are characterized by what H. L. A. Hart calls "limited altruism." See *The Concept of Law* (Oxford: Clarendon Press, 1961), 190.

lic goods are to be provided at all, in what priority, and in what amounts, but if public goods are to be provided at all, there must be some decision-making system or rule which chooses the goods to be provided. There is only one decision rule that insures that no one is forced to pay for unwanted public goods—unanimity. By giving every member of the group a veto, we could be sure that no one would be coerced into paying for goods they did not want. Under majority rule, for example, half the community may have to pay for unwanted public goods in addition to being coerced into paying for the goods they do want. In adopting any decision rule other than unanimity, then, we subject members of the community to a "double" coercion.[37]

Although a unanimity rule would reduce coercion imposed by unwanted public goods, it entails and even maximizes other costs. The cost of decision-making itself is increased considerably, because the time and effort required to reach decisions are considerably greater. The behavior of juries under a unanimity rule is an example of these decision-making costs in a context where there is only one decision to make, and by only twelve persons. While a small group may be able to "afford" a unanimity rule, in larger groups the costs may become prohibitive, to the point of making decision-making practically impossible. Most important, and most relevant to the present concern, unanimity increases the probability and therefore the costs imposed by the inability of groups to reach decisions. Because there is a high probability in any large group that someone will want to veto a decision, it is those who are in most need of decisions, that is, in most need of public goods, who suffer the most. Those who are "coerced by the market" remain without public goods, without provision for their needs, and they, too, are subject to a double (perhaps triple) form of coercion.[38]

---

[37] For a general discussion of the problems of decision-making systems, see James Buchanan and Gordon Tullock, *The Calculus of Consent* (Ann Arbor, Mich.: University of Michigan Press, 1962).

[38] For an excellent analysis of the power of elites in creating "nondecisions," see Peter Bachrach and Morton S. Baratz, "Two Faces of Power," *American Political Science Review,* LVI (1962), 947-52. For an empirical analysis of the difficulty in getting (even trivial) decisions made for the poor, see Michael Parenti, "Power and Pluralism," *Journal of Politics,* XXXII (1970), 501-530. An interesting analysis of the inability or unwillingness of political systems to respond to issues such as air pollution is

Of course no modern democracy operates under unanimity rules, but rather with various forms of "majority-rule" combined with various schemes for representation. One justification for majority-rule as a decision procedure is that if public goods are to be allocated, decisions must be made, and majority rule is more consistent with "political equality" than any other rule. Under unanimity, one person's power may be equal to the rest of the community, since one person may veto any decision. Hence, while unanimity decreases the costs of unwanted decisions, it increases political inequality.[39] If no modern democracy operates under unanimity, few operate under majority rule. In the United States, the intricate system of checks and balances, federalism, decentralization, plural elites, bargaining, negotiation, compromise, "muddling through"— all the features of our system which are so often applauded—approximate a unanimity-decision rule to a striking degree.[40] Our political process generally works so that any important elite, organization, or individual will have a veto, they will not be coerced by unwanted allocations of public goods. If a decision to build a hospital is never made because each elite affected by the decision may exercise a veto, those who need the hospital are coerced, for they may suffer extreme deprivation—they will lack adequate medical care.[41]

If the resolution of a social problem requires the provision of public goods, and if there is no political agency capable or willing to deal with the problem, most likely as not the problem will go unresolved. "The rich man's dog DOES drink the milk that undernourished children require and will continue to do until the jurisdictions in which they live intersect in a single authority with the ca-

---

contained in Matthew Crenson, "Nonissues in City Politics," in Marvin Surkin and Alan Wolfe, eds., *An End to Political Science* (New York: Basic Books, 1970).

[39] I do not mean to imply that other arguments for democratic decision procedures, such as the moral significance of participation, carry no weight. I only mean to suggest that these procedures *can* be justified in different terms.

[40] This is of course precisely what Calhoun had in mind in his principle of "concurrent majorities."

[41] This is what happened with regard to a public housing project in Chicago, as described by Martin Meyerson and Edward C. Banfield, *Politics, Planning and the Public Interest* (New York: Free Press, 1955).

pacity and value structure needed to make changes."[42] As Meehan suggests, if the socioeconomic systems of a society are incapable of providing for human needs and wants, "the only possible agency for coping with such moral problems is government."[43] There must be a system willing to exercise coercion, willing to take the milk away from the rich man's dog and give it to the starving child, and there must be a decision-rule which allows this coercion to occur without the rich man's consent. It must be both involuntary and coercive.

Earlier in this paper I indicated that the size of a political community made both consent and voluntary provision of public goods impossible, implying that perhaps Plato and Rousseau were correct about the need for small political communities. Here we encounter one advantage of large political communities, for increased size may make possible more equitable distribution of wealth and greater provision for human needs. If Alabama were to secede from the nation, any attempt to provide for the needs of black and white Alabamans would run into difficulty. Alabama is a poor state. By increasing the size of the political community we increase the potential for greater internal transfers of wealth, although other political factors may negate this potential. This is not to say that large political communities are always preferable, as this must be evaluated in terms of several criteria. I do not, however, agree that "justice in its highest form requires the small state. . . ."[44] Consent, yes. Participation, perhaps. Community and fraternity, probably so. But not distributive justice, neither welfare, nor equality.

There is a tendency for political philosophers to consider the justification of political coercion as a strictly political matter, one which involves only the relationship between individuals and their polity. I have argued that the justification of political coercion may well lie (at least in part) in the ability of the political system to resolve and respond to social problems that it did not directly create. When Robert Paul Wolff argues that "neither majority rule nor any other method of making decisions in the absence of unanimity can

[42] Eugene Meehan, *Value Judgment and Social Science* (Homewood, Ill.: Dorsey Press, 1969), 87.

[43] *Ibid.,* 88.

[44] Wilson Carey McWilliams, "Political Arts and Political Sciences" in Philip Green and Sanford Levinson, *Power and Community* (New York: Vintage Books, 1970), 367.

be shown to preserve the autonomy of the individual citizens,"[45] he fails to take note of the autonomy denied to many citizens by the failure of government to act, and act coercively. If we persist in defining coercion in strictly political terms, we will always conclude that by minimizing governmental coercion we have thereby minimized the total coercion experienced by any citizen. As I have argued, this view is mistaken, for the choice is often not one of more as opposed to less coercion, but a choice as to which social system applies the coercion and which persons or classes of persons will be coerced.[46]

V

If it is possible to provide a justification of political coercion along these lines, it still makes sense to ask why any individual is under an obligation to comply with the polity's directives. Why is one "bound" not to "free ride," that is, accept the system's public goods without incurring the costs? As I argued in Part I, there is a difference between claiming that an activity is justified or moral, and claiming that persons had obligations to perform it. It could be argued that since the collective enterprise which produces public goods is justified, and since its operation requires the obedience of all members, then all must obey. This argument is plainly false, for a collective enterprise need not depends upon absolute obedience from all members. A political system may function quite well with considerable deviance from its norms. A stronger argument can be derived from the "generalization principle," that the maxim "I should free ride when possible" cannot be generalizable to the entire community without contradiction. If everyone acted on that maxim there could be no community, hence the maxim is not a valid moral principle.[47] Unfortunately, this argument contains a fatal weakness, for the maxim "one should free ride when it is un-

[45] Robert Paul Wolff, "On Violence," p. 607.

[46] In systems analysis vocabulary, I am arguing that the justification of political coercion focus on "outputs" rather than "inputs," as the consent theory suggests. On the evaluation of political systems in terms of outputs, see J. Roland Pennock, "Political Development, Political Systems, and Politician Goods," *World Politics*, XVIII (1966), 415-434.

[47] For a detailed discussion of this principle see Marcus Singer, *Generalization in Ethics* (New York: Alfred A. Knopf, 1961).

likely that such acts will endanger the community" is generalizable without contradiction, and therefore does not, in itself, tell use why we have an obligation not to "free ride."[48]

If we cannot demonstrate that citizens have political obligations to a coercive system along these lines, and if there are no political obligations which can be derived from consent, are there no political obligations at all? John Rawls has suggested that the usual terms in which this problem is considered are misleading, because our political obligations are now owed to the state or its officials, but are obligations

> . . . owed to our fellow citizens generally; that is, to those who cooperate with us in the working of the constitution. . . . That it is an obligation owed by citizens to one another shown by the fact that they are entitled to be indignant with one another for failure to comply.[49]

Although the state employs coercive power in enforcing its norms, it is our fellow citizens who are often enraged at disobedience, be it "criminal" or "civil."[50] While the state punishes tax or draft evaders, it is our fellow citizens who must foot the bill, or more important, who will be called to serve in their place. It is clearly not "fair" to expect others to obey those laws which provide benefits for oneself without doing the same for them.[51] But why do I have an obligation to refrain from doing what is unfair? I doubt that this is a coherent question, for to say that something is unfair in this context

[48] For a most interesting quantitative discussion of the "free rider" problem see Norman Frolich and Joe A. Oppenheimer, "I Get By With a Little Help From My Friends," *World Politics,* XXIII (1970), 105-20.

[49] John Rawls, "Legal Obligation and the Duty of Fair Play," in Sidney Hook, ed., *Law and Philosophy* (New York: New York University Press, 1964), 10. While I think it can be said that persons have obligations arising from "fairness," I would not want to argue that such acts as not reporting for induction into the army, while unfair, are necessarily immoral. In fact, they may have another justification which "outweighs" any obligations to their fellow citizens arising out of "fairness."

[50] For a treatment of the distinction between criminal acts and civil disobedience see Hugo Bedau, "On Civil Disobedience," *Journal of Philosophy,* LVII (1961), 653-665.

[51] Even when it can be claimed that persons do have political obligations, there may be moral reasons which could justify particular acts of disobedience, although some reasons which are commonly advanced may not be adequate. To say that an obligation may be overridden, however, is to acknowledge that there is an obligation, and that is all that I claim here.

is to give a good reason for not doing it, *is* to give good reasons why those who do not should be subject to blame; *is* to say that there are obligations not to do it. Even though the relationships are not experienced directly or in very personal terms, citizens do have a special relationship with each other by virtue of their contributions to a collective enterprise. The relationships between citizens of a political system are relationships of mutual dependency, because the actions of one citizen may and often do have both direct and indirect consequences upon other citizens. It is a relationship which is not entered voluntarily, but which serves certain important and morally justifiable purposes, and it is a relationship in which it is appropriate to say that persons have obligations toward each other. When I speak of political obligations, then, I am not speaking of the obligations of a citizen to his leaders or representatives, but of the obligations of citizens to each other.

The argument that I have developed in supporting the claim that persons do have political obligations even when the state is coercive, assumes that political coercion is used for certain purposes. If political coercion is not used to provide for the needs and wants of certain classes or races, and if political coercion is used to support the position of certain groups within a society at the expense of others, these different groups may well have obligations of varying intensities. If the coercive powers of the state do not provide for the legitimate needs of black citizens, and if political coercion does not serve to reduce the total coercion to which blacks are subject, it could be argued that black citizens do not have the same kinds of obligations that do white citizens. Although the notion of "differential political obligations" has never been a part of liberal theory, it is a notion which I find plausible and reasonable, and would suggest that it certainly deserves our serious consideration.

I have argued that the claim that because one consents to a political system it is therefore not coercive, and that therefore one has political obligations does not stand up for several reasons: first, even if there were consent the system would not therefore be uncoercive; second, in modern political communities there is no consent which approximates the kind of consent a theory of political obligations would require; third, it is not the case that if there were no consent there would be no obligations. I also argued that the claim that because membership in the state is involuntary, coercive, and without consent that therefore one has no political obligations does not stand up for several reasons: first, it is possible to have obligations in involuntary and coercive systems; secondly, the terms in which coercion are usually defined are misleading, concealing important ideological and class biases; thirdly, political coercion can be justified in terms of "public goods" and can be used to reduce total coercion in a society; fourthly, that if political coercion can be justified it is possible to support the claim that persons have political obligations by a principle of "fairness."

Although the arguments contained in this paper are not entirely new, most philosophical treatments of political obligation seem to assume what I have denied. I think the problem is that we do not have a political vocabulary which allows us to discuss these problems without great strain. Our political vocabulary is largely a borrowed one, our moral concepts being generally derived from our face-to-face relationships. The emotional impact of the remote relationships of a political system have never been sufficient to generate a new and more appropriate vocabulary. We have continued to use inappropriate concepts and theories, often with one of two consequences: we attempt to justify important moral relationships in inappropriate terms (for example); or we may recognize that the concepts are inappropriate and concluded that there are no important moral relationships. When we confront head-on, the problem of our inadequate and inappropriate political vocabulary, significant political philosophies will again be developed. In no case is this more true than in the very complex relationship between political coercion and political obligation.

13

COERCION AND INTERNATIONAL POLITICS: A THEORETICAL ANALYSIS

Donald McIntosh

INTRODUCTION

This paper consists of two parts. First, there is a theoretical analysis of the idea of coercion and its relation to other forms of influence. Second, this definition is applied to the area of international politics. Although the discussion in the second part will bear on factual matters, the main purpose of this paper is purely theoretical. The rather free and impressionistic discussion is aimed to show how the concepts developed here work out when applied to international affairs, rather than to advance or defend empirical propositions.

A concept is a tool by which reality may be understood and dealt with. As with many other tools, sharp concepts tend to do the most effective job. An attempt at definitional precision has therefore been made, and for this purpose I have drawn heavily on the modern theory of games and decisions. The underlying frame of analysis rather than the substantive conclusions of this theory will be employed. In contrast to the usual approach, the use of this highly precise and, I think, potentially fruitful frame of reference will be speculative and philosophical, not technical and prescriptive.

Although the concepts used here are developed in game theoretical terms, by way of orienting the reader, it might be useful at the start, to compare them to the very similar typology used by Max Weber. He divided the compulsions whereby stable social order is maintained into two broad types: "external means" and "inner justifications." By "external means" he meant such compulsions as military power, economic might, and the manipulations of the legal or bureaucratic experts: in short, the compulsions of the sword, the purse, and the pen. Also included as external means are the constellations of mutual interest which lead men to enter voluntarily into cooperative associations.

Such external means, Weber felt, are rarely a sufficient base on which to support a stable social and political order. They need to be supplemented by an "inner justification," an acceptance of the social order, with its rules and rulers, as inherently rightful and just, to which obedience is morally obligatory quite apart from questions of personal advantage or disadvantage.

In this paper, the concept of ideology will be developed as a kind of "inner justification" very similar to the sense used by Weber. Even closer to Weber's views will be the treatment of coercion, which in nontechnical terms will be defined as influence through the use of external means, where by "external means" is meant exactly what Weber meant.

This is a much broader definition of coercion than is usually employed. While coercion is generally seen as operating through external means, these means are often thought to be confined to the threat or use of some instrument of force or violence. The use of wealth or technical expertise to influence others is not usually thought of as coercive. Even farther from conventional usage is the treatment of the essential or defining relations in economic exchange and voluntary associations as coercive. Before undertaking a precise definition of the idea of coercion, therefore, a brief outline of the reasons for the unusual approach taken here will be presented.

In part, our definition of coercion springs from purely technical considerations. From a game theoretical point of view, it is more natural and comfortable to operate with a broad rather than a narrow meaning. For example, coercion is generally thought to operate through "negative sanctions," that is, through threat of injury or deprivation of some kind. In contrast, using "positive sanctions," that is, rewards or benefits, to influence others is not normally regarded as coercive. The distinction between benefit and injury, however, does not spring readily from a game theoretical framework, but instead requires a somewhat elaborate construction. More fundamentally, game theory treats an actor as confronted with a set of options or alternatives, which are ranked in order of preference. As between any two alternatives, it is not a question whether one involves an injury and the other a benefit, but simply which alternative is preferred. In this and several other instances, when expressed in game theoretical terms, the usual definition of coercion seems to be unnecessarily complex and to involve distinctions not important or germane to the central issues.

But more substantive considerations have also led to the novel definition of coercion used here. The question of whether or not to consider economic influence as coercive is central in this respect. Clearly, some forms of economic influence seem to be coercive in the common-sense usage. Thus, for one nation to threaten to cut off an import vital to another by refusing to trade seems to be coercive, as does threatening to foreclose a mortgage on a reluctant debtor. Numerous instances of similar uses of apparently coercive economic influence are easily cited. In such cases, the issue of whether or not actual force is used or threatened seems secondary.

If we admit that some forms of economic influence are coercive, where do we draw the line? Suppose, for example, we define as coercive all injurious economic influence, and as noncoercive all beneficial economic influence. The trouble is, many economic relations appear to fall within both categories. For example, take a contract between a landlord and a sharecropper. From one point of view, both benefit from the relationship, which is hence, on the supposition we are discussing, noncoercive. From another point of

view, however, the landlord may be in such an advantageous bargaining position that he can impose highly unfair and exploitative
terms. From that point of view, the relationship is injurious to the
sharecropper.

By extension of essentially this point, the entire set of institutions
defining the free contract and the open market have been held to be
beneficial to one class, but injurious to another. To make an even
more fundamental point, just as the transferral of an economic good
or the performance of an economic service confers a benefit, so the
refusal to transfer the good or perform the service may constitute
an injury. The question of harm or benefit is a pseudo question in
this context. What matters is control over the valuable good or service. Hence it appears inadequate to make our definition of coercion
hinge on the question of benefit or harm. What is crucial is control
over some instrument which is capable of influencing the behavior
of others.

The term "coercion" tends to have a pejorative connotation.
Hence it is most often used to describe influence wielded by one's
opponents. Reinhold Neibuhr has argued that economic influence is
the characteristic weapon of the middle class, while the lower
classes, perforce, must rely on violence. It is a sign of class bias, he
says, to regard the former as morally superior to the latter. The true
moral questions turn not on the type of instrumentality employed,
but the purposes involved and the results obtained.[1] The distinction
between coercive and noncoercive influence should not turn on a
distinction between "good" and "bad" forms of influence.

In sum, to define the influence of force as coercive and economic
influence as noncoercive, is to make the definition hinge on an unimportant and ephemeral difference and, possibly, to reveal a class
bias. Economic influence is best regarded as a form of coercion.

What distinguishes an economic exchange from highway robbery
is not that benefits rather than harms are conferred, for we do not
account this distinction of more than superficial worth; nor that the
relationship is one of equality, for economic exchanges may be very
unequal; nor finally that coercion is not mutual, for even a robbery
may be a mutually coercive event (for example, "You may have

---

[1] Reinhold Niebuhr, *Moral Man and Immoral Society* (New York:
Charles Scribner's Sons, 1955).

my wallet, but I will not give you my wrist watch without a struggle"). It is the regulative context of property rights, and the existence of the market, which sets the price more or less independently of the relative power of the actors, which marks economic exchange off from other coercive relations. In the international arena, where property rights between states are both less well defined and less secure, and where a market system may be much less developed, the distinction between voluntary economic exchange and highway robbery may be more difficult to make.

Once economic relations are defined as coercive, we can no longer exclude any relationship which involves an exchange of services, or where the performance of a service is used to influence the behavior of another. For example, an alliance between two states can be regarded as an agreement to exchange services, and hence to involve coercion. This idea may be extended to all voluntary association, indeed to any organization, to the extent that the members of the organization are motivated not by any inner justifications, but only by desire for some benefit or fear of some harm.

Thus, what is crucial to coercion is the presence of some instrumentality, some external means, which can be used to influence the behavior of others. Such instrumentalities will be called sanctions. A sanction may be an act of force or the threat of force; it may be the transferral or the refusal to transfer an economic good; it may be the performance of a service or the refusal to perform a service. The transaction may be one-way or two-way. War, for example, involves an exchange of negative sanctions, while economic trade involves the exchange of positive sanctions. The defining property of coercion is control over some such instrumentality, and its use to influence the behavior of others in desired ways.

A THEORY OF COERCION

Definitions

The following account is an interpretation of the definitional framework (not the substantive conclusions) of game theory.[2] The

[2] The treatment in this section is based on my more detailed and comprehensive account in Donald McIntosh, *The Foundations of Human Society* (Chicago: University of Chicago Press, 1969).

theory proper is purely mathematical, and capable of many different interpretations. The one developed here is, I believe, consistent with the one used by von Neumann and Morgenstern, but goes considerably beyond it. Those familiar with game theory will be readily aware of these departures, or, as I would rather have it, extensions. Those not so familiar must bear in mind that they are by no means getting a standard interpretation of the theory.

For conceptual simplicity, we will imagine only two actors, A and B, in interaction. Later we will enquire what is the significance if these two actors are nation-states, rather than other organizations or individuals.

Each actor is considered to have open to him a number of alternate *strategies*, or programs of action. Each such program consists of an elaborate plan, providing a discrete and separate course of action for every foreseeable contingency, in the sense that an organizational program or a computer program provides for such contingencies.

A given strategy by A coupled with a given strategy by B constitutes an *interaction pair*. The *result* of an interaction pair may be conceived of as the sum total of events which ensue when A and B put their strategies into effect. In the normal case, there are a myriad possible results. These constitute the *interaction field* for A and B, which contains all the possible interactions between the two.

The actors prefer some possible results to others, and indeed are assumed to be able to rank the results and probabilistic combinations of results into a clear order of preference.

An actor, however, cannot choose a result, for the result also depends on the choice of the other. He can only choose his strategy. The question thus becomes, "Which strategy will yield the most preferred result?" This is the problem of the nature of rational action in situations with other actors influencing the field, to which the bulk of game theory is devoted. However, here the question of rational choice will concern us only peripherally. We are not mainly concerned with what strategies will yield the most preferred result, nor with the circumstances under which actors will or will not choose such strategies. It is the structure and contents of the interaction field that will receive the major attention.

As stated, an interaction field is a sum total of possible results. Each such result may be conceived of as a complex totality of events—a segment of the flux of reality. One can talk about reality, however, only by the use of abstract concepts. We will talk about the possible results of the field in terms of the values of a set of elements, in the form of variables and constants. A *variable* of the field is any element which changes in value from result to result according to (as a function of) the strategies chosen by the actors. A *constant* of the field is any element which does not change according to their strategies.

These definitions may be illustrated by an example. Suppose A and B are two armies prepared for battle. Their *strategies* are the various detailed battle plans available to them. A *result* is a particular possible battle which will occur when A and B choose a particular *pair of strategies*. The *interaction field* consists of all possible battles between the two armies (all possible results), and all probabilistic combinations of such results. The terrain and the weather are *constants* of the field (since they are unaffected by the behavior of the armies). Note that although the weather may vary, it will vary in the same way for every possible battle, and in this sense is a constant. The disposition of the armies, their maneuvers, the casualties they suffer and inflict, the territory they occupy, are *variables* of the field.

We now possess the vocabulary with which to define coercion (coercive influence). Suppose that A has the power to determine the value of variable x of the field (that is, the value of x is a function of A's strategy), and that the choice of strategy by B is influenced by the structure or pattern of variation of x in the field. In that case, A is capable of exercising coercive influence over B, and his power over x is the coercive sanction which enables this influence.

This definition is not as simple and straightforward as might appear at first glance. It contains a number of difficulties and ellipses, and a more detailed treatment is necessary to unfold its full meaning.

Control over Sanctions

A sanction is any variable of the field whose value is significant to the preferences of one actor and is controlled by another. It is thus necessary to enquire what is meant by control over a sanction.

Just as any result of the field is the product not of a single choice by A (or B), but rather of a choice by each, so in general the value of a variable is determined by the choices of more than one actor. For the most part, A cannot uniquely determine the value or the range of values of a variable without regard to what B does.

This conforms to common-sense observation. Almost every individual lives in a social environment, and his ability to accomplish almost anything from breathing to flying depends on the cooperation or at least the noninterference of those with whom he interacts.

This is hardly less true of the nation-state. It is difficult, for example, to imagine very much that even a powerful nation like the United States could accomplish if this accomplishment were actively and ardently opposed by all the other nations in the world, acting in concert. We will therefore assume that the category of independent power over the value of a variable, in the sense of ability to determine the value of the variable regardless of what the other actors may do, is for all practical purposes empty. In speaking of the control of sanctions by a nation-state, therefore, it is necessary to operate under some sort of assumption as to how the other states are to be expected to behave. Thus, if we say that within a decade China will be capable of building and using a large navy, there is an implicit assumption (among others) that the United States, the Soviet Union, and Japan will not initiate full scale hostilities the moment China starts to build the first ship of her navy. It is meaningless to talk of the capabilities of a state apart from a set of express or implied assumptions of this kind.

Game theory normally operates under the assumption of the rationality of the actors. From the point of view of purely theoretical analysis, this is undoubtedly the best approach; but at a lower level of abstraction, and when speaking of nation-states, this assumption appears to be unwarranted. This is less because nation states frequently behave irrationally than because the very idea of rationality becomes slippery when applied to state policy. Suppose, for example, that we treat state policy as the outcome of the interaction of a number of actors, each with a different set of purposes, with the actors changing for each policy decision. Even under the unlikely hypothesis that each of the actors always behaves rationally, it would seem hard to say anything about the rationality or irrationality of state policy itself.

We will therefore adopt another assumption, namely that nation-states behave the way they behave. To put the matter less paradoxically, we will assume that the forces that produce state policy can in principle be known, and hence that in principle it is possible to foresee the behavior of a state in a given situation. It is possible that in a given situation a state may behave rationally. The assumption is that, if so, this can be forseen. When we say therefore that nation A has the ability to do x, we mean that it could, if it wishes, do x, given the expectable behavior of the other states with which it interacts.

It follows from this approach that even a state that is "weak" from the point of view of economic resources, weapons, skills, etc., could have a very substantial amount of sanctions at its disposal if it could expect to have its undertakings actively supported by stronger states, while a state that is "strong" in terms of such factors might have a very low capability to have and use sanctions if it found itself thwarted at every turn by a strong hostile coalition.

The Effectiveness of Sanctions

It has been pointed out that to possess a sanction, in the sense of being able to employ a coercive means, is not necessarily to be able to influence the behavior of others. The effectiveness of a sanction depends on other things besides its size or weight. A threat of violence or an offer of money will affect different actors differently, because they fear violence and desire money to different degrees. Furthermore, to possess a sanction is not necessarily to be willing to use it, because of the costs involved.

Finally, the structure of the interaction field itself may block the employment of an otherwise powerful sanction. For example, suppose that A possesses a weapon that is capable of killing B but not of inflicting lesser injury. If what A needs from B is his cooperation in some task, the weapon will be an ineffective coercer because its employment will block the attainment of precisely what A wants. Supposing, instead, that A wants some object that B possesses, the weapon then becomes a highly effective means of coercion. Thus, the structure of the situation will often determine the effectiveness or ineffectiveness of a given coercive instrument.

The matter may be stated as follows: Suppose that A has two

strategies, a_1 and a_2, which are identical in every respect, except that in a_1 he employs or threatens (promises) to employ a given sanction in a given way and in a_2 he does not. Let us then examine the strategy that B would employ in response to (or in anticipation of) first a_1, then a_2.

If B's strategy is the same for each case, then the sanction in question is totally ineffective. Assume, however, that his strategy is different for the two cases, and that the response to a_1 is b_1 and the response to a_2 is b_2. Then the difference between b_1 and b_2 is the effect of A's coercion on B's behavior.

This formulation reveals the relative nature of positive and negative sanctions mentioned earlier. Suppose that B prefers the result a_1b_1 to the result a_2b_2, while A prefers a_2b_2 to a_1b_1. Then A will use the sanctions at his command by employing strategy a_2, which will "*force*" B to adopt b_2 (his preferred strategy once A has chosen a_2). Since a_2b_2 has a lower preference ranking for B than a_1b_1, A is employing a negative sanction.

On the other hand, suppose that both A and B prefer a_1b_1 to a_2b_2. Now A will refrain from a_2 and instead choose a_1. The result, a_1b_1, as compared to a_2b_2, will be mutually beneficial. In this case, A's choice of a_1 *induces* B to choose b_1, that is, it has the effect of a positive sanction on B. The issue of whether a positive or negative sanction is involved turns, not on the nature of A's control over the results of the field, which is the same for both instances, but rather on whether A's and B's preferences conflict or harmonize.

In the example it was assumed that only A had a sanction at his disposal, but in practice this must be considered unusual. Usually there is an exchange or interplay of sanctions. The balance of coercion depends, first, on the relative control that each exercises over the results of the possible strategies of the other; second, on the extent to which the controlled variables are significant to the preferences of the other; and third, the extent to which the controls possessed by each, and the preferences of each, combine to affect the behavior of the two.

I have elsewhere worked these ideas out in greater detail, and in a more formal way.[3] Perhaps, however, the discussion here has

---

[3] *Ibid.*

served to indicate the general meaning of the term "effectiveness of a sanction" from a game theoretic point of view.

Coercion and Legitimacy

Coercion has been defined so broadly that the question might arise whether there are any other forms of compelling influence. The existence of such other forms, however, becomes readily apparent if we glance at the general formula for deliberate action that emerges from an examination of the theory of games and decisions. In schematic outline, human action consists of the following steps:

1. Assessment: the actor examines what strategies are available to him and the other actors, and what the results of the possible combinations of strategies would be. In other words, he inspects the contents of the interaction field.

2. Evaluation: the actor ranks the results of the field in order of preference.

3. Choice: the actor chooses the strategy that will, he thinks, yield him a more preferred result than any other strategy.

4. Execution: the actor puts his choice into effect.

We are examining the ways in which one individual can influence the choices of another. So far, we have considered only one possibility, the case whereby control over the results of the field is used to influence the choices of others. But other forms of influence are possible.

First, it is often possible to influence the assessment that an individual makes of the field by providing information, either true or false, about the contents of the interaction field. Such information may influence the process of assessment or change assessments already made in such a way as to affect the individual's choice. The term "propaganda" fits this type of influence very neatly.

Another possibility is that one actor might be able to change the preferences of the others. It must be borne in mind that coercion affects only the results of the possible strategies of the others. As to the various possible interaction pairs, the preferences of the individuals are presumed to be constant throughout. Here, we are raising the possibility of affecting not the results but the evaluation of the results.

It is strange that game theorists have not heretofore considered this kind of influence, for it springs to mind as a logical possibility upon an examination of the frame of analysis employed. Once the possibility is discerned, examples are readily at hand.

Charismatic leadership utilizes this kind of influence. The followers *identify* with the leader—that is, they adopt the preferences of the leader, whose evaluations then become decisive for their choices of action. Charismatic leadership thus involves an entirely different form of influence from coercion.

Plato distinguished two main types of influence, coercion and persuasion. He developed a third type, however, as an indispensable foundation of any viable state. The guardians (the ruling class), he felt, must be loyal to the state not because of fear of retribution or desire for gain, but because they identify with the state. They must feel

> . . . the sort of concern that is felt for something so closely bound up with oneself that its interests and fortunes, for good or ill, are held to be identical with one's own.[4]

The education of the auxiliaries must be such that

> . . . they might take the color of our institutions like a dye . . . indelibly fixed, never to be washed out by pleasure and pain, desire and fear, solvents more terribly effective than all the soap and fullers earth in the world.[5]

Thus, an individual can identify not only with another individual but with a social whole, whose rules will then govern his behavior with an internal, not an external, force. This is the kind of inner justification treated by Weber in his theory of legitimacy.

Legitimacy, for Weber, is a group phenomenon. If a command from A to B is regarded as legitimate by the latter, then both must be members of a social group which has defined the command as legitimate. Such social groups are not only formally or informally organized into cooperative systems of action, they are also held together by psychological forces of group solidarity and social cohesion: the social group is not only an organization, it is also a community, bound together by ties of group identification.

[4] Plato, *The Republic,* 412b.
[5] *Ibid.,* 429.

To put this point in game theoretic terms, if a system of legitimacy operates successfully, strategies or results which are prohibited are assigned a low preference ranking by the members of the group, while strategies and results which are prescribed have a high preference ranking.

One can argue that the principal function of the system of legitimacy of a group is to regulate the coercive relations among the members. At least it is striking the extent to which such regulation invariably occurs within stable systems of organized social interaction. The nation-state is no exception to this generalization; indeed the defining property of a state, according to Weber, is its possession within a territory of a monopoly of legitimate violence. Only the state has the right to use this most extreme form of coercion, the coercion of last resort, and frequently only in specially defined ways and instances.

The regulation of coercion within states applies to the use of both positive and negative sanctions. In general it is illegal for one person deliberately to injure another, and a major part of any legal system consists of an elaborate definition of what does and does not constitute injury in a legal sense and what processes are to apply when deliberate injury occurs. The law of course does not prohibit or restrict all negative sanctions, but it does forbid the use of most of those negative sanctions that are considered morally wrong or reprehensible by the members of the society.

We have seen that typical positive sanctions are the transfer of valuable goods and the performance of valuable services. Hence the regulation of positive sanctions is to a considerable extent nothing but the regulation of the economic life of the society, including the laws pertaining to property and exchange.

In sum, if we examine for any state the formal and informal rules and regulations that define what is legitimate and what not, we will find that a large part, perhaps the vast bulk, of these systems of legitimacy consist of regulation of the use of sanctions in the interactions among the members of that society. On the whole, the power struggles that pervade any state operate within the boundaries and through the channels provided by this system.

The state enforces the rules of legitimacy by sanctions, up to and including violence. To cite the passage from Hobbes quoted in Professor Riker's article, covenants may not be valid without the sword, but within states, while violence may be the cutting edge, it is the legitimacy of the sword that provides the handle by which it may be used effectively.

Ideology

So far we have used the phrase "system of legitimacy" as a general term, covering any set of standards or rules of behavior that are internalized through group identification and form or influence the preferences of the members of the group. It is now necessary to be more precise.

A *social norm* is an informal standard of behavior internalized through identification by the members of a particular social group. Every social group is characterized by its own normative standards. As held by most sociologists, a defining property of a social norm is that it is enforced by the members on each other by the use of sanctions, both negative and positive. Here at the level of the basic building block of systems of legitimacy, we already see the presence of coercive elements.

Law is a more or less formal and rational system of legitimacy. In general it is supported by and reflects the social norms of at least the predominant groups in society. Where an act does not violate a social norm, a law against it is often enforceable only with difficulty, if at all.

An *ideology* is an intellectualization of the social norms of a group. The norms are organized into a more or less coherent set of principles that are justified as morally right by arguments and statements couched in terms of general principles of morality and justice, and buttressed by broad claims of a factual nature.

In other words, an ideology is a rationalization of the social norms of a group[6] in the double sense: first, that it justifies these norms, and second, that it is worked out into a more or less coherent view of the world.

---

[6] In the language of the theory which I have developed elsewhere, an ideology is the rationalization of the general will of a group. McIntosh, *op. cit.* My debt to Karl Mannheim should be evident in this section. Mannheim, however, lays great stress on the effect of the institutionalization of values (rationalization is only one aspect of institutionalization). This very important question is not treated here. Karl Mannheim, *Ideology and Utopia* (New York: Harcourt Brace and Company, 1949).

This rationalization of the social norms enables their communication as a coherent set of ideas and hence enables the firmer control of the members of the group as well as provides a means of influencing persons outside the group, either by winning converts or by influencing them to conform to the ideology. The transformation of the social norms of a group into an ideology enables the influence of these norms to spread beyond the boundaries of the social group. (Ideology has this in common with law.)

Historically, religious beliefs and doctrines have been the most important forms of ideology. As such they are always to be identified with specific groups of people. Modern times have seen the growth of secular ideologies. Nationalism is the political ideology of a nationality, liberalism of the bourgeoisie, communism of the Communist Party, etc.

COERCION IN INTERNATIONAL AFFAIRS

The Contrast between National and International Politics

In contrast to politics within states, the relations between states are not governed by any well-defined and effective system of legitimacy. The conclusion sometimes drawn from this is that coercion plays a greater and more decisive role in international relations. From the point of view of the broad definition of coercion adopted here, however, this does not appear to be the case. It has been suggested above that the normative system of society and the institutional structures built on this system do not eliminate coercion, but instead regulate its form and pattern of operation. What marks off national from international politics is the form and organization, not the amount, of coercion.

As against domestic politics, with its firm and extensive controls over the use of coercion, the coercive relations between states are largely unregulated, whether this coercion takes the form of exchanges of positive sanctions, as in alliances (exchange of services) and trade (exchange of goods); exchanges of negative sanctions, as in war; or international "politics as usual," with its various and shifting mixture of positive and negative sanctions. In this section, we will focus on these coercive relations. Later, we will enquire whether important noncoercive influences can be found. Meanwhile, for the sake of the discussion, it will be assumed that relations between states are purely coercive.

Coercive influence can be classified in many ways. Since our theory emphasizes the role of sanctions (coercive instrumentalities), it seems logical to classify coercion according to the sanctions employed. It will be recalled that a sanction is a course of action that will affect the environment or situation of another actor in a way that is significant to his preferences. What is crucial is control over the results of the field. From this point of view, either the employment or the nonemployment of a coercive instrumentality may be regarded as a sanction.

Looking at international affairs, it is convenient to divide sanctions into three types: violence, the transferral (or nontransferral) of valuable goods, and the performance (or nonperformance) of valuable services. As a negative sanction, violence is force applied to the person of another in such a way as to produce a result that he would not have chosen of his own volition, or to cut off a course of action that he would have or might have preferred to take.

Violence may be a positive sanction, as with surgery. To cut a person's hair is violence used as a negative sanction if the person does not want his hair cut, a positive sanction if he does, and not a sanction at all if he is indifferent on the question. In the broadest sense, a "service" is the performance of any positive sanction. It is more convenient, however, to define a service (or disservice) as any sanction that does not constitute violence or the transferral of a valuable good, that is, as a residual category.

To cite some examples, the defining aspect of war is the exchange of violent negative sanctions, although normally other sanctions also come into play. International trade involves the exchange of positive sanctions in the form of the transferral of goods. A treaty granting mutual privileges to foreign embassies is an exchange of services.

The residual category of services conceals a type of coercive influence that is of the greatest importance within political systems, but does not play a significant role between states. I have elsewhere termed this form of influence "political power."[7] This form of influence may be defined briefly as follows:

[7] McIntosh, *op. cit.*, Chap. 8, 13.

Following general usage, political authority may be defined as the successful exercise of the right to govern. The effectiveness of political authority rests first on the community's sense that the authority is legitimate, and second on the sanctions that the person in authority can evoke and exercise in case of noncompliance. In other words, authority rests on a combination of "inner" and "external" (coercive) influences.

The influence of an office may greatly exceed its authority. This is because political authority not only *rests on* sanctions, but itself *constitutes* a sanction. Through the artful use of his authority and position, a governor can often influence people to behave in desired ways, even where he has no authority to do so. For example, the authority to make appointments may be used as a sanction to induce campaign contributions. Political power is thus the effective use of political authority as a sanction.

This kind of influence has received heavy emphasis in Richard Neustadt's *Presidential Power*.[8] It plays a decisive role within political systems. In contrast, since the members of one nation do not normally have authority over the members of another, political power does not play a role in the relation between states, except to a minor degree with respect to international organization; for example, the Secretary General of the United Nations is sometimes able to exercise some influence on international events by virtue of his office. The growth in the extent and importance of international organization may see the gradual expansion of this category as a mode of influence in international affairs.

The contrast between coercion in national and international politics is not always so sharp as it might seem from the analysis so far. The differences are most striking if we look at states with firm, stable, and well institutionalized systems of legitimacy, where the maintenance of political order is an easy task. As Machiavelli put it,

> Hereditary states, which are accustomed to the rule of the line of their prince, are much more easily maintained than the new ones for it is sufficient for the prince not to transgress the customs of his predecessors and to meet emergencies.[9]

[8] New York: John Wiley and Sons, 1960.
[9] Machiavelli, *The Prince*, Chap. 1.

As for ecclesiastical states,

> . . . they are supported by time-honored laws of religion, so powerful and of such nature as to leave their princes always in authority whatever kind of policy they may follow, and whatever sort of life they may lead.[10]

The contrast becomes less sharp, however, when it comes to states where the system of legitimacy is poorly developed, as in new states, or where internal stresses have weakened the bonds of legitimacy. In *The Prince,* Machiavelli's advice is directed to the head of a "new" state in the sense of one where the established regime has just been overthrown. It is here that the coercive element comes to the fore and must be played to the hilt. For this reason the book has been called a better primer for the international than the national politician. This special context also explains, I think, why Machiavelli's treatment is very different in *The Discourses,* where the discussion presupposes more stable institutional systems.

The Limits of Military Power

The main consequence of the lack of government on the international level is the much greater role played by violence. This is by no means simply a question of the greater incidence of violence, if indeed there is more violence between states than within them. Since war is the ultimate resort in international politics, the possibility of its happening must at all times be provided for, even when it does not occur. This necessarily affects the bargaining position of the nations by giving the greater leverage to the militarily strongest nations. In contrast, within states, where the expectation of violence does not exist, because of a firmly seated system of legitimacy, other factors may have relatively greater weight.

Considerations such as this have led some thinkers to the conclusion that all power in the international arena derives directly or indirectly from the military equation, and that political and economic factors assume importance only as they derive from or have an impact on the capacity of states to make war. A balance of power, according to this view, must be understood as ultimately a military balance.

---

[10] Machiavelli, *op. cit.,* Chap. 11.

While questions such as these cannot be settled by abstract analysis alone, the theory developed here seems to cast doubt on an exclusively strategic (military) perception of the play of power in the international arena. Applying this theory to the use or threat of military force, the ability to exercise military influence rests on the following factors.

1. Military power over the field: the mission capability of a state, in terms of the physical effects which can be produced, given the manpower, equipment, training, morale, etc. of the armed forces of the state, in the light of the expected responses of the other states to the development or employment of these sanctions.

2. The relative desirability of the results of the employment of military force, in terms of a cost/gain analysis.

3. The degree to which the employment of these sanctions, and the consequent results, affect the preferences of the other states.

4. The structure of the field: that is the actual configuration of possible strategies and results.

The following brief discussion will illustrate these points.

The military power of a nation-state is not an individual capacity, like muscular strength or the ability to run fast. It is rather a relational thing, and must be measured in the context of the resources, opportunities, and preferences of all of the nations involved.

In assessing the role of military power in international affairs, it is necessary to take into account both the possible reluctance of nations to undertake the last resort, as well as the existence of sanctions that may be effective quite apart from the military equation. So, the starting point in understanding U.S.-Soviet relations is not the military balance, but the deep reluctance of both powers to take any step which might risk a full-scale military confrontation. So also, militarily weak nations can often wield a great deal of power, especially over allies over whom they can hold themselves as hostage. The United States has had a good deal of experience with this kind of ally.

Clausewitz's dictum that politics is the continuation of war by other means bears on the question of the decisiveness of military power. Contrary to the usual interpretation, the implication of this saying to me is that war consists not wholly of military action, but is rather a resolute struggle for advantage between nations by use of any means at hand. Such a struggle need not be carried out by military means, nor need the underlying military balance be decisive. It can be argued that the "cold war" between the United States and the Soviet Union from 1948 to 1962 is a case in point. The reluctance of both main powers to risk a military confrontation pushed political and economic factors to the fore. The eventual "balance" and resulting *détente* must be understood primarily in terms of progressive political and economic stabilization on both sides of the Iron Curtain.

Finally, the expectation of violence is not always present in the relations between states, for example, as between France and Great Britain in recent decades. The military situation between them tells us little about the important questions between them. Much more pertinent is the network of economic relations, centering about such questions as the Common Market and the economic system within the former British empire.

In short, while the military factor on the whole is undoubtedly the most important single coercive influence in international politics, it appears by no means always decisive and may in some instances play a minor role in comparison with other factors. In analyzing international events, the full range of positive and negative sanctions available to the nations must be taken into account, without assigning any priority in advance. The pervasive way in which the various forms of influence shift, interpenetrate, and interact, tends to justify the broad definition of coercion developed here.

Alliances

From the point of view of the logic of action, there appears at first to be no significant difference between the interactions of states at war with each other, and of allies. Only after the discussion has developed will such a difference emerge. In terms of game theory, the interactions of both allies and belligerents fall into the category of imperfectly competitive games, where the interests of the actors partly conflict and partly coincide (unless one can conceive of allies whose interests coincide completely, or belligerents whose interests diverge completely).

Abstractly, allies and belligerents cannot be distinguished sharply from one another. Two states may be at war yet not exchange blows for years, while much scuffling occurs among allies (even including hostilities) when the alliance remains in real and active force. Cooperative behavior often occurs between belligerents, as when they mutually refrain from escalating the level of hostilities, or from using certain kinds of weapons or tactics, while on the other hand the terms of an alliance may be strongly influenced, even dictated, by force of arms. The distinction is one of degree. There is relatively more violence and a higher expectation of violence between belligerents, and a relatively greater degree of cooperation between allies. To put the matter another way, war (hot or cold) is primarily an exchange of negative sanctions, while an alliance is mainly an agreement to exchange positive sanctions. The relative nature of the distinction (discussed earlier) between positive and negative sanctions makes it clear that the difference between alliance and war is neither so sharp nor so deep as it is often thought.

One may speak of an implicit alliance if it is highly probable that two or more states will behave cooperatively in certain circumstances. Thus, historians have pointed out that an implicit alliance existed between Great Britain and the United States during much of the nineteenth century, even though this fact was not widely appreciated by U.S. statesmen.

To focus the discussion, assume that two states, A and B, have little to fear from each other but much to fear from a third state, C. The military defeat of A or B by C would render the other even more vulnerable. Here, it is plausible that A and B would come to each other's aid in the event that one was attacked, even if no explicit agreement existed. The alliance is built into the interaction field.

Several advantages accrue, however, if A and B sign a defensive alliance against C. First, the alliance might clarify under precisely what circumstances A and B would come to each other's aid. Second, the publication of the alliance might have a deterrent effect on C (although secret alliances also have their uses). Third, although no nation can be expected to honor an agreement which turns out to be distinctly to its disadvantage, still many are reluctant to renege, and the existence of the document might exert an independent force in marginal cases.

The defensive value of the alliance between A and B will probably be increased if they plan for coordinated action in case of war (for example, a joint high command), or undertake coordinated precautionary action. For example, A and B might agree to lay railroad tracks of the same gauge, but different from those of C. In the event of war, this would facilitate movement of troops and material between A and B, and hinder such movement from C.

The scheme of analysis employed so far is insufficient to handle the kind of interaction introduced by this simple example, because what is involved is coordinated, not unilateral, action. It has been supposed so far that each individual chooses his own strategy, but here we have a case of two actors jointly choosing a strategy pair, presumably after consultation and discussion. We have moved from the idea of individual choice of strategies to group choice of strategy sets, which in a coordinated way involves one strategy for each actor. To a certain extent, A chooses B's strategy, and B chooses A's strategy.

It seems reasonable to assign the term "government" to the process whereby groups choose coordinated strategy sets. Coordinated group action requires government. Hence, insofar as an alliance involves such action, it constitutes or involves a rudimentary form of government.

While governmental institutions generally have a strong effect on the nature and patterns of coercive relations, it appears doubtful that the governmental aspect of alliances has had much impact in this regard. The governmental apparatus is too elementary, and firm systems of legitimacy are lacking. However, when we come to an organization such as the United Nations, especially if we take into account its affiliated and associated organizations, we have moved a modest but real distance along the road from the simplest coordinating alliance toward a full scale government. The independent impact of such forms of organization on the play of coercion in international affairs might not be negligible.

Coercion and Ideology in International Politics

There is a second area in which our distinction between national and international politics has been overdrawn. Just as systems of legitimacy within a nation-state may be weak, causing coercive relations to move toward the characteristic forms of international politics, so the forces of legitimacy are by no means always to be discounted in the international arena. This is especially true of a special form or principle of legitimacy called ideology.

There is a *prima facie* case that ideology has a great influence on international politics. States often use ideological appeals and programs as instruments of state policy; all that is required is to distinguish the cases in which ideology has been an effective instrument from those in which it has been ineffective. Also, as the men who control decisions within the state apparatus belong to certain social groups, their decisions can be expected to reflect to a greater or lesser extent the ideology of these social groups. Thus, ideology would seem to operate in the international arena both as a means by which statesmen influence the preferences of others, and also as an influence on the statesmen themselves in forming their preferences.

Despite this *prima facie* case, many theorists of international politics have tended either to minimize the importance of ideological factors as a separate element or to deny them altogether. It is worth considering some of their arguments.

Some theorists treat the propagation of an ideology as a question of the manipulation of symbols. Just as certain physical acts—say, pointing a gun at a person—produce certain responses, so the proper combinations of symbols can be used to evoke desired responses. Hence, ideology is simply another coercive instrumentality, like guns or butter.

This approach, however, ignores the difference between symbol and thing symbolized. The words employed by the ideologist are symbols that stand for certain ideas. Of most significance is not the impact of the symbols *on* the individual, but the effect of the concepts they stand for *within* the individual. The distinction developed here between coercive and ideological influence, as employing external and internal means respectively, is hence valid.

Another approach that tends to minimize the importance of ideological factors emphasizes the role of coercive factors—threats and promises—in the spread of an ideology. From this point of view, an ideology is something imposed by the politically successful, rather than itself used to gain political success.

A variant of this view treats a given population as having a more or less stable set of expectations. They will support governments or programs which they feel have met, or will meet, these expectations and reject those which they feel have not, or will not meet these expectations. The role of ideology is to convince people that their expectations have been or will be met. Since an "expectation" is a form of preference, this approach assumes that preferences are more or less stable, and that the role of ideology is to get people to think their preferences are being or will be met, rather than to change these preferences. The "revolution of rising expectations" is not a matter of changing preferences, but of becoming aware of better ways of satisfying existing preferences. Hence, ideology is essentially a form of propaganda (treated briefly above).

Clearly, both variants of this argument contain strong elements of truth. However, the ubiquity of coercive elements in ideological programs is no proof that ideology does not have an appeal independent of its coercive backing, and general observation seems to support this view. As pointed out, it is characteristic (in the sense of being a defining property) of social norms that they are enforced by external sanctions, but few sociologists take this to be a denial of the crucial importance of the internalization of norms.

On the second point, it is often the case that an ideologist will tailor his case to meet the existing preferences of his audience. This is evident even in the epistles of Paul himself, the greatest ideologist of Christianity; but this does not gainsay the revolution in values produced by Christianity. It is more germane to enquire to what extent ideologies operate by changing preferences, and to what extent by appealing to existing preferences. It appears common for both factors to operate together.

In sum, these two objections operate to temper possible excessive claims as to the magnitude of the influence of ideology in international affairs, rather than to challenge its existence.

Finally, we come to what may be regarded as the "realist" critique of views emphasizing the role of ideology in international politics. Realists tend to hold that except in moments of absent-mindedness or aberration, states pursue their national interest. The national interest consists mainly in the military security and economic welfare of the nation. States may be divided into two types: satisfied and dissatisfied. Satisfied states adopt the defensive policy of protecting what they have, while dissatisfied states attempt to enlarge their territorial and/or economic base. In the main, the policy of a state is directed by its strategic position and its economic situation and problems. The form of government and the prevailing ideology do not affect matters a great deal. For example, the foreign policy of the Soviet Union would have been much the same if the Czar or Kerensky had stayed in power, and the underlying conflicts of interest between Russia and China could not long be obscured by the fact that both have a communist form of government.

This brief summary does not of course do justice to the variety of forms that realism has taken, nor to the depth and subtlety of some of the arguments advanced in its favor.

When this broad stream of writings is viewed as a whole, however, a central theme does emerge. That is the exhortatory quality of the literature. Such theorists as MacKinder and Haushoffer, Mahan and Spykman, Morgenthau, Kennan, Kissinger and Kahn, different as they are from each other, all urge that certain policies be adopted and others rejected. This of course is most striking in the most famous work of the greatest of all the realists, Niccolo Machiavelli. *The Prince* is devoted to advice to rulers, and ends with an impassioned plea for the unification of Italy. The suspicion arises that realism itself is essentially an ideological position.

The key to understanding any ideology is to identify the social group whose values and interests (preferences) it reflects and promotes. On the supposition that realism is an ideological position, we do not have far to look—the group consists of members of the state apparatus, those who govern: in the case of international politics, the professional statesmen.

At first this might seem implausible, for a government is an organization, which is a different thing than a social group. But studies of organizations have shown that they quickly become social groups, in the sense that bonds of group solidarity develop, forming the soil for the growth of a system of social norms peculiar to members of the organization.

Modern theories of organization lead us to suppose that governments and subgroups within governments will form separate and distinctive systems of norms. For the purpose of examining what preferences different governmental groups might have in common, one must look at the objective interests of the state apparatus itself, quite apart from the purposes it is supposed to serve.

The state is the supreme authority, and within a territory possesses a monopoly of the right to use the supreme sanction. That is, legally, and by and large in fact, its rightful decisions take precedence over the decisions of any other individual or group within the territory, and it alone has the right to employ violence to enforce its rules and decisions. The central interest of any state apparatus, as a state apparatus, is to achieve and maintain this supremacy. Domestically, its central problem is to maintain its legitimacy; abroad, its central problem is military security. The latter in turn depends to an important extent on the firmness of its legitimacy and the wealth of the nation. Hence the pursuit of wealth and the development of national resources must be an important goal of state policy.

It appears, then, that realism speaks for the interests of the state apparatus and for those who identify their interests with the interests of the state apparatus, namely the government. Its ideological character lies in two assertions, one of value and one of fact, which tend to conceal the actual nature of the "interests of state" it advocates.

First, realism tends to equate the interests of the state apparatus with the interests of the members of society at large. But this equation may not be valid; in fact, it is always untrue to some extent. While the security of the state apparatus may be genuinely to the interests of the citizens, it cannot be their only interest. If the maximization of the state security is the overriding goal of state policy, then other interests must necessarily suffer. To put the matter as bluntly as possible, the state will survive any successful war, no matter how devastating, which is more than can be said of many of its citizens (including members of the government). The security of the state and the security of its citizens are two entirely different things.

Indeed, the very existence of the state may not be to the interests of its citizens. By the Hellenistic era, for example, the city-state had outlived its usefulness to its citizens, most of whom were better off after the Roman Empire had replaced it as the supreme political unit. The comparisons between the city-state in the Hellenistic era and the nation-state today are sobering. In sum, the overwhelming emphasis that realism accords to considerations of state security seems in fact to reflect the interests of the state apparatus, as defined by members of the government, rather than of society at large.

Second, realist thinkers tend to assert that in fact state policy almost always assigns the highest priority to considerations of state security. This view may be questioned on several grounds.

The members of a government will in general hold the preferences of the social groups from which they came when they entered governmental service, alongside the preferences they pick up by the process of political socialization after they enter. Governmental policy may reflect in part this first set of preferences.

Even if the government does not share sentiments which are widespread in society, it may be politically expedient to be sensitive to such sentiments. Thus, those who set U.S. foreign policy have seemed by and large to regard Israel as something of a nuisance, but public opinion (or at least the Israeli lobby) has forced a moderately pro-Israeli policy. The realist may denounce such policies as departures from the principles of national security, and as pandering to public opinion or special interests, but he would be unrealistic to assert that this kind of thing does not happen, and with some frequency.

New regimes seem often to be more "ideological" and less "realistic" than long established ones. It takes a while, apparently, for the socializing effect attendant upon running the government to make itself felt.

On a more fundamental level, it seems difficult if not impossible to supply a clear-cut, operationally relevant meaning to the concept of state security. Suppose we begin by defining state security or "interests of state" as the secure maintenance of the authority of the state apparatus in its territory. Now the government, as the group of men who occupy the offices in the state apparatus, constitutes a social group with its own interests, which will always differ to a greater or lesser degree from the interests of state. For example, they can be expected to refuse to recognize those instances when a change of government (new men in office) will serve state security.

Furthermore, the government is divided into subgroups, each of which has its own special interests, which it tends (usually sincerely) to confuse with state security. The navy, for example, can be relied on to feel that national security requires a larger fleet, while the air force will think that what is needed is more aircraft.

Thus, the idea of state security appears to have a doubtful political relevance. What is actually operating are the motivations of the men who fill the governmental offices, motivations that will vary importantly according to the position which they occupy in the state apparatus, as well as the social strata from which they are recruited. State policy is not the outcome of a search for state security, but of a complex political struggle among conflicting elements. The result is often a set of policies which a disinterested observer would have difficulty in relating to state security. For example, it would seem necessary to view policy formation in this light in order to understand Soviet policy leading up to the Cuban missile crisis, or the U.S. policies which led to an ever deeper commitment in Indochina.

The difficulty of relating actual state policy to the concept of state security is compounded by the fact that while the concept of state security may be clear in the abstract, the problem of determining which of the concrete policy alternatives available to the governors will most further state security is so complex, and depends on so many unknowns and intangibles as to defy solution, even if the governors were to approach the problem from this point of view (which they do not).[11]

A number of realists have argued, and with considerable force, that there is no such thing as a national interest or a general welfare.[12] What we are presented with, they argue, is nothing but a welter of conflicting partial interests. The idea of a national interest is an empty abstraction, both irrelevant in application and problematic in meaning when applied to actual policy problems. In this, however, they are hoist with their own petard, for exactly the same point can be made about the concept of state security.

SUMMARY

Coercion is best defined broadly as the use of sanctions to influence the behavior of others. Narrower definitions, which depend on such distinctions as those between force or absence of force, the willingness or unwillingness of the coerced, positive or negative sanctions, unilateral or mutual influence, are unsatisfactory either because the line is impossible to draw clearly or because the distinction turns on an unimportant question.

A game theoretical definition of coercion suggests that three independent factors are involved: (a) control over the results of the

---

[11] The point of view argued above is developed in detail in Warner R. Schilling, "The Politics of National Defense, 1950," in Schilling, Hammond, and Snyder, *Strategy, Politics, and Defense Budgets* (New York: Columbia University Press, 1962).

[12] For example, Charles A. Beard, *The Idea of the National Interest* (New York: Macmillan Company, 1934).

strategies of the coerced, (b) the preferences of both coercer and coerced with respect to the controlled variables, and (c) the effect of these preferences on the behavior of the coerced.

Noncoercive influence can include influence over another's assessment of the situation (propaganda) and influence over the preferences of another, which is involved in the operation of charismatic leadership, social norms, law, and ideology. The relationships among the latter three were indicated.

Coercion as here defined does not appear to play a larger role in the international than in the national arena. It is true that violence and the threat of violence play a comparatively greater role in international politics, but this is a matter of degree and is not always true. War and alliance involve essentially the same kinds of coercive interactions, except that alliances may involve a rudimentary form of government. The realist view that states do not, or ought not, allow ideological consideratons to play an important role in policy formation was challenged on the grounds that realism itself is an ideological doctrine.

There does, however, seem to be one fundamental difference between the way in which coercion operates on the national and the international arena. This does not concern the relative amounts of coercion, nor the kind of coercion. In both arenas, influence consists of a complex interplay of coercive and noncoercive factors. Within states, however, the use of coercion is regulated by the system of legitimacy, which prohibits and prescribes coercion in such a way that it forms a coherent organized pattern. In contrast, while noncoercive influences, especially similarity of ideology, may enable a considerable degree of cooperation between states, they do not act to organize coercion in this way. On the national level, coercion operates according to a set of coherent normatively defined rules. On the international level it does not.

14

BARGAINING AND BARGAINING TACTICS

Robert Jervis

In most periods, war has paid for the state that won. To inflict high costs on the opponent a state had first to defeat its army. And only one side could do that. For the superpowers the situation is different today.[1] Each side can protect itself only by destroying the adversary's strategic nuclear weapons, and this ability is no longer a prerequisite to the ability to destroy the adversary. When neither side has the first-strike capability needed for defense and both sides have a second-strike capability for deterrence,[2] even if

I wish to thank Robert Axelrod, Alexander George, and Glenn Snyder for comments on an earlier draft of this essay. The Center for International Affairs provided financial suport.

[1] For the purpose of abstract analysis of bargaining relationships, we shall be concerned with a bipolar world in which there are only two actors possessing significant nuclear capability.

[2] Thomas Schelling, *Arms and Influence* (New Haven: Yale University Press, 1966), 1-34, and Glenn Snyder, *Deterrence and Defense* (Princeton: Princeton University Press, 1961), 9-30.

one side could "win" a war the loser could inflict extreme punishment on the winner. Mutual second-strike capability implies not overkill but mutual kill.

Before discussing some of the implications of this situation we should blur the distinction just drawn by indicating the ways in which nonnuclear war imposes high costs on the winner. If it were true that war in the past always paid for one side, there would have been many more wars. Only moral restraints and the fear of losing would have inhibited states from attacking. In fact, the winner always paid a price in terms of the human and material resources consumed. These could outweigh the expected gains, especially in eras in which the defense had the advantage over the offense. That such costs usually bore more heavily on the loser than on the winner, and indeed were often a major reason why the loser conceded defeat (as in the case of Russia in the Crimean War), should not obscure the fact that conventional war, like nuclear war, is not a zero-sum game. The side that loses less than its opponent can still lose more than it gains and more than it would have lost had it made the concessions necessary to avoid the war. Indeed, industrialization and the growth of the ability of the state to pour huge amounts of resources into war would probably have made this condition the rule rather than the exception, even had nuclear weapons not been developed. Norman Angell was right[3]—World War I did not pay, even for the winners. If in 1914 the Entente powers had known the costs of the war, they surely would have made concessions rather than fight. And even had technology favored the offense and the war not bogged down in a bloody stalemate, this conflict would not have paid for the winner unless either of two conditions were met. The winner would have had to hold out moderate terms or develop means of ending the loser's efforts to resist, for example by conquering all of its territory or by using as a hostage the enemy's population that it held. For the Germans to have taken Paris in 1914 probably would not have had the same decisive effect that it had had in 1871. As Hitler learned, even conquering all of France would not have automatically ended the struggle.

The Allies took the lesson of World War I to heart, and their realization of the costs of another war contributed to their refusal to stand firm until it became clear that Hitler's ambitions were unlim-

---

[3] *The Great Illusion* (London: Heineman, 1910).

ited. World War II paid for Britain and France not because their gains in the war outweighed their losses, but because the losses that would have been incurred by allowing Hitler to dominate Europe were higher still. And taking into account both the costs of fighting and the risk of losing, only a person like Hitler who was willing to run very high risks (or who placed an unusually high valuation on making gains) would have followed the policy he did. These costs would have deterred most decision-makers, as they deterred the German generals.

A second kind of cost often incurred by the winner in the pre-nuclear era is diplomatic. A successful war could convince other states that the winner, by virtue of his intentions and/or capability, was a menace to the system and had to be met by a united front. Thus, after Bismarck waged three successful wars his sincere protestations of satisfaction with the *status quo* were greeted with a skepticism that hindered his efforts to maintain peace.

Undesired changes in the combatants' domestic systems constitute a third kind of cost that may be incurred by states that win a war. Russia was on the winning side in the First World War. After the Napoleonic wars the conservative powers believed that wars involved a risk of revolution that outweighed most potential gains. Similarly, in 1936 Harold Nicolson opposed going to war with Germany over the latter's occupation of the Rhineland, even though "we shall win and enter Berlin. But what is the good of that? It would only mean communism in Germany and France. . . ."[4]

Finally, even without nuclear weapons states were often able to increase the costs of war to the other side above those incurred by the clash of military forces. Blockades, employed by Britain in World War I and by the central government in the Nigerian civil war, not only weaken the adversary's military position in a number of ways (for example, diverting resources from military uses, lowering the morale and even the physical strength of the troops), but also increase the cost of conflict to the other side, perhaps to the point where it prefers making concessions to continuing the war.

Another possibility for the side which cannot gain its objective on the battlefield is to subvert the opponent's government or to

---

[4] Harold Nicolson, *Diaries and Letters 1930-1939* (New York: Atheneum, 1966), 250.

weaken its society to an extent that threatens, if not the other side's social order, at least the future of its government. While such weakening is often a by-product of engaging in a costly or losing war, it is not beyond the direct manipulation of foreign powers, as German policy toward Russia in World War I showed.

Conventional bombing can also impose high costs.[5] The United States, unable to defeat the insurgency in South Vietnam, did not have to use nuclear weapons to force the North to pay a price for remaining in the war. And the fear of bombing was a pervasive influence on British and French policy in the 1930s even though Hitler never threatened such a policy and lacked both the capability and the intention of carrying it out. Although Britain and France were confident that they could win an eventual victory, they thought the price of the destruction of their cities was too high to pay unless the alternative was the certain domination of the Continent by Germany.

The possession of a second strike capability by both superpowers thus has not created the ability of the loser to punish the winner, but by increasing the scale and certainty of such punishment it has been made a prime influence in world politics. Since a large-scale war cannot pay for either side, many crises now resemble the game of Chicken rather than Prisoner's Dilemma. In Prisoner's Dilemma two men caught by the police are being questioned in separate rooms and so cannot communicate with each other. As each knows, the police have firm evidence that they committed a minor crime and suspect—correctly—that they also participated in a major one. However, only if one or both men confess can the police prove the latter charge. So if neither confesses both get a light sentence for the minor crime. If one confesses to the major crime while his partner remains silent, the former gets a pardon for both crimes and the latter receives a heavy sentence. If both confess and plead guilty to the major crime, each gets a sentence that is heavier than if both had kept silent but lighter than if only his partner had turned state's evidence. In the game of Chicken two teenagers drive their cars toward each other, trying to make the other give way. If both swerve

---

[5] See the discussion of blockades, subversion, and conventional bombing in John Herz, *International Politics in The Atomic Age* (New York: Columbia University Press, 1959), 96-108.

at the same time they suffer an indignity which is minor because it is mutual. If one swerves and allows the other to continue going straight ahead, the former pays the high price of being shown to be chicken. If neither swerves each pays the still higher price of being killed. The pay-offs for these games are shown in the figure below, with the terms "defect" (from the coalition with the other player) and "stand firm," or "cooperate" (with other player) and "back down" added to show the obvious twin-headed international analogies.

Although the Prisoner's Dilemma is often discussed to show how rationality can lead to an outcome that does not maximize the participants' self-interest, the point here is somewhat different. On any single play of the game each actor prefers to stand firm (confess) no matter what his partner does. In Chicken, on the other hand, each actor prefers to do the opposite of what he thinks his partner will do. He would like to stand firm (go straight ahead) and have

Prisoner's Dilemma

	Keep silent (i.e., cooperate and back down)	Confess (i.e., defect and stand firm)
Keep silent (i.e., cooperate and back down)	−2, −2	−20, 5
Confess (i.e., defect and stand firm)	5, −20	−10, −10

Chicken

	Swerve (i.e., cooperate and back down)	Go straight ahead (i.e., defect and stand firm)
Swerve (i.e., cooperate and back down)	0, 0	−10, 10
Go straight ahead (i.e., stand firm and defect)	10, −10	−50, −50

his partner back down (swerve). But if he thinks his partner is going to stand firm, he will, unlike in the Prisoner's Dilemma, back down.

Aspects of international relations can be seen in these frameworks. In both pre-nuclear and nuclear crises each actor's first choice is to stand firm and have his opponent retreat. But in the pre-nuclear era actors were often willing to stand firm even though they thought their adversaries would do likewise. They often preferred a war to a retreat. Each side might calculate that it would win the war or believe that the costs of not fighting were high enough to justify a war in which it had only a small change of victory. This is not to claim that in all instances of war in the pre-nuclear era both sides preferred war to retreat. Some pre-nuclear crises terminated in war because each side, although preferring a retreat to a war, incorrectly believed that the other side would back down if it stood firm. For example, Hitler might not have invaded Poland had he known that Britain and France would not only declare war, but refuse to make peace after Poland had been conquered. But most wars were not the inadvertent result of bluffs that were called. Although the calculations may have been crude and shortsighted and based on wildly incorrect beliefs about the costs of fighting and backing down, such calculations as there were often pointed to war. The mutual destructiveness of nuclear war has changed this. No issue, with the possible exception of each side's maintenance of its political and social system, could be worth a high risk of a major war. In any crisis each side will be willing to stand firm only if it thinks the other will back down. Thus the game of Chicken is much more relevant than it was in the past.

Certainty as to whether an adversary will stand firm is rare. Statesmen have to deal in probabilities. The estimate of the probability that the adversary will retreat—when combined with the costs of a war, the costs of a unilateral retreat, the advantages gained if the state stands firm and the adversary retreats, and the pay-offs if both states retreat—determines whether the state should back down or stand firm. Assuming that the actors have only two choices (to retreat or to stand firm), that they must simultaneously decide what to do, and that the pay-offs are known, we can use the equation which holds when the expected value of standing firm equals that of retreating in order to calculate how certain the actor must be that the adversary will back down if the actor is to make a rational decision to stand firm.

Under this condition:

probability that the other will retreat, multiplied by the pay-off if you stand firm and he retreats		probability that the other will retreat, multiplied by the pay-off if you retreat and he retreats
+	=	+
(1—[probability that he will retreat]) multiplied by the costs if you stand firm and he does not retreat.		(1—[probability that he will retreat]) multiplied by the costs if you retreat and he does not retreat.

Taking the pay-offs from the chicken game in figure 1.

$$p\,(10) \;+\; (1-p)(-50) \;=\; p(0) \;+\; (1-p)(-10)$$
$$p \;=\; .80$$

Thus, the actor should stand firm if he thinks that the chances are better than four out of five that the adversary will back down. Of course this does not determine the probability of the adversary's standing firm, although (as we will discuss later) the adversary's equation contains valuable evidence about his intentions.

The point of setting up this equation is not to claim that decisions on whether to stand firm can be made an exact science, but rather to show how a state can increase its chances of prevailing.[6] The risk that the state is willing to run is increased, and the degree of certainty that the state requires before it will stand firm therefore decreased, by behavior that increases the pay-off that accrues from standing firm, or decreases the pay-off (that is, increases the costs) of retreating. The actor is more likely to stand firm if any of the following conditions are met: a) the value to him of the issue at stake increases, b) the cost of war decreases (both of these increase the pay-off of standing firm), c) the cost of a stalemate in which both

[6] For an analysis in a similar vein see Glenn Snyder, " 'Prisoner's Dilemma' and 'Chicken' Models in International Politics," *International Studies Quarterly*, 15 (March 1971), 66-103.

sides retreat increases, and d) the cost of a unilateral retreat increases (both of these increase the cost of retreating). But while policies that meet these conditions make the state more apt to stand firm, they also increase the chances of a war resulting from both sides standing firm. For the state to be able to stand firm and yet avoid war it must convince the adversary to retreat.

Because the adversary's decision is influenced by his belief about what the actor will do, anything that leads the former to think that the latter is more apt to stand firm will increase the actor's chance of peacefully prevailing. Thus an actor who increases his incentives for standing firm will want to communicate this to his adversary. Some tactics, like making a commitment to stand firm, both change the state's incentives and, if successful, communicate this to the other side. But the state can also represent or misrepresent its beliefs about its pay-offs without at the same time altering them. Thus the state will want to exaggerate its perception of the costs of retreating and the gains of standing firm. Similarly, by changing the adversary's pay-offs the state can increase the chances that the former will decide to retreat even though the adversary's estimate of what the state will do is unchanged.

However, some methods of either changing pay-offs or misrepresenting one's beliefs about them raise what can be called the problem of symmetry. It will not help the actor to increase his incentives for standing firm or increase his costs of retreating if he simultaneously alters his adversary's incentives in the same direction. In a real game of chicken played between two young men courting the same girl, it would not help one of them to invite the girl to witness the contest. Although he would have greater reason to show his bravery, so would his rival. Symmetry similarly complicates some strategies of commitment. By pledging his reputation for living up to his word, the actor increases his cost of retreating. But if the adversary expects to engage in future conflicts with the actor, commitment also increases the pay-off to the adversary of making the actor back down. For a state to stress that its prestige or reputation for living up to its word is involved in a particular conflict increases the incentives of the other side to stand firm if the latter has an interest in damaging the state's prestige and reputation.

The most obvious way to change the pay-offs in an asymmetrical fashion is to reduce the cost of war to oneself and increase it to the adversary. In the past, additions to the state's military forces accomplished this end, but when both sides can maintain second strike capability less change is possible. However, the state may be able to gain at least a slight bargaining advantage by pretending to believe that the results of a war will not be disastrous to it. A country can understate the level of physical destruction it expects or can claim that this damage would be partly outweighted by seeing the new world constructed along lines it favors. Many Chinese and early Soviet statements should be seen in this light.[7] But now the scope for manipulating these perceptions is relatively slight, and thus the importance of other factors in the equation, particularly the value of the stake and the cost of unilaterally retreating, are elevated.

The state will gain a bargaining advantage if either or both sides believe that a retreat on the issue in question will trigger events that harm the state but do not help its adversary. For example, the cost of retreating can be increased by commitment, although this may involve the disadvantage of symmetry. Alternatively, the state may claim to believe that the resolution of many issues is related to the present conflict. People who believe in domino theories are more apt to stand firm. Of course, for this reason the state does not want its opponent to believe in such theories, and it is hard to hold to the view that dominoes will fall but that the other side does not know this if the theory gives the other side's actions a large role in making the dominoes fall. But if the state can argue that it believes a retreat will have wide repercussions irrespective of the other's actions, it can make this advantageous claim. In a related manner, the cost of retreating can be both stressed and increased by tying the specific issue to a general principle about which the actor feels strongly. To avoid a symmetrical increase in the opponent's incentives, the actor must select a principle that is more important to him than to the opponent. Thus management's chance of prevailing in a dispute with labor is increased if it can tie an issue to the principle of "management's right to manage," and the union's chances of success are greater on those issues which it can convincingly claim are related to its right to speak for all the workers in the plant.

[7] George Quester, "On the Identification of Real and Pretended Communist Military Doctrine," *Journal of Conflict Resolution,* 10 (June 1966), 173-79.

As Schelling has pointed out, a similar logic dictates that a state can gain strength through weakness. If backing down would mean the disruption of a state's economy or the overthrow of its government, it has an incentive to stand firm that is not likely to be matched by its opponent (unless, of course, the other side places a very high value on destroying the state's regime). To create these imbalanced incentives the state may place itself in a situation in which a retreat will encourage third parties to make claims against it. A clause in the Japanese peace treaty "gives the United States certain claims if subsequent Japanese territorial concessions to other powers are more favorable."[8] This increases the cost to Japan of concessions to the Russians without creating a corresponding incentive for the Russians to stand firm (unless the Russians feel it is in their interest to have Japan make concessions to other countries). For this reason, a most-favored-nation policy can make it more likely that a state will refuse to cut its tariffs. Similar arguments can be used by women in refusing to give sexual favors.

Often the decisive factor in bargaining, because it makes the cost of retreating and the gains from standing firm much higher for one side than for the other, is the unequal value the states place on the issue at stake.[9] Peaceful resolution of conflict is more apt to occur on issues about which the states do not feel equally strongly, provided that each has a rough idea of how strongly the other feels and that the state with the smaller incentive for winning does not for any extraneous reason have to pay a prohibitively high price for losing. The latter condition would not be met if the state that did not highly value a stake had, out of rashness or miscalculation, strongly committed itself to stand firm. While this state would then

[8] Thomas Schelling, *Strategy of Conflict* (New York: Oxford University Press, 1963), 159.

[9] This point has been neglected in much of the strategic literature. Recent studies are rectifying this error. See Stephen Maxwell, *Rationality in Deterrence* (London: Institute of Strategic Studies, Adelphi Papers, No. 51, 1968); Alexander George, David Hall, and William Simons, *The Limits of Coercive Diplomacy* (Boston: Little Brown, 1971); James King, *Limited War and Escalation* (unpublished paper); Steven Rosen, "A Model of War and Alliance," in Julian Friedman, Christopher Bladen, and Steven Rosen, eds., *Alliance in International Politics* (Boston: Allyn and Bacon, 1970), 223-32; Glenn Snyder, "Bargaining Tactics and the 'Critical Risk-Credibility' Model," *op. cit.;* and Brent Scowcroft, "Deterrence and Strategic Superiority," *Orbis* 13 (Summer 1969), 450.

not care about the intrinsic value of the issue, it would be apt to stand firm because of the costs of losing.

The fact that there are almost no issues on which the superpowers feel equally strongly is a key element in maintaining the stability of the present international system. And a lack of comprehension of this point led U.S. decision-makers into one of the greatest blunders of the postwar period. American policy in Vietnam was based largely on the belief that since we could inflict more punishment on Hanoi and the Viet Cong than they could on us, they would give up. This overlooked the fact that the fate of South Vietnam, although important to the U.S., was far more important to the other side. Thus the other side was willing to absorb far more punishment than America was, and the fact that the U.S. could hurt it more than it could hurt us did not, as American decision-makers originally believed, lead the other side to concede.

When both sides realize that one of them values the stake more than the other, the former has a major bargaining advantage. For this reason clear and objective determinants of the differential value of an issue are of great significance. For example, the good harbors situated in the part of the Oregon territory that was in dispute between the U.S. and Britain before 1846 were of more value to the U.S. than to Britain because of the abundance of harbors in the area under undisputed British control and the absence of harbors in American territory. The British knew this, realized that it strengthened American resolve, and so were more willing to make concessions. Similarly, the Finnish threat to resist Russian demands for control of the nickel mines in northern Finland in 1940–41 was made more credible by the plausible claim that allowing the Soviets to run the installation would undermine Finnish political control of this area, if not of the whole country.[10]

For this reason a state may want to exaggerate the importance to it of the issue and overstate how strongly it feels. While the U.S. obviously feels strongly about its special position in the Caribbean, it is possible that it not only capitalized on but exaggerated its concern to gain bargaining advantages during the Cuban missile crisis.

[10] Frederick Merk, *The Oregon Question* (Cambridge: The Belknap Press of the Harvard University Press, 1967), 167; H. Peter Krosby, *Finland, Germany, and the Soviet Union, 1940-1941* (Madison: University of Wisconsin Press, 1968), 94.

And Russia may overstate her dissatisfaction with the *status quo* in Berlin. The scope for this tactic is larger in cases in which the powers lack long-standing positions, and these obviously tend to involve areas, such as the Congo, in which neither superpower has a vital interest. However, this tactic, like so many others, entails a risk. If the state is forced to retreat on an issue about which it has exaggerated its concern, its adversary is likely to lower its estimate of the state's resolve and expect the state to retreat on other issues about which the state claims to feel strongly.

The incentives to overstate the value of the stake and the costs of retreat have contributed to the inflation of rhetoric. Not only is it hard to take decisive action in the Cold War, but strong words make it less necessary to do so. However, this new style of diplomacy may make it more difficult for states to explore possible compromises.

The logic of the bargaining equation also dictates that states minimize their adversaries' costs of retreating. This can involve persuading the other side that its estimates of these costs are incorrect. Labor often tries to convince management that the latter has overestimated the cost of the fringe benefits demanded by labor. Or the actor can actually reduce the other's cost of retreating, usually by decommitting the adversary. To do this the state can act as though it did not hear the other give any commitments, knows that they were meant only for domestic audiences, or believes that they were issued as the result of bureaucratic infighting and do not represent official policy. To reduce further the adversary's costs, the state can stress that the issue is unique and that the state will not expect retreats from the adversary in other conflicts. However, while such tactics make it more likely that the state will prevail, they reduce the value of victory if the state expects to engage in a continuing series of conflicts with the adversary. Indeed, this fact will make the adversary more apt to respond favorably because it may infer that if these tactics are used the state does not have designs on other of the adversary's values.[11]

Symmetry creates problems with those methods of reducing the adversary's cost of retreating that also reduce the actor's cost of

---

[11] For a further discussion of this topic see Robert Jervis, *The Logic of Images in International Relations* (Princeton: Princeton University Press, 1970), chap. 8.

backing down. So states may want to avoid tactics that mutually lower the value of the issue at stake, or provide a way out of the dispute that makes it equally easy for both sides to make concessions. For example, if the U.S. had tried to lower the costs to the Soviets of retreating in the Cuban missile crisis by arguing that the missiles did not change the balance of power, it would have simultaneously lowered the cost of retreating for the U.S. So the U.S. instead made it easier for the Russians to retreat by tentatively agreeing not to invade Cuba and allowing the Russians to claim they were complying because their missiles had accomplished their mission.

The state can increase the chances that the adversary will retreat by reducing the advantages the latter would gain if it stood firm. For example, the state may claim that if it is forced to retreat on this issue it will do something to harm the adversary in another arena. The fact that the U.S. responded to the North Korean attack on the South by quadrupling its defense budget may have decreased the value to the Russians of standing firm in later crises by making them fear that a victory would be met by another spurt in arms spending. The severe punishment the U.S. has inflicted on North Vietnam, although not great enough to make that country accede to the American demands, has lowered the net value to the North of prevailing. And if the North believed a similar American response would be triggered by their supporting guerrilla wars in other parts of South East Asia, they could be deterred from doing so even if they thought such wars would be successful. Again, to be most effective these measures must not simultaneously reduce the state's gains from standing firm. Thus an effort to make the adversary retreat by convincing him that a victory would not affect the outcome of other disputes would reduce both sides' incentives and so would not produce a bargaining advantage.

All the tactics discussed so far deal with changing or misrepresenting beliefs about pay-offs. In addition, actors can alter or misrepresent their beliefs about their own and their adversary's resolve or general willingness to run risks.[12] Since each side wants to stand

---

[12] Since an actor's resolve depends on the subjective costs and advantages of alternative courses of action, this factor could be incorporated into the pay-offs. However, since it is a general and important influence on bargaining outcomes, it should be singled out for special attention.

firm if and only if it believes[13] that the other will back down, each can try to convince its adversary to retreat by establishing its bravery, foolhardiness, or inability to calculate. Thus actors may try to convince others that they are not rational.[14] They can act as though they do not understand the risks they are running. Or they can try to show that they have a particularly high tolerance for danger and pain. The other side of this coin is that each actor will try to make the adversary believe that he thinks the latter does not have high resolve. Such a belief would make the actor more likely to stand firm, and therefore if the adversary thinks the actor holds this belief he is more likely to retreat. So a state may claim that its adversary has a decadent domestic political and social system and so will not run risks. Or it can argue that previous international behavior has shown the adversary to lack resolve. The adversary's past retreats can be seized on, the extent of prior risks run can be minimized, and the number of previous commitments broken and values sacrificed can be exaggerated. This may conflict with the versions of these events that the state propagated at the time. Thus, before the Russian pressure on Berlin eased it was in America's interest to minimize the degree of Russian concern and commitment. But after Russia withdrew her challenge, America could gain a bargaining advantage in later conflicts by claiming to believe that this episode showed that Russia would not stand firm even when there were strong incentives for her to do so. When an event has not been preceded by extensive bargaining it is easier for the state that retreated to put forth a view of the incident that suits its future interests. The fact that the U.S. did not try to deter the Russian invasion of Czechoslovakia allows America to claim that it believes that Russia knew that this action did not entail high risks and so did not lead the U.S. to revise its estimate of Soviet resolve.[15]

This analysis can be carried through the familiar he-thinks-that-I-think-that-he-thinks cycle. State B is more apt to back down if it thinks state A thinks it will back down. Therefore, A will not only try to raise the costs of war to B and lower B's gains of prevailing

---

[13] The degree to which the actor must believe this is given by the bargaining equation.

[14] Schelling, *Strategy of Conflict, op. cit.,* 17-18, 149.

[15] For a further discussion of this and related tactics see Jervis, *op. cit.,* 197-216.

and costs of retreating, but also will try to show B that A believes that B's pay-offs make it unlikely that B will stand firm. If B believes that A holds this view of B's pay-offs, B will think it more likely that A will stand firm and so will be more apt to retreat. Thus, even if A cannot influence B's pay-offs, he will want to have B believe that A holds certain views about these outcomes. To proceed one step further, B will think A is more likely to stand firm if B believes that A believes that B believes the version of both states' pay-offs that A is propagating. In other words, A is more likely to stand firm if it feels the stake is more important to it than to B. It is still more likely to stand firm if it believes that B shares this view. If it thinks B knows that A knows this, it gets further benefits, and so on through the cycle.

In summary:

Tactic	*Effect*
Changing A's pay-offs to increase the costs of retreating and the incentives for stand-firm.	A more likely to stand firm.
Changing B's pay-offs to decrease the costs of retreating and the incentives for standing firm.	B less likely to stand firm.
If B believes A's pay-offs have been changed in this way.	B less likely to stand firm.
If A successfully communicates to B that A believes the pay-offs have been changed in this way.	B less likely to stand firm.
If A believes that it has successfully communicated to B that the pay-offs have been changed in this way.	A more likely to stand firm.

This analysis indicates why objective and subjective measures of national power are peculiarly intertwined in the Cold War. The belief that something contributes to a state's ability to stand firm is self-fulfilling. If either actor believes that one side has a bargaining advantage in a given conflict, then that side does indeed have an advantage. If it is believed that a state can safely stand firm in a dispute, then the chances are greater that it will stand firm and that its adversary will retreat.

The most important current application of this principle concerns the question of whether, as long as both superpowers have a second strike capability, nuclear "superiority" (that is, the ability to do more damage to the other side than it can do to the first) has any influence in disputes. It may be true, as is often alleged, that such capability could not possibly be of aid in any conceivable war, does not add to the meaningful options the state has, and thus that it should not lead a decision-maker who was even minimally rational to stand firm when he would not do so if both sides had equal capability. However, if the decision-makers of the state which has "superiority" do not accept this analysis and instead believe that this capability does indeed help them, they will be more likely to stand firm. If the other side believes that this is the view of the first side, it will be more apt to retreat. And if the first side thinks that the second understands its belief, its willingness to stand firm will be reinforced. In addition, of course, if the second state thinks that the first's "superiority" will influence the course of a war, it will be more apt to retreat. And the first state will be influenced by the knowledge of this belief.

Thus there are two separate cycles following from each side's views of the usefulness of "superiority." In the hypothetical example just given they reinforce each other, but this is not automatically true. The state which has "superiority" is more apt to stand firm if it thinks superiority matters and if it thinks its adversary thinks it matters. The adversary is more likely to retreat if it thinks superiority is meaningful and if it believes that the state holds this position. These four beliefs are independent and any combination of them is possible.

The importance of the decision-makers' views and the consequent impossibility of rendering an objective judgment as to the utility of "superiority" may partially account for the internal contradictions in some analyses of this question. Many people believe that neither the U.S. nor the USSR can possibly achieve a first strike capability, and that as long as both have a second strike capability it does not matter which side has more missiles. McGeorge Bundy, for example, argues that Polaris submarines by themselves provide sufficient deterrence.[16] But the same people who hold this view also believe that it is important to reach an arms control agreement in order to halt the strategic arms spiral. To predict such an arms race implies that the decision-makers believe that bargaining advantages accrue to the side that has the greater strategic capability.[17] And to fear this arms race implies that the side that is "ahead" may act rashly. If decision-makers felt that both sides were assured of a second strike capability and that more strategic weapons would do no good, there would be no strategic arms race and no need to reach an arms control agreement. However, as long as one side believes there are advantages in having a greater strategic capability, or believes that the other side believes it, or believes it in its interest to try to make the other side believe it believes it, then there are real incentives to increase strategic forces.

[16] McGeorge Bundy, "How to Wind Down the Nuclear Arms Race," *New York Times Magazine* (Nov. 16, 1969), 152. "The neglected truth about the present strategic arms race . . . is that in terms of international political behavior that race has now become almost completely irrelevant." (Bundy, "To Cap the Volcano," *Foreign Affairs*, 48 [Oct. 1969], 9). A similar position is taken by Hans Morgenthau, "The Four Paradoxes of Nuclear Strategy," *American Political Science Review*, 58 (March 1964), 23-35.

[17] Alternatively, an arms race could result even if the decision-makers feel the extra weapons do not help them in international politics if they have little control over the military. But neither Morgenthau nor Bundy takes this position.

15

COERCION IN POLITICS AND STRATEGY

John W. Chapman

To both political and strategic theorists it may seem at first sight that the place of coercion in politics and in strategy is radically different. We do know that politics may be predominantly either persuasive or coercive. But has not the purpose of genuine political thought—as distinguished from that form of political thinking that we call ideological—been to design institutions that would minimize the need for coercion, and by so doing to place coercion itself in the service of freedom and social rationality? Is not the ultimate justification of political and legal coercion that without it moral freedom and other goods cannot be had, and so the possibility of an even greater freedom—which anarchy is said to promise—is only a dangerous illusion? Strategic thought and action, on the other hand, presumably has to do with coercion essentially, with its rational uses, with how to use force economically, or with how best to resist and deflect coercive intentions and actions.

We tend to think of strategy as the art of imposing one's will on adversaries or enemies; an analogy with the game of chess readily comes to mind. But politics is, or at least at its best should be, the art of eliciting a general will, the formation of a moral balance or consensus. The aim of politics is integration of apparently conflicting interests in the light of a common appreciation of justice. The strategist aims at dislocation, disintegration, and defeat of real opponents. Hence political and strategic activity seem irreducibly different.

My purpose is to show that this way of thinking about politics and strategy is no longer adequate. It is a way of thinking that arose in a legal civilization, in which nations came to organize themselves as sovereign states. These nations shared a common political culture and were locked in a balance of power. Our strategic tradition derives directly from our political tradition; the purpose of military coercion was the preservation of political independence and security. Now, however, the new weaponry and technology have imposed on the world a condition of political interdependence much more intense than that to which we have been accustomed. Essentially different political cultures have been brought into competition and into question. The legal and individualistic culture of the West confronts the more ethical and communitarian political traditions of the East. And in between stands ambiguous Russia, neither wholly Western nor wholly Eastern, and regarded as a threat by both. In this situation new forms of coercion have become possible, forms of coercion that are essentially political rather than military. We are in fact living through a revolution in strategic thought and analysis, the outcome of which is already becoming clear, namely, a unification of political and strategic theory. In our technically unified world we can no longer afford to think of politics and strategy as separate and distinct spheres of theory and activity. We sense and feel that a more unified way of thinking is required; we do not know yet what this is to be.

INCONGRUITY IN STRATEGIC THINKING

Signs of the coming unification of political and strategic theory are already here in abundance. Strategic thinking and language have become politicized. To describe what they are talking about, strategic theorists now quite properly and casually use many concepts that are obviously political in nature, such as policy, will, belief, art, signal, and escalation. They speak of national strategy, indirect strategy, political value and balance, crisis management, blackmail, compellance, coercive persuasion, coercive diplomacy, coercive escalation, coercive warfare, and revolutionary war. They speak not only of deterrence and limited war, but also of containment, strategic responsibility, political parity, and moral balance or consensus. That strategic conceptions have become increasingly political in their derivation is, I think, plain. However, this is not to say that strategic thought and analysis have become as thoroughly political as they may need to become. The unification of political and strategic theory so far remains partial and incomplete.

Our strategic thinkers continue to use an array of analogies when they wish to characterize the nature of their studies. Some hold that strategy is like economics, that strategic theory is essentially an application of economic theory; and there surely is an economic dimension to strategic thinking. However, others compare strategic behavior to bargaining or even to fencing, and they too have captured an important aspect of strategy. Still others speak of strategy in terms of systems design or as a form of diplomacy. As compared with the military clarity and simplicity of classical strategic thought, modern thinking has become patently complex, and our thinkers, despite their analytical acuity, seem somewhat bemused. They are fully aware that strategy no longer has to do with war plans only, that it has somehow become deeply political in nature; they seem less certain as to the origins and the significance of this momentous development.

I shall begin by looking at important tendencies in contemporary strategic thinking that suggest its incomplete political awareness. Then I shall examine the political thought and experience of modern times, ultimately with a view to their comparison with the shape of strategic thought and with emergent patterns in world politics. It is our concern with the political implications of nuclear weaponry that has given our strategic thinking its political cast, and all of our strategists recognize that military plans and political policies are almost entirely interlocked. However, the new weapons have structural as well as policy implications, and my thought is that we may learn something about their structural implications from our domestic political experience. Moreover, in a world composed of disparate political cultures, these structural implications may take the form of political processes that are profoundly disequilibrating in their impact on these cultures.

Most of what I have to say about our political and strategic experience may be easily grasped by keeping in mind those two concepts basic to political theory and analysis, the concepts of structure and process. For the novelty of strategy in our time is that it is concerned not so much with the efficient use of military force or potential as it is with the design of postures and configurations of force for the purposes of shaping and using, or averting or controlling what are essentially political processes and deeply coercive in nature. To think of strategy as having to do only or mainly with coercive policies is an indication of an imperfect understanding of our situation.

STRATEGY AS POLICY SCIENCE

What is contemporary strategic thinking all about? What is it exactly that our strategic theorists think they are doing? They are not quite sure themselves. For example, Bernard Brodie is inclined to take a rather classical view of the strategist's work. Strategy is comparable to economics in that it is involved with the effective allocation and use of military resources to attain political ends that are pretty much given. One wonders how appropriate this military-means and political-ends form of thinking is in today's world.

General André Beaufre also invokes the economics analogy to explain his conception of strategy, and yet more than any other contemporary thinker, he considers strategy to have become thoroughly political and hence must be devoted to understanding coercion as a total phenomenon. He recognizes that a strategy must be based on a political diagnosis, and so it is doubly disconcerting when the General compares strategic activity to fencing. Just as he appears to be on the verge of dealing with the political implications of the world's strategic structure, Beaufre veers off to reflections on the ideological nature of politics. Throughout his work, General Beaufre thinks of strategy as the dialectic of opposing wills, and he assumes that in the world today essentially similar systems confront one another. His concepts of "wills" and "systems" prevent him from seeing that the strategist must take account of differences in political culture and the asymetrical strategies to which these differences give rise.

Raymond Aron is prepared to equate strategy with the total conduct of a nation's foreign policy, a clearly politically expansive interpretation of the strategic art. Rather more narrow is Thomas Schelling's conception of strategy as the art of coercion based on the threat or the infliction of pain. In a brilliant piece of political analysis, Alexander George, with his eye on the policy maker, displays the uses and limitations of coercive diplomacy. Other strategic thinkers, such as Klaus Knorr, make much of the role of will in the exercise of military power, an emphasis that is to be contrasted with George's specification of the situational constraints on the use of power.

Michael Howard regards classical strategic thinking as finished, for now the strategist has to deal with the interdependence of strategy, international relations, and technologies. But Howard thinks that General Beaufre goes dangerously too far in his insistence upon the political dimensions of strategy, to the point where he would reduce policy-making to strategic planning.

Many thinkers advise that to be effective, coercive threats must be coupled with inducements in the form of credible offers, that is to say, that in the world as it is coercive and persuasive policies should be tightly linked. Alexander George even speaks of coercive persuasion, an expression which in itself fuses the political and the military dimensions of policy.[1]

[1] These observations are based on the following works. Bernard Brodie, *Strategy in the Missile Age* (Princeton, N.J.: Princeton University Press, 1965); *Escalation and the Nuclear Option* (Princeton, N.J.: Princeton University Press, 1966); "Strategy," *International Encyclopedia of the Social Sciences*. André Beaufre, *An Introduction to Strategy,* trans. R. H. Barry (New York: Praeger, 1965); *Strategy of Action,* trans. R. H. Barry (London: Faber and Faber, 1967). Raymond Aron, "The Evolution of Modern Strategic Thought," in *Problems of Modern Strategy: Part One* (London: The Institute for Strategic Studies, February 1969). Thomas C. Schelling, *Arms and Influence* (New Haven, Conn.: Yale University Press, 1966). Alexander L. George, David K. Hall, and William E. Simons, *The Limits of Coercive Diplomacy: Laos, Cuba, Vietnam* (Boston, Mass.: Little, Brown, 1971). Klaus Knorr, *On the Uses of Military Power in the Nuclear Age* (Princeton, N.J.: Princeton University Press, 1966); *Military Power and Potential* (Lexington, Mass.: D. C. Heath, 1970). Michael Howard, *Studies in War and Peace* (London: Temple Smith, 1970). Some of the
(continued)

Now it seems to me that what these differing perspectives on strategy all have in common is the notion that strategic planning is essentially a policy science. As Henry Kissinger once said, "It is the task of strategic doctrine to translate power into policy."[2] This statement is certainly correct as far as it goes, and it may well be that strategists naturally tend to assume a policy science stance, for they are in the business of giving advice on what to do. It would be a mistake, however, to confine strategic theory and analysis to the perspective of policy science.

That strategic thinking has become politicized in itself suggests the appropriateness of ways of thinking that are fundamental to political theory and political science. Furthermore, the very concept of policy science seems to convey a sense of deliberateness and rationality, even a sense of security and manageability, whereas recognition of the political dimensions of strategy should alert us immediately to unpleasant possibilities. Trends and processes that are political in nature, unlike their social and economic counterparts, tend to be volatile and subject to collisions and conjunctures, reversals and discontinuities. This is the case even in well ordered polities. In a world where ideologies clash and cultures differ, and where polities press upon one another, some of which are marked by grave internal tensions, one must anticipate even more serious volatility.

As contrasted with the policy orientation toward strategy, a more thoroughly political appreciation of our strategic situation may help us to avoid surprises as well as to engineer outcomes.

THE POLITICAL SIGNIFICANCE OF WEAPONRY

As I see it, the deployment of nuclear weaponry has given to world politics a strategic structure or framework that comes to something more than the constraints imposed by considerations of balance of power, and that comes to something rather less than the

---

political dimensions of strategic analysis are dealt with in my "American Strategic Thinking," *Air University Review* XVIII (January-February 1967), 25-33, and in my "Political Forecasting and Strategic Planning," (WP-70-3; Holloman AFB, N.M.: Office of Research Analyses, OAR, May 1970; also in *International Studies Quarterly,* September, 1971).

[2] Henry A. Kissinger, *Nuclear Weapons and Foreign Policy* (New York: Harper & Row, 1957), 7.

constraints upon political processes that we associate with the concept of sovereignty. If we compare this strategic framework, bipolar nuclear stability, with the constitutional and legal framework of a sovereign state, perhaps it may best be regarded as a condition of imperfect sovereignty.

What are the political implications of this condition? In particular, what are the processes, especially the coercive processes, that are distinctive to and encouraged by this new strategic structure? Beyond identifying these processes, we need to ask whether they are self-equilibrating and mutually neutralizing, or if not, whether they are subject to control and how much. In the politics of national states there is a tendency for coercion to be displaced by persuasion. Is a similar tendency at work in our imperfectly sovereign world, or must we expect discontinuous and possibly even sudden changes as national threat advantages operate in a shearing rather than a canceling manner?

These are the sorts of questions that I hope a comparative examination of our political and strategic experience will help to answer, and the answers should take us further down the road toward the needed unification of political and strategic theory.

THE MORAL CONSEQUENCES OF SOVEREIGNTY

Let us start with an analysis of what is perhaps the most important structural innovation in Western political experience, the introduction and consolidation of sovereignty. What this did was to put an end to the preemptive instabilities that Hobbes had recognized as the crucial feature of the "state of nature."

The invention of sovereignty amounted initially to a centralization of coercion, to a monopolization of legitimate violence and threat of violence; and this meant that men and groups no longer had to resort to coercion or compulsion to protect themselves against one another. Strategically speaking, the sovereign became the only member of society to possess "Type II Deterrence," to use Herman Kahn's nomenclature.[3] That is to say, the sovereign could

---

[3] "Type II Deterrence is defined as using strategic threats to deter an enemy from engaging in very provocative acts, other than a direct attack on the United States itself." Kahn, *On Thermonuclear War* (Second Edition with Index; Princeton, N.J.: Princeton University Press, 1961), 126.

deter not only direct attacks against himself and his government, the equivalent of having Kahn's "Type I Deterrence." The sovereign could use his military forces also to deter provocative or coercive threats or actions by any other member of society against another. "The greatest triumph of the Tudors was ultimately successful assertion of a royal monopoly of violence both public and private, an achievement which profoundly altered not only the nature of politics, but also the quality of daily life."[4] Later governments acquired a police force, analogous to Kahn's "Type III Deterrence," when use of the army to control public disturbances proved to be overwhelmingly impractical.[5]

Although Hobbes himself apparently had expected the beneficial consequences of sovereignty, beyond security, to be mainly economic, other developmental processes were unleashed as well; and these political and moral processes culminated in the complementary ideas of democracy and justice, in Rousseau's conception of the state in which justice was the expression of the will of its citizens and not merely the dictate of a modernizing sovereign. As T. H. Green was later to argue against Hobbes, "will not force" was the basis of the state.

Coerciveness was not, of course, abolished immediately from the relations of men, neither by the installation of sovereignty nor by growth toward constitutional democracy. Some men were more coercible than others, and so coerciveness remained in the form of what John Rawls analytically refers to as "threat advantage." And the threat advantages possessed by some enabled them to distort in practice conceptions of justice in their favor. But in the course of time, in some fortunate countries, more egalitarian conceptions of justice arose as power became equalized through political organization and economic development. As differentials in threat advantage reduced, politics became less coercive and more persuasive.

---

[4] Lawrence Stone, *The Crisis of the Aristocracy* (Oxford: Oxford University Press, 1965), 200.

[5] According to Hans J. Morgenthau, "The search for a modern police force was the result of this dilemma, foreshadowing the dilemma with which the availability of nuclear weapons confronts modern nations in their relations with each other." "The Police in Their Political Setting," in his *Truth and Power: Essays of a Decade, 1960-70* (New York: Praeger, 1970), 293-314, p. 300. For continental experience with police, see Brian Chapman, *Police State* (London: Pall Mall Press, 1970).

The original centralization of coercion in the sovereign thus ultimately led to its minimization, and coercive politics were replaced gradually by processes of persuasion, negotiation, and bargaining —the competitive politics of pluralism—all more or less informed by common conceptions of justice. In the longer run the creation of the sovereign state had made possible the emergence of constitutional democracy and the pragmatic and cumulative politics with which that form of government is associated and which it fosters. In an even longer view, these developments were the fulfillments of the principle on which Western civilization is grounded, individual freedom under law.

REVERSION TO IDEOLOGY AND COERCION

Hobbes had also expected that his recommendation would put a stop to the menace of ideological "fits" and warfare, and he further expected that the European sovereigns would competitively enforce upon one another responsible and liberal behavior. Constrained by the dynamics of the balance of power, their strategic ambitions would be mutually frustrating and yet salutary in encouraging their devotion to economic advance and their respect for individual freedom. In these hopes of Hobbes we find our greatest disappointments. For a time, as he had expected, both political and economic rationality advanced together. But in the twentieth century, economic and cultural disparities combined to generate national ambitions that were ideologically charged. International competition ceased to promote political and economic liberalism; instead it brought ideological panic.

The return of ideological thinking and coercive politics began with the tensions connected with industrialization and democratization. The reaction to economic liberalism took the form of anti-individualistic ideologies, those of socialism and nationalism, and the latter brought down Hobbes' European system in the catastrophe of the first world war.

The European nations, locked into strategies of preemptive mobilization, stumbled back into the state of nature and hence found themselves in a war that none desired. The trench and the machine gun ruined Napoleonic concepts of strategy, and the spirit of nationalism submerged von Clausewitz's theory of war in the doctrine of attrition, the political purposelessness of which could not bring the fighting to a halt. Only exhaustion could accomplish that. War had escaped from control by political purpose, and the sovereigns could not heed von Schlieffen's voice, that should his plan fail to bring swiftly a decision against France, then the only responsible thing to do was to negotiate an end to hostilities.

In the outcome, the first world war fostered even more deeply illiberal forms of political thought than had the internal divisions and despairs of the nations. The discipline that the war had imposed on the nations was in itself sufficient to incline men toward socialism. Moreover, those countries that had been revealed as hopelessly backward determined to catch up with the rest. In Russia communism in practice became a program for coercive industrialization, and Mussolini's brand of fascism was in many ways an effort to bring Italy into the twentieth century. The appearance of a dynamic communism in the Soviet Union provoked an amalgamation of nationalism and socialism in Germany, and these coercive ideologies collided in the second world war.

Looking back, the meaning of our political experience comes down pretty much to this. Liberal political theory and practice had as their objective the reduction of political and legal coercion to that minimum essential for moral freedom and economic growth, and where conditions were favorable these aims were achieved in the form of societies whose values—individual freedom, economic rationality, and justice—were in stable equilibrium.[6] However, the free play of market forces was experienced by many as oppressive, and to them socialism appeared to be the road to freedom. Such was Marx's message, and it is noteworthy that he put little stock in coercion; he was no Jacobin. Rather he thought that the advance of industry itself, combined with his understanding of the dynamics of capitalism, would bring about a change of character and consciousness naturally and rather spontaneously. For Marx the socialist revolution was a process and not an event. Marxism did not take hold in those societies in which the liberal equilibrium had become established. But it did have great appeal for a society whose political culture was more deeply religious and ethical in content than those

[6] On the liberal equilibrium of values, see my "Natural Rights and Justice in Liberalism," in D. D. Raphael, ed., *Political Theory and the Rights of Man* (London: Macmillan, 1967), 27-42.

of Western Europe, a society more in need of a vision than ready
for an equilibrium. And so it was Lenin, determined to bring his
nation to the fore, who divorced socialism from democracy and
made that ideology indelibly coercive.[7] The chain reaction against
liberalism inevitably followed.

For Lenin, political thinking became, as it was also later to become for Hitler, a form of strategic thinking, the point of which was
to manipulate, or to blackmail and coerce, or if need be to destroy
your adversaries. For adversaries were enemies, quite beyond persuasion or conversion to your vision, and bent upon your own destruction. This ideological conversion of political into strategic
thinking constituted not only a revolution in Western political
thought; it marked the beginning of that fusion of coercive intent
and nationalistic sentiment that erupted in the second world war;
and it meant the demise of military rationality and classical strategy. Lenin's desertion from Marxism amounted to a militarization
of political thought. This is the revolution that the arrival of nuclear
weaponry is now reversing as strategic thinking becomes embedded
once again in political philosophy and analysis. The ideological
warfare of the first and second world wars marks an interlude between our imperfectly sovereign world and the world of Hobbes
and classical strategy.

A WORD ON CLASSICAL STRATEGY

By classical strategy[8] I mean the way of thinking about the
uses of military power that arose in European civilization as that
civilization became organized as sovereign states. Classical strategy
does not constitute a kind of universal strategic logic. It is rather a
special strategic tradition, one that could arise only in the context of
Western political philosophy and organization. In the East, where
societies lacked the legal rigidity peculiar to the West, effective
strategies were and continue to be both more protracted and moral

---

[7] "That ideology might be used to hold a great party tightly together, to
justify its elimination of all rivals, and to impose its will on the people
generally—this idea of it is not Marxist but Leninist." John Plamenatz,
Ideology (London: Macmillan, 1971), 141.

[8] See Michael Howard, "The Classical Strategists," in his *Studies in War
and Peace*, 154-83.

in nature, as the careers of Mao and Gandhi demonstrate.[9] A sovereign state, especially an industrialized one, provides a target for military action, its capitol, that is lacking in semisovereign and backward societies. Classical strategy is the military philosophy of liberalism.

Unlike the coercive ideologists, Lenin and Hitler, the classical strategists (by whom I mean not only thinkers of the last century such as Henri Jomini and Karl von Clausewitz, but also men of the twentieth such as Basil Liddell Hart) were occupied primarily with the rationally limited uses of coercion and force. Ideological warfare would have horrified them as much as it did Hobbes; they took for granted a Europe that had a common political culture. Military history and, in the case of Clausewitz, Hegelian philosophy were sources of inspiration. Napoleon's campaigns in particular came in for intensive scrutiny. Classical strategy is the theory of the uses of professionalized and controlled violence in the service of political purpose. Clausewitz took a dim view of the use of guerillas, so effective against Napoleon in Spain, and he did not encourage escalation to extremes.

The strategic art consisted in pulling off a decisive battle for a reasonable political objective, as Marlborough had done at Blenheim, as Napoleon was to do time and time again, and Bismarck after him. Except for Liddell Hart, the view was that strategic operations were a direct and concentrated business. Unlike the continental strategists, he favored an indirect approach, more coercive than compulsive, the aim of which was to dislocate and paralyze the enemy rather than to attempt a Napoleonic knock-out. His models were Scipio against Hannibal and Sherman in Georgia, not the Franco-Prussian War.

This is to say that classical strategy was essentially military or operational strategy, the employment of force or coercion, directly or indirectly, to impose your will upon an opponent. Military capabilities were conceived as means to directly envisaged and specific political ends; war was the continuation of policy. The existence of

---

[9] On Mao, see Scott A. Boorman, *The Protracted Game: A Wei-Ch'i Interpretation of Maoist Revolutionary Strategy* (New York: Oxford University Press, 1969), and for an analysis of Gandhi's techniques of moral coercion, see Arne Naess, *Gandhi and the Nuclear Age* (Totowa, N.J.: The Bedminister Press, 1965).

these capabilities provided the context for diplomacy, and from time to time these capabilities would be brought into play when coercive threats proved insufficient, and the issue could be settled, or the balance maintained or restored, only through compulsion. Strategy was thought of as the coercive servant of politics, not as the coercive framework that shaped and directed political forces. Military power served to protect and to advance national interests, and since a prime national interest was political independence, power need not even be used if it could but be astutely manipulated, as it was by that nation which for so long held the balance, Britain.

Classical strategy went bankrupt in the first and second world wars and was finally rendered obsolete by the new military technology. From a strategic point of view, World War I may be regarded as the result of the failure of Type I deterrents, which led to a thoroughly unclassical war of attrition, sustained by nationalistic emotion. In this perspective, the second world war was brought on by the failure of deterrence Types II and III to withstand and refute Hitler's blackmailing strategy. It also became a war of attrition, prolonged by ideological impulse and fear. These were not the sorts of war that Hobbes or Hegel or Clausewitz had had in mind.

The lessons of the world wars were not lost on American strategic thinkers, and since the end of World War II and the coming of the atomic bomb they have had two objectives uppermost in mind: To avoid strategic configurations that would prompt preemptive attack, and to avoid exposure to atomic blackmail. The strategies of deterrence and containment added up to a grand strategy of controlled political evolution, a strategy in which we are relying upon political dynamics to accomplish the objective of an ideological transformation of the adversary. Both this objective and the manner in which we seek it are quite foreign to the world of classical strategy and its reliance upon military power and potential within the bounds of a common political culture. Although we were not fully aware of it at the time, the formulation of the strategies of containment and deterrence amounted to a recognition of the imperfectly sovereign nature of the world, and in such a world the presence of Type I deterrents means there is no place for Napoleonic strategy. Operational strategy is displaced by planning for deterrence and calculation of the political implications of strategic configurations.

THE POLITICAL IMPLICATIONS OF STRATEGIC CONFIGURATIONS

Despite the inclination to think of strategy as a policy science, an inclination that accords well with the Western strategic tradition, in fact contemporary American strategic thinking increasingly resembles Western political philosophy in that it is concerned with the ways in which structures shape processes, in this case with the ways in which strategic configurations may influence both military and political dynamics. Our new strategists are much closer in their modes of thought to Hobbes and Hegel than they are to Napoleon and Clausewitz; they are analytic designers, political forecasters and engineers, not generals. Although the classical concept of strategy lingers on in their definitions of the art, it has not in practice greatly influenced what our strategic theorists have done.

Given the presence of nuclear weapons, the first task of strategy was to prevent war, not to plan for or to wage it. Hence the remarkable development of the theory and practice of deterrence. Here I have in mind in particular the work of Albert Wohlstetter and his associates and successors at the RAND Corporation.[10] Their objective has been to design a strategic configuration that was militarily stable and to maintain such a configuration.[11] So far, through close attention to the strategic implications of emerging technologies, in this endeavor we have been successful. Mutual deterrence at the strategic level is the foundation of which I have called imperfect sovereignty; the world consuls dare not attack one another, and no one dares attack either of them.

In the job of designing against nuclear coercion and blackmail we have become less resolute. Apparently the American public and politicians have found it easier to grasp the notion of strategic nuclear deterrence than they have the concept of the political implica-

---

[10] The formative statements are: A. J. Wohlstetter, F. S. Hoffman, R. J. Lutz, and H. S. Rowen, *Selection and Use of Strategic Air Bases* (R-266; Santa Monica, Calif.: The RAND Corporation, April 1954); and A. J. Wohlstetter, F. S. Hoffman, and H. S. Rowen, *Protecting U.S. Power to Strike Back in the 1950's and 1960's* (R-290; Santa Monica, Calif.: The RAND Corporation, 1 September 1956).

[11] See Wohlstetter, "Theory and Opposed-Systems Design," XII *The Journal of Conflict Resolution* (September 1968), 302-31.

tions of strategic confrontations, although the essentials of the theory of atomic blackmail were set forth over a decade ago[12] and have since been thoroughly elaborated. The concept of minimum or finite deterrence appealed to many. In fact, we were prepared to engage in what was tantamount to an act of unilateral disarmament by permitting the Russians to go for and to achieve a posture of strategic parity.

But in the nuclear era it may not be good enough only to design against the direct use of strategic weapons, to forestall a general war by maintaining a credible Type I deterrent. If our grand strategy is to be successful, we must seek political independence and integrity for our allies and for ourselves, and that means we must also prevent the coercive use of nuclear weapons to deny their potential for blackmail. In a world of imperfect sovereignty, defeat is far more likely to come in the form of political and moral disintegration than in an atomic holocaust. Our strategists have understood that coercion was more to be feared than compulsion, and so they broke with our strategic tradition but failed to carry the public with them.

ON THERMONUCLEAR WAR REVISITED

At this stage of the analysis it will be useful to look again at Herman Kahn's *On Thermonuclear War*. The significance of that book does not appear to have been appreciated at the time of its publication. Rather, people were stunned by Kahn's willingness to contemplate nuclear war and to analyze its consequences. Perhaps because they continued to think of strategy in classical terms they did not attend to what Kahn was really trying to say, that nuclear weapons had brought into the world a new form of warfare, the meaning of which could be discerned in Hitlerian blackmail.

As I now see it, Kahn, an instinctive Hobbesian, was so worried by the coercive implications of unfavorable strategic configurations that he was prepared to advocate what amounted to the acquisition of full world sovereignty by the United States. And he doubted whether we would have the will requisite to do so.

---

[12] On blackmailing, see Daniel Ellsberg, *The Art of Coercion: A Study of Threats in Economic Conflict and War* (Boston: Lowell Institute, March 1959), and his "The Theory and Practice of Blackmail" (P-3883; Santa Monica, Calif.: The RAND Corporation, July 1968).

Should the Soviet Union obtain a position of superiority, Kahn reasoned, and all this required was that we fail to maintain adequate Type II deterrence, the political consequences would be dire. "The accommodations by the threatened nations would be close to automatic." The Soviets would have ". . . an almost incredible advantage at some bargaining tables." If all the United States has is a Type I deterrent, that is, if we assume a posture of minimum or finite deterrence, then it will be possible for the Soviet leaders to engage in convincing blackmail, and therefore, Kahn said, ". . . it is absolutely essential that we do not allow a position to develop that tempts such action." Looking ahead, he thought that, "Because we may have so little Type II Deterrence, it will not be necessary for the Russians to threaten or blackmail our allies; the threat will be automatic and dominate even 'friendly' negotiations." The purpose of Kahn's attempt, early in the book, to persuade people that a nuclear war could be fought and survived becomes clear when we read that ". . . mutual belief in the automatic annihilation theory is an open invitation to Munich-type blackmail."[13]

Kahn's evaluation of the coercive uses of military power flowed directly from his appreciation of the structured nature of nuclear confrontation, that deterrence is not only a matter of degrees but also of dimensions. "The main objective of our military forces is to protect ourselves and influence others. This is sometimes forgotten. In particular, we do not really want to destroy the enemy; we want to coerce him." Kahn was not yet thinking in terms of the concept of controlled or coerced political evolution; his strategic concept is not yet that of ideological transformation, but he is on the way. "We attempt to *regulate* his behavior by having effective Type II and Type III deterrence."

Doubts about our resolution and our understanding of the dynamics of coercion had earlier led Kahn to say, ". . . I strongly suspect the necessary efforts are not going to be made." If we did not make the effort necessary to regulate the behavior of the Russians, then an unpleasant conclusion followed. "I think we can expect much firmer, confident, and imaginative behavior, if not audacious and reckless conduct, from Khrushchev and his successors than we had from Stalin."[14]

---

[13] Kahn, *op. cit.,* 98, 98, 287, 463, and 562.
[14] *Ibid.,* 302, 302, 160, and 348.

In the event, Cuba 1962, this turned out to be a remarkably accurate prediction. Since then, however, the Russians have been more circumspect and cautious, except for their invasion of Czechoslovakia in 1968, and even that may be interpreted as an act of caution, the purpose of which was to prevent a drastic shift in the political balance of power. Later we shall ask why this has been the case and whether we may expect their caution to continue.

In retrospect it seems to me that if Kahn had gotten his way, if we had indeed constructed and maintained the full range of deterrents that he recommended, then the United States would have achieved a position in the world comparable not to that of a Roman Consul, but to that of an Hobbesian sovereign. Our power would have functioned widely, deeply, and almost automatically to deter coercive threats and behavior. I do not mean, of course, nor did Kahn say, that our strategic superiority would or could be used to impose upon others our political principles and practices. Political maturity cannot be imposed; it can only be fostered.

Given the form of sovereignty that Hobbes and Kahn had in mind, we could have relied with confidence upon the operation of those economic, political, and moral processes that had been central in Western history. We could have anticipated that ideological erosion and transformation would have proceeded in an unhindered fashion as strategic constraints released pluralizing forces.

The way would have been open for the emergence in the world of what Henry Kissinger refers to as a new "moral balance."[15] As ideological compulsions weakened and declined, it might have been the story of from Hobbes to Rousseau and beyond all over again, and it yet may be. But it must be apparent to both political and strategic theorists that Kissinger's Rousseau has no robust *Leviathan,* upon whose shoulders to stand. In consequence the American program for controlled evolution has met with audacious resistance from the Soviet Union, offensively in Cuba in 1962 and defensively in 1968 with the invasion of Czechoslovakia. Ironically, our essentially Marxist aspiration has been countered by a Leninist resort to coercion.

[15] Henry A. Kissinger, *American Foreign Policy: Three Essays* (New York: W. W. Norton, 1969), 81. "Our goal should be to build a moral consensus which can make a pluralistic world creative rather than destructive." *Ibid.,* 84.

IMPERFECT SOVEREIGNTY AND COERCIVE POLITICS

American failure to adopt a fully Hobbesian strategic posture—and it may have been only a dream of Kahn's, not a real option—has meant the domination of world politics by two divergent processes that have yet fully to work themselves out in what may prove to be a dangerously disequilibrating manner. The unhappy truth may turn out to be that imperfect, consular sovereignty is not just a slower road to the political and moral benefits that full sovereignty has to offer, to Kissinger's new moral balance. Although the military balance between the consuls at present is stable, the political balance is not stable and it would be imprudent to expect it to become so.

Imperfect sovereignty, by which I mean the absence of truly effective Types II and III deterrent forces, has resulted in forms of military and political activity that are deeply coercive; to the analysis of these pressures and processes much of recent strategic thinking has been devoted. On the other hand, our retention of Type I deterrence not only ensures bipolar nuclear stability; this strategic configuration releases and provides scope for the operation of important developmental forces that impinge on the Soviet Union as coercive pressures. We are in a situation that is a kind of contest in which the superpowers are both using and defending themselves against coercive pressures for the purpose of altering the political balance, and ultimately the moral balance, of the world. The world's strategic structure encourages coercive forms of politics that must be understood and mastered if there is to be any chance at all for the erosion of ideology in the direction of an international general will.

In this contest, the position of the Soviet Union would seem to be peculiarly difficult. From the West there comes steady pressure for greater economic rationality, and with it implications for democratization and accommodation. From the East come political antagonism and cultural revolution, and these pressures cannot but impede liberalization. It would seem that whichever way the Soviet Union leans, the political balance tips against her. Accommodation with the West and acceptance of Western political culture mean deeper alienation from China and further loss of command over communist movements, even as the Soviet Union would itself become a more dynamic and powerful society. On the other hand, ideological competition with and neutralization of China means retardation of economic growth both in the Soviet Union and in Eastern Europe along with further decline in political attraction for the West. The signs of indecision that the Soviet leadership displayed in the Czechoslovakian affair may well be the product of these competing coercive pressures to which they are exposed. The Soviet Union is in a situation that encourages her acquisition of strategic strength to compensate for her political weakness, and in our imperfectly sovereign world strategic strength provides the basis for pursuing a coercive politics of blackmail. In the older world, the world of classical strategy and balance of power politics, the stronger nation could expect the others to unite against her. In the nuclear era, even without the use of overt and explicit strategic threats, the acquisition of strategic strength holds out the hope of fragmenting the opposition and inducing individualized accommodation.

THE THEORY AND PRACTICE OF BLACKMAIL

An understanding of coercive politics depends first of all on an appreciation of the nature of blackmail, on a grasp of the ways in which threats and commitments are interrelated in what is essentially a bargaining process. Convincing blackmail depends upon presenting the victim with an acceptable combination of threats and offers, and upon persuading him that his failure to comply will surely bring execution of the threats, costly though this may be to the blackmailer. Blackmailing and resistance to it bring into life a host of Machiavellian impulses including deception, pretence, manipulation of image, reliance upon reputation, displays of determination and motivation, and sheer skill at cumulative intimidation, that is, coercive escalation that does not provoke eruption. Our strategic analysts, in their exploration of the dynamics of blackmail, have gone far toward elaborating a theory of political coercion. Machiavelli has joined Hobbes and Rousseau on the political stage.

The transformation of American strategic thinking into a theory of coercive politics owes much to the inspiration of Hans Speier and

Thomas Schelling, who advanced respectively the concept of the political value of nuclear weapons and the conception of diplomacy as the art of coercion. Landmarks in the evolution of this aspect of strategic thought include the following contributions. Fred Iklé analyzed the ways in which the very process of negotiation involves changing expectations and changing values attached to outcomes. He showed how Stalin and his successors, from a position of manifest weakness, managed to con and to persuade the West of the depth of their commitment to Eastern Europe. Their success is an illustration of the blackmailer's art at its finest; the victim gives in not so much because of the intensity of the threat to which he is exposed; rather, he complies because he has been persuaded to accept the blackmailer's estimate of the stakes.

Apparently, successful pretence on the part of the Russians led them to attempt political coercion through strategic deception, and when this move failed to bring political gains in Berlin, Khrushchev tried to tip the political balance by installing missiles in Cuba. He argued that their purpose was defensive only. That time we did not accept Russian evaluations of the situation, called their bluff, and forced their retreat with threats that in the end amounted to an ultimatum.

Khrushchev's techniques of strategic decption were laid bare by Arnold Horelick and Myron Rush, who also introduced the concept of political parity, an important way of operationalizing the concept of the political value of weaponry. Political parity differs from military parity to the extent that there is a disparity between the opponents' levels of critical risk, a concept which had been developed by Daniel Ellsberg. A lower level of critical risk exposes one to blackmail by the adversary, even though one may possess in reality strategic superiority, let alone a measure of marginal superiority. Willingness to take chances confers a threat advantage which Khrushchev attempted to exploit in Cuba. Real superiority, both strategic and local, skillfully deployed and escalated, enabled his defeat.

More recently Robert Jervis has exposed the significance of reputation and image and the ways in which these are anchored and manipulated, along lines that Schelling had marked out. And finally Alexander George and his associates have demonstrated the dependence of coercive diplomacy, in its defensive form at least, upon the structure of the situation in which this strategy is attempted.[16]

Beyond doubt the work of these strategists has greatly advanced our understanding of the nature of coercive policies and processes, and to that extent they have much reduced the dangers that could otherwise arise from ineptness or misanticipation in the face of overt blackmail. Still, our understanding of the dynamics of coercion remains incomplete, and given the coercive pressures to which the Russians are being subjected, vast uncertainties lie ahead.

Although Horelick and Rush had been inclined to think that it would be reasonable for the Soviets to accept a position of strategic inferiority, instead they have chosen to attain strategic parity, even though we did not employ our superiority in an offensive manner. This means that they have in actuality obtained a position of political superiority, given our presumed differences in levels of critical risk. That is to say, the Soviet leaders have acquired what is surely a superb opportunity for blackmail. And yet they have not resorted to manifest blackmail to anything like the extent that one might have expected from the perspective of Kahn's *Thermonuclear War*. Rather, they have elected to build up their strategic forces, to probe, and to expand their global capabilities, as they continue to try to disengage us from our European allies.

It may be that overt blackmail in the shape of strategic threats no longer seems an attractive option. Affluence, including nuclear affluence, may incline one against taking the kinds of chances that Khrushchev was once prepared to take. Or it may be that the Soviet Union is simply prepared to go about improving its image and to rely upon disintegrative forces within both the United States and the

[16] Consult the following: Hans Speier, "The Political Value of Arms," in his *Force and Folly: Essays on Foreign Affairs and the History of Ideas* (Cambridge, Mass.: The M.I.T. Press, 1969), 32-49; Thomas C. Schelling, *Arms and Influence;* Fred Charles Iklé, *How Nations Negotiate* (New York: Harper & Row, 1964); Arnold L. Horelick and Myron Rush, *Strategic Power and Soviet Foreign Policy* (Chicago, Ill.: University of Chicago Press, 1966); Robert Jervis, *The Logic of Images in International Relations* (Princeton, N.J.: Princeton University Press, 1970); Alexander L. George, *et al., The Limits of Coercive Diplomacy.* For a history of the period under review, see George H. Quester, *Nuclear Diplomacy: The First Twenty-Five Years* (New York: Dunellen, 1970).

Western alliance. Blackmail that is slow and subtle and that points toward changing attitudes may be much more effective than threats which galvanize the intended victims. In this process, when the final crystalization comes, when the political balance shifts and accommodation seems rational, there are no moments of crisis at which these outcomes would be starkly seen for what they are and hence forestalled.

Moreover, the Soviet leaders must be impressed by the results of that ingenius combination of brute and moral coercion, that astute blending of Mao and Gandhi, developed by the North Vietnamese. "That the liberals are now in a state of complete intellectual disarray is one of the great successes of revolutionary war in world strategy. That a defeat in Vietnam could lead to disruption of American society, and consequently of the Western alliance, could make that particular revolutionary war one of the decisive wars of history."[17] In view of this possibility or prospect the sensible thing for the Soviet Union is to take it easy, to negotiate about but not to reach a strategic settlement, to continue to build and to deploy but not in so menacing a manner as to create a determined response by the United States, and to work toward that day when the United States, despite its possession of a secure second strike capability, can clearly no longer guarantee the nuclear security of Western Europe. Thus the Soviet leaders could hope to extricate themselves from that disagreeable choice between having to lean either to the West or to the East and so avoid a shift in the political balance against themselves by shifting it against us.

And yet it is precisely American disunity and apparent lack of resolve and will that may lead the Soviets to underestimate our determination to preserve our political independence and that of our allies. They could be tempted into a return to more coercive tactics, especially in Western Europe and against NATO.[18] It could be very tempting to replace strategic pressures with strategic threats if a crisis of legitimacy should arise in the USSR. In this conjuncture

[17] Sir Robert Thompson, *Revolutionary War in World Strategy: 1945-1969* (London: Secker & Warburg, 1970), 158.
[18] See Malcolm Mackintosh, "Clues to Soviet Policy," *Survival* XIII (January 1971), 25-29; reprinted from *US News & World Report,* November 2, 1970.

of coercive processes, the leaders, given their political superiority, could shift from a strategy of slow to sudden coercion, from a politics of fear to a politics of fright.

TOWARD A CRISIS OF LEGITIMACY

In addition to blackmail in all its various shades, in addition to direct aggression and resistance to it by means of coercive diplomacy, and that most insidious of all forms of coercion, the shaping of attitudes and values through fear, coerciveness in still an even more subtle sense is characteristic of the world's strategic environment. For our strategy of restrained containment and controlled evolution is really an effort to place the Soviet Union in a situation that is present leaders must experience as coercive. From our point of view, it may seem that we are merely counting upon natural processes of economic, political, and ideological development to bring about an eventual accommodation. Indeed, it could be argued that in the pursuit of this strategy we are not only extrapolating from Western experience to the world but are also acting in accordance with a Marxian appreciation of the relative unimportance of direct political action as compared with the political transformations that may be expected to follow upon economic and social development.

From the standpoint of the Soviet leadership, however, these processes, which may be summarized in the concept of modernization, must appear as constraints that impell them toward reconsideration and realignment of their political, economic, and ideological objectives. If their indirect strategy, to use General Beaufre's terminology, amounts to gaining concessions and accommodations through fear, ours consists in the exploitation of indefeasible vulnerabilities. Restrained containment threatens the integrity of their empire, the cohesion of their political culture, and ultimately the very legitimacy of their regime.

These forms of coercion that we are using against each other are obviously and essentially different, as different as the political theories of Marx and Lenin, or as different as modernization is from blackmail. These coercive processes constitute asymmetrical threat advantages and as such do not neutralize and mutually offset one another. They do not encourage the competitors toward that moral balance or consensus of which Henry Kissinger speaks. Rather, reliance upon blackmail, on the one hand, and modernization, on the other, could upset, perhaps even in a convulsive manner, the world's political balance, a prospect which no nation can envisage with equanimity.

In the first place, our comparative restraint, our defensive posture, has had the paradoxical effect of promoting the dissolution of the Soviet empire and, indeed, the disintegration of monolithic communism. We simply did not hinder the pluralizing tendencies that exist within all modern or modernizing societies. Without an external threat, the threat of rollback as it used to be called, it has proved impossible to preserve unity in Eastern Europe other than on a coercive basis. Moreover, the unconstitutionalized regimes in Eastern Europe have been forced to cultivate nationalistic sentiment and liberal yearnings in order to gain popular support, and so far the Russian leaders have felt impelled to suppress these tendencies, quite rightly seeing them as inconsistent with the preservation of their own political monopoly. Leninism has proven to be inconsistent not only with the imperatives of economic rationality but also with Marx's internationalism.

Secondly, the strategy of containment has bought time for the internal contradictions of the Soviet Union itself to evolve and to intensify. Both the position of the Party and the vitality of its ideology are compromised by the pressures of competitive modernity. Economic liberalization would seem to be required if the Soviet Union is to keep up with the pace of dynamic economies, a point which Hobbes would relish, and yet greater reliance on the market strikes at the status of the Party and is incompatible with its ideological claims and professions. One cannot but think that some more flexible and competitive form of politics is necessary for the restored dynamism of the Soviet Union. Now that the job of coercive industrialization has been done, and a once-and-for-all gain achieved, the Party and its leaders need new roles and a new political formula.

In a very real sense what we have done through our policy of containment is to galvanize the energies of Europe and to set the example of Japan against the Soviet Union and her reluctant dependents. By doing so we have turned Russian national interests against the interests of the Party and its élite. Our aim has been not only to get from them responsible behavior, to deter blackmail and open aggression. Our larger goal is the ideological and political transformation of the Soviet Union, for this is the prerequisite for a new world order. However, to turn a nation against its government is a revolutionary enterprise. We are provoking a crisis of legitimacy, the intensity of which could be fateful. Unless some Soviet statesman can devise a political formula that will resolve internal tensions in an orderly manner, the present political balance could collapse in an ideological panic as Eastern Europe erupted against its Communist regimes. Desperation in Moscow would be dangerous for all, for some would surely recommend a reversion to strategic threats, perhaps even an invasion of Western Europe, although these measures could accomplish no rational political objective. At least the men in Moscow need fear no direct attack from the United States, against which they would feel compelled to preempt. For our part, to bring our strategy of controlled evolution to a successful conclusion we will require sufficient strategic and tactical strength to deter or to control desperate actions.

We have blocked Soviet ambitions toward Western Europe, to which they have responded not by reverting to direct intimidation, despite their presumed position of political superiority. Rather they continue to press for a conference on European security, the point of which would be to get the United States out of Europe and so to secure its domination. They have also embarked on a flanking maneuver through the Middle East, and they are going into the oceans. Their ascent to parity has been rapid, one would think more rapid than their military security required. It remains to be seen whether the Soviets are seriously interested in the limitation of strategic arms.

What does this pattern of behavior mean? The Middle Eastern venture does pose a real threat, both military and psychological, to the security of Western Europe and accords well with their basic strategy of fear. Owing to their geopolitical position, however, the Soviets' naval expansion seems rather less compelling; in any form of coercive showdown we could lock and bolt their exits to the oceans. One senses in their naval operations a political adventure, an effort to buttress shaky legitimacy through the manufacture of prestige. But a naval challenge to the United States makes no contribution to the solution of the contradictions that have arisen in the Soviet state. At most it can only postpone for a while the coming crisis of legitimacy and delay somewhat the day when Russians themselves, as some are already trying, will wish to participate in the debate on the ideas in terms of which world order will be constructed.[19]

Perhaps the key to the intentions of the Soviet leaders may be found in their attitude to strategic arms limitation, and here we must consider the political implications of a strategic settlement. A settlement would mean their abandonment of coercive politics, a renunciation of the strategy of blackmail. It would mean a tacit reversal of the Czechoslovakian invasion. For henceforth they would be committed to a strategy of political competition rather than political coercion. This choice would imply commitment to full modernization of Soviet society, including the introduction of competitive politics, a sort of planned conversion of their political culture, in the course of which no legitimacy crisis need occur. Hence settlement would be a decision of momentous consequence, so momentous in fact that one cannot but wonder whether the present leadership has the nerve and the imagination required to take it.

On the other hand, not to settle, especially if this is combined with a decision to go for strategic superiority, would reactivate the arms race, a race which the Soviet Union could not hope to win unless the United States were to falter badly. And it would be a race in which the Soviet leaders' reluctance to modernize would place them at a serious disadvantage. Their personal and Party interests would come even more deeply into conflict with Russian national interests; the inescapable crisis of legitimacy would be upon them.

[19]Soviet prospects, political and strategic, are appraised in the following works: Arnold L. Horelick, "Fifty Years After October: Party and Society in the USSR" (P-3630; Santa Monica, Calif.: The RAND Corporation, September 1967); Allen Kassof, ed., *Prospects for Soviet Society* (New York: Praeger, 1968); Samuel P. Huntington and Clement H. Moore, eds., *Authoritarian Politics in Modern Society: The Dynamics of Established One-Party Systems* (New York: Basic Books, 1970); Thomas W. Wolfe, *Soviet Power and Europe, 1945-1970* (Baltimore, Md.: Johns Hopkins Press, 1970), and "Impact of Economic and Technological Issues on the Soviet Approach to SALT" (P-4368; Santa Monica, Calif.: The RAND Corporation, June 1970); and Hanson W. Baldwin, *Strategy for Tomorrow* (New York: Harper & Row, 1970).

FROM COERCION TO COMPETITION

I conclude from this review of our political and military experience that the fundamental reason why strategic thinking has become politicized, and why strategic and political theory have become increasingly unified, is this: In our imperfectly sovereign and tightly interdependent world, what is at stake is the world's political balance. It could not really be otherwise. For the co-sovereigns cannot use military compulsion against each other, only political coercions. The political not the military balance was at issue in the Cuban missile crisis, and that was the only time that we were prepared to escalate to nuclear war. We gave that ultimatum because we would not accept so sudden and so drastic a shift in the balance against us. To accept it would have meant not merely the defeat of our strategy of controlled evolution; it would have meant the ascendancy of the Soviet Union. Again it was the political and not the strategic balance that was threatened by the policies of Alexander Dubček. Once it became clear that he had lost control of the situation, the Soviet leaders had no alternatives other than to invade Czechoslovakia or to accept Western ascendancy, shockingly sudden in its arrival.

That the political balance is at stake has important implications. It means, first of all, that our situation is more precarious and more revolutionary than many would suppose. In this respect many of the concepts that we use to describe that situation such as cold war, arms race, détente, national security, or sufficiency, seem outdated and misleading; they convey a sense of political stability that may have been appropriate in the era of classical strategy, but is no longer appropriate to ours. After all, the revolutionary transformation of a society amounts to a shift in its political balance. The introduction of sovereignty itself was not only a decisive alteration of a military balance in favor of the sovereign; it was also a shifting of the political balance in his favor, the outcome of which was a change in the character of politics, or political culture. We are standing on the verge of a comparable change. It is a revolutionary transformation of world politics that we must contemplate and anticipate and endeavor to control as best we can. It is mistaken to think of our situation as one in which gradual and evolutionary processes are dominant; the situation is much more thoroughly political and volatile, and composite socioeconomic concepts like modernization cannot be applied to it without obscuring its inherently explosive nature.

Hence it is premature, at best, to think of the world as moving smoothly toward, converging toward, or being guided toward a new moral balance or consensus. This would be to confuse our condition with that of a sovereignly organized society. In a condition of imperfect, duopolistic sovereignty, based on nuclear deterrence, the co-sovereigns are able to bring against each other coercive pressures of an unprecedented intensity. This is the significance of the Cuban and Czechoslovakian crises. In this perspective, Mao's cultural revolution may also be seen as a form of coercive politics, the point of which was to protect Chinese political culture by paralyzing the Soviet Union, by preventing, or at least hindering, its political transformation and economic resurgence. Given his previous efforts rapidly to advance the economic development of China, a political interpretation of the revolution seems warranted, for it has cost much by way of China's economic growth.

We cannot any longer think of coercion as we have been wont to, in terms of actions or policies only. Governments act and pursue policies or strategies. But a strategic configuration, like a political or constitutional structure, generates those more massive and pervasive systemic tendencies that are known as processes. These systemic tendencies, although strategic in their origins, are essentially political in their bearing and nature. They provide not only the context for action and policy but also serve to give these direction and significance. Their presence accounts for the increasingly political nature of strategic thought and analysis, for the unification of strategic and political theory.[20]

[20] Political and strategic forecasting virtually force this unification. See, for examples: Alexander L. George, "The 'Operational Code': A Neglected Approach to the Study of Political Leaders and Decision-Making" (RM-5427-PR; Santa Monica, Calif.: The RAND Corporation, September 1967); Wayne Wilcox, "Forecasting Asian Strategic Environments for National Security Decisionmaking: A Report and a Method" (RM-6154-PR; Santa Monica, Calif.: The RAND Corporation, June 1970); and my "Political Forecasting and Strategic Planning," *International Studies Quarterly,* September, 1971.

The processes generated by our strategic structure reveal themselves as coercive forms of politics, which are in fact ways of riding them with the aim of upsetting the world's political balance. The concept of policy is inapt for understanding either our methods or our objectives.

The Soviet Union aspires to hegemony in Europe, not through conquest but through accommodation inspired by fear. Her success would mean not only her relief from the competitive pressures to which she is presently exposed; it would have an impact on American political unity and culture far more severe than the disruption produced by the Indochinese war, for it would shatter belief in the viability of the liberal conception of political authority. Political hopes and orientations would be decisively, and perhaps irreversibly, realigned throughout the world.

Our objective, on the other hand, is not merely the deterrence and containment of the Soviet Union and China; ultimately the objective we seek is the political transformation of those societies, a liberalization of their political cultures. As for the Soviet Union, we would force her from her strategy of coercion onto the path of political and economic competition, the outcome of which may be foreseen. If we can but manage a transition from coercive to competitive politics the gains for all would be immense; no real national interest would be damaged. For China there would be security far greater than that which she can hope to obtain from the possession of an insecure retaliatory force. For the Soviet Union the transition would mean not only economic vitality, but also and perhaps even more importantly, an end to her long cultural silence. For Europe, freedom from repression in the East, and in the West, respite from divisive fears and the chance to move from functional towards political unity. In truth, the costs of coercive politics are extremely high, just as high as Hobbes had said.

In this light the difficulty is that the strategies now being pursued by the United States and the Soviet Union are shearing strategies. The coercive processes on which we are riding do not neutralize each other. Although the target of each is the other's political culture, the threat advantages possessed by the adversaries are different, and what is even more ominous, these advantages are on the increase. We threaten the political integrity of the Soviet Union and its empire, and the longer the Party aristocracy delays liberalization the more explosive will become both internal and external pressures upon them. They are countering with grinding pressure on the Europeans and threaten our political disorientation. A clear way out of this state of nature exists: strategic settlement. For this is the only available strategic configuration that would force each of the co-sovereigns to consult and to foster their permanent interests, many of which would turn out to be common interests.

"ENDEAVOUR PEACE"

If my analysis of our situation in its essentials is correct, it means that new and systemic forms of coercion have come into the world. Their novelty consists in a peculiar duality, for while their source is strategic their ultimate import is cultural. Little in our previous experience, either political or military, seems relevant to their understanding, and to their analysis the standard categories of international relations—balance of power, foreign policy—will seem inadequate. We noticed an incongruity between our strategic theory and our strategic practice.

My thought is that these new forms of coercion are best understood in structural terms, as unique forms of coercive politics. For they are the joint product of the new weaponry and the unevenness of Western political development. If it were not for the weapons the Western alliance would not be confronted by divisive blackmail and fear; if it were not for the political and economic retardation of the Soviet Union we could not anticipate its transformation. And if we were not locked together by the weapons we both could contemplate a much more orderly evolution of our political systems. As it is, the paradoxical effect of the weapons has been to stabilize the military balance between us, and at the same time to render ever more delicate and precarious the political balance. It would have been far better if our military and our political interdependence had not intensified so swiftly and dramatically, for that is what has exposed our cultures to the threats of disorientation or transformation.

The systemic, dynamic, and asymmetrical nature of the coercive forces at work in the world renders an alteration of its political balance inevitable. The only question is whether this alteration is to be convulsive or planned and managed. Nuclear blackmail can be resisted and defeated, modernization cannot. Moreover, the stark irrationality of blackmail is revealed in its cost to the blackmailer, economic retardation and cultural sterility. This is no real cost, for economic and cultural vitality are precisely what we have to offer as an inducement to accommodation. Hence it would be folly beyond all belief, an unthinkable abdication of historical responsibility, if at this point the United States were to falter in its determination to preserve the political integrity of Western Europe against encroaching fear or desperate fright. It is equally unthinkable that a great country, claiming inspiration from Marx and Lenin, should permit its leaders to play out a losing hand. For only its domination of Western Europe could ensure the survival of the Soviet Communist Party, and that cannot be had.

In the West once again there has arisen a situation in which systemic compulsions conflict with human interests. This is a revolutionary situation as Hobbes and Rousseau and Marx would all allow, and they all correctly inferred that humanity would prevail against coercive deformations. Hobbes' solution to the conflict was the sovereign, and this time the sovereign sits not upon a throne but in holes in the ground, an impersonal and imperfect sovereign to be sure. But the message is still the same: the first law of nature is to endeavour peace.

INDEX

Index